Hip-Hop Genius 2.0

Hip-Hop Genius 2.0

Remixing High School Education

Ten-Year Anniversary Edition

Samuel Steinberg Seidel
Tony Simmons
Michael Lipset

ROWMAN & LITTLEFIELD
Lanham • Boulder • New York • London

Published by Rowman & Littlefield
An imprint of The Rowman & Littlefield Publishing Group, Inc.
4501 Forbes Boulevard, Suite 200, Lanham, Maryland 20706
www.rowman.com

86-90 Paul Street, London EC2A 4NE, United Kingdom

British Library Cataloguing in Publication Information Available

Library of Congress Cataloging-in-Publication Data

Names: Seidel, Samuel Steinberg, 1978–, author. | Simmons, Tony, 1960–, author. | Lipset, Michael, 1987–, author.
Title: Hip hop genius 2.0 : remixing high school education / Sam Steinberg Seidel with Tony Simmons, Michael Lipset.
Description: Second edition. | Lanham : Rowman & Littlefield, [2022] | Previous edition c2011. | Includes bibliographical references and index. | Summary: "Through stories about the professional rapper who founded the first hip-hop school and the aspiring artists currently enrolled there, Hip-Hop Genius delivers a vision for how hip-hop's genius can lead to a fundamental remix of the way we think of teaching, school design, and leadership"—Provided by publisher.
Identifiers: LCCN 2021033734 (print) | LCCN 2021033735 (ebook) | ISBN 9781475864304 (cloth) | ISBN 9781475864311 (epub)
Subjects: LCSH: High School for Recording Arts (St. Paul, Minn.) | Teenagers with social disabilities—Education (Secondary)—Minnesota—St. Paul. | Hip-hop—Influence.
Classification: LCC LD7501.S9246 S45 2021 (print) | LCC LD7501.S9246 (ebook) | DDC 373.776/581—dc23
LC record available at https://lccn.loc.gov/2021033734
LC ebook record available at https://lccn.loc.gov/2021033735

With appreciation to all our parents: Shirley, James, Samuel, Adria, Steve, Nancy, Dicky, Kathleen, David, Diana, and John.

Contents

Foreword 2.0

"It's a Banger!"

Gloria Ladson-Billings

Like many people who came up with a variety of new habits during the global pandemic known as the coronavirus or COVID-19, I came up with my own secret obsession. Along with baking copious amounts of banana bread and bingeing on streaming services (shout out to Netflix, Amazon Prime, Own, and Hulu), I found a YouTube channel developed by a set of twin brothers from the Gary, Indiana, area—Tim and Fred Williams. The 22-year-old African American young men's channel is titled "TwinstheNewTrend," and they use the channel to react to all manner of music from the '50s, '60s, '70s, '80s, and '90s. Because they grew up in their grandparents' strictly religious household, the only music they regularly listened to was gospel music. On their channel they listen to rock, R&B, country, late '80s and '90s hip-hop, and even opera (at least Pavarotti has caught their attention).

The young men's reactions are so genuine and enthusiastic that they now have close to 1 million subscribers. Even former President Obama is a subscriber and did a session with them on YouTube. The first time they listened to Stevie Wonder they could not contain their excitement. Their response to Phil Collins' classic, "In the Air Tonight" went viral and actually landed the Phil Collins song back on the Billboard charts. Dolly Parton was clearly tickled at the response to her classic, "Jolene." However, the reaction that got me hooked on the twins was Boyz II Men's "End of the Road." The boys demonstrate excitement about so many aspects of the song—the harmony, the vocal prowess of singer Wanya Morris, the passion, and the acapella ending. So impressed with the twins' reaction, I have used it in scholarly presentations to suggest it is exactly this kind of reaction every teacher would love to have from students.

I point out to education researchers and teachers that the twins are astute at moving across linguistic registers, they describe the song using similes and metaphors. They display facility with what might be considered "standard" English and musical terminology, describing listening to the track as "mandatory" and expressing surprise by asking, "They goin' a capella?" When the twins finish listening and reacting to a song they love, they often refer to it as a "banger."

The denotation "it's a banger" is exactly what I have to say about Sam Seidel's *Hip Hop Genius*. When I first read it in 2011, I thought, "Now this is the book for teachers who are intimidated by hip-hop education!" More precisely, it was the book for teachers who are intimidated by hip-hop and have no idea how to integrate it into their pedagogy. Instead of expecting teachers to go through four decades of hip-hop discographies, this book exposed us to the elements of hip-hop that could help teachers move away from "using hip-hop" and toward "being hip-hop." Seidel's notions of flipping something out of nothing, staying fresh, and being creative in the face of scarce resources became an important rubric for making sense of the pedagogy that was working for students in urban classrooms where I spend my research life.

One of my former students is a high school teacher who kids describe as "corny," but they love coming to his class and they work harder for him than any of their other teachers. His work is a great example of "flipping something out of nothing." Although he is assigned to teach courses in world and U.S. history, he developed an elective course on global health and poverty. There was no such course at the high school level so there was no ready-made textbook. The teacher began contacting various authors, activists, health experts, government and policy leaders, and anyone he could locate who had something to say on the course topics. The students read an amazing array of texts. Their teacher told them that a teacher who didn't "let" them read entire books didn't respect them! This tactic worked well with students for whom "respect" is one of their highest values. His students were given the opportunity to talk with people like then Secretary of Education Arne Duncan, MacArthur Genius grant winner and health activist Paul Farmer, World Bank President Jim Yong Kim, Equal Justice Initiative Founder and death penalty crusader Bryan Stevenson, and Professor and media commentator Marc Lamont Hill. The students had these experiences because their teacher was willing to flip something out of nothing. His class is always oversubscribed and students who struggled in traditional classes seem to thrive in his class.

Another former student provides a powerful example of "staying fresh." At his school he noticed that the Black boys were constantly in trouble. They were the ones detained, suspended, or expelled. The pattern was so pronounced that he approached his principal with a "fresh" idea. He asked if the principal could assign him a classroom of just Black boys. Instead of making it a punitive class he told the students they were a part of a manhood class and he regularly told them how special they were and how they were a part of an exciting educational experiment. Within a month the referrals of

Black boys dropped precipitously, and the boys became more invested in their schoolwork. This teacher was being hip-hop by keeping it fresh.

I met a third teacher who worked as a dean in a "school of last resort." Its students were those who had experienced nothing but school failure. If they did not "succeed" in this environment, they were likely to drop out of school altogether. This teacher was actually a hip-hop artist and one of the regular activities he did with his students was to begin the day by asking them, "What is the last thing you listened to on your mobile device or iPod and why?" This prompt was one that worked for all of the students because every one of them was connected to their devices as they filed into the school each day. This teacher was being creative in the face of limited resources.

At another time, the school principal asked this teacher to take on the development of a Saturday school for the students who were habitual truants. The teacher felt that was just the opposite of what the students wanted. The ones who did not come regularly were being asked to come even more. But again, the teacher was hip-hop by saying to the students, "Saturday school ends at noon and I head into the studio at 12:05. Those who are here and on time can come in with me." That declaration convinced many of the students to attend the Saturday school where they produced a video with spoken word, dance, and singing. It was a wonderful example of being creative in the face of scarce resources.

Reading *Hip Hop Genius* and observing wonderful teachers all over the country convinced me that my own work on culturally relevant pedagogy (Ladson-Billings, 1994; 2009) needed to remixed (Ladson-Billings, 2014). Although I was convinced that the major principles of culturally relevant pedagogy—student learning, cultural competence, and critical conscious-ness—would stand the test of time, I realized that I was missing an important element of culture—youth culture. In hindsight, I recognized that while doing my work in elementary classrooms afforded me some important research conveniences—one teacher in a self-contained classroom, it also limited my ability to see the power and influence of youth culture, particularly, hip-hop culture.

While it is true that youth culture (and in this case, hip-hop culture) is sufficiently powerful enough to influence younger students (i.e., elementary aged students consume youth culture), youth and young adults produce that culture. The work that Seidel's book does demonstrates how that culture can both be incorporated into and transform teaching and learning. The point is not to look for some catchy hook to capture students' interests in traditional curriculum and instructional strategies. Hip-hop culture can and should be the vehicle through which teachers think differently about themselves, their students, and their work. It is designed to disrupt the notion of teaching as transmission to teaching and learning as a site of construction where teachers and students "build" together.

Reading this new edition provides another generation of teachers with an opportunity to recognize the power and influence of a culture that has demonstrated its power and longevity. Through developing two courses focused on hip-hop at the undergraduate college level, I have been able to influence a number of students of color to pursue teaching as a career. When they realized that teaching could be a place where they could embrace hip-hop they pursued teaching in cities like Milwaukee; Detroit; Columbus; and Washington, DC, as well as rural Louisiana. The beauty is that the very notion of hip-hop is genius and Sam Seidel has reminded us once again in this second edition.

REFERENCES

Ladson-Billings, G. (1994). *The dreamkeepers: Successful teachers of African American children.* San Francisco: Jossey Bass

Ladson-Billings, G. (2009). *The dreamkeepers: Successful teachers of African American children*, 2nd *Edition.* San Francisco: Jossey Bass.

Ladson-Billings, G. (2014). Culturally relevant teaching 2.0 aka the remix. *Harvard Educational Review*, 84, 74–84.

Foreword 2.0

D Smoke

I wanna bypass my struggles and life's mazes and make it
Through the rubble get a couple of scratches and scars to 'member
the days when . . .
I had my face in my palms but never let it hit the pavement.

—Chiz, 1985–2011

The hood is water. It's the source of life, creativity, and talent for every industry and art form. It is my firm belief that true creativity is born out of necessity, and therefore it abounds in our ghettos. The innate resilience of oppressed people has proven generation after generation that nothing can keep people from growing, overcoming and, ultimately, thriving.

In all my experience as an educator, my success in producing student outcomes has always been predicated on one core principle: students are not blank slates but complex individuals with a wealth of experiences. Furthermore, the breadth and magnitude of their experience, although often traumatic, still increases their ability to draw connections and imagine solutions. However, this powerful process of converting trauma into learning potential *should be* the responsibility of the teacher to facilitate. Unfortunately, the students are often the ones who are expected to code switch, to go the extra mile to access information foreign to their cultural experience. Teachers, for far too long, have blamed students for their own inability to structure lessons in a way that identifies and incorporates students' experiences, languages, and cultures into their lessons in authentic ways.

I had the distinct privilege of teaching for an academy that understood these principles and based their practices on forward thinking philosophies. During an interview for a job at High School for Recording Arts I was asked questions that no other school had asked me before in all my years as an educator: "What life skills are not taught in schools that should be a part of all curriculum?"

To that question I responded, "Financial literacy."

I was then asked, "What are the students interested in?"

The most obvious response was "Music."

As a then "aspiring" musician, I had become well aware of the complexities of pursuing one's life dreams. I had to dabble in all of the peripheral skills of design, accounting, time management, communication, video production, and so many more in order to realize my own dreams. My endeavors had pushed me to the limits, a point where I had to apply everything I had ever learned in order to accomplish the goals I had set out for myself. And at my breaking point I found a beautiful reality, that my love for music could drive me into any career path. Engineers build and design hardware used to put on major tours, doctors give us clearance to travel to foreign countries. Ex-military soldiers accompany us on tours to ensure our safety. Dancers add motion to our sounds. Businessmen negotiate mutually beneficial contracts to help distribute my music to the masses. Lawyers defend my best interests. Managers organize my time and make sure I'm compensated fairly and journalists help to document the journey.

My dreams are a window into everything the world has to offer. Understanding this, acknowledging the creative passions and artistic interests of students is the avenue into introducing them to countless career pathways. Fortunately, we live in an age where this is no longer conjecture or theory, but factual information based on studies that have been performed and continue to perfect a progressive educational practice.

It is my absolute pleasure to write this. You've chosen wisely to explore the intersections of hip-hop and education. You've chosen to learn what it means to stimulate and inspire our innovators and untapped talent. For this, I salute you.

Foreword 2.0

David "TC" Ellis

Maybe it was like how some people don't like to look in the mirror or hear their own voice . . . or maybe I was too busy at the time. For whatever reason, making myself read a draft of *Hip Hop Genius* before the original edition came out was a struggle for me. I went back and forth with Sam four times. He was like, "David, you gotta read this shit! Have you read it?!"

A couple times I said to myself, "Next time he asks, I'm just gonna tell him I read it," but then I settled down and binged the whole thing in two or three days. I was amazed.

I read sections thinking, "This is what we do?"

And then as I kept reading it turned into: "*This* is what we *do!*"

Holding that book in my hands was an aviation experience. It reminded me of my experiences as an airplane pilot. You start on the ground. Everything is at a familiar scale. As you take off, the scale starts to shift. It's a different perspective from the cockpit looking down at a whole city than it is when you're down on the street. Reading *Hip Hop Genius* for the first time let me see the school from a different elevation. While I knew hip-hop music and culture, and I knew what was happening in schools, and I knew what we were doing at the High School for Recording Arts, the text in these pages let me see how what we're doing was iconic and is contributing to these massive things that are happening.

Sometimes when you're in the game, you look at it like it's a game. You don't realize the impact you're making. It's like being with Prince—having grown up with him, throughout his whole trajectory and mine, I couldn't fully see the impact. *Now* I see it. When he died it finally came home to me like, "Damn, this mufucka's an icon of the world and I had an opportunity to be with him, chop shit up, and parlay it into family, respect, community, and education." Prince changed the world. And rolling with him I got to bring something to that whole era of music and the Minneapolis sound. It is really hard to see that when you're in it—it's just part of your regular day. But there are these moments that let you see it. Prince's passing was one of those moments for me. Aviation experiences.

In the time since *Hip Hop Genius* first came out, it's been gratifying to see that the book has given other people an overview, pictures, stories, kind of like it gave me. Maybe others experience it from the opposite direction though—they've been flying even higher over the whole landscape and this book brings them down to an elevation where they can start to make out more details on the ground. The buildings, roads, and people they see are our studios, learning models, and students. For me it reveals a broader perspective of the landscape; for them it reveals the texture of the terrain. I remember reading a review online where someone was talking about how relatable the book was and how it gave them a glimpse into the reality of urban America and the challenges of education. I feel good about that. I want people to think about this shit. I want them to understand what we do.

I was particularly proud of George Clinton's reaction. He commented to me about how much he enjoyed the book one night when we were out at dinner. In that moment, I saw how it all stitched together—his music, the school, and the book. It's so flow-orientated. None of it is constructed or rigid. It's all free-flowing. It can transition between worlds—and that's an essential part of learning. Society doesn't value it enough and it's really a snub to learning. They'll put people in rows trying to teach them how to make music like George Clinton! When he'll tell you straight up, "If you hear any noise, it's me and the boys." The way you make music is you gotta get in the band—*just get in there!* You're looking at some of the most genius mathematicians and scientific interpolators anywhere. They communicate with their eyes and instruments. They can have a guest come up that they've never made any music with and have it all end with a perfect crescendo—how do you do that?

A lot of people in education value the outputs—they elevate student work that comes from that same flow, but they don't understand the spirituality, math, science, or other competencies that go into producing it. George Clinton does it with his music. Tony and I have done it with the school. Sam did it with *Hip Hop Genius*. The book is special because it brings together George Clinton with the school with the origins and evolutions of hip-hop culture. It's the same energy from the same source. What Kool Herc did with the turntables, what kids did with linoleum on street corners—we did that with the school. This is that. That is this.

Acknowledgments
The Ten-Year Anniversary Edition

We would especially like to thank the members of the HSRA community involved in this project directly—Joey Cienian, Walter Cortina, Morgan Welch, Haben Gebreghergish, Tiki Blackmore, and Amanda Galloway—each of whom contributed in their own ways. Joey, thank you for your swift ability to succinctly and accurately capture the nature of the High School for Recording Arts' growth over the last 10 years. Walter, thank you for bringing a tenacious exuberance to this project. Minnesota and now the readers of this book will be better for your work and for you sharing your story. Haben, thank you for supporting Walter and Jon in telling Walter's powerful story and for being a beacon of teaching excellence in a school system that often diverts incredible teachers away from the students HSRA serves. You choose HSRA every day and you choose our students every day, and for that we are grateful. Tiki and Amanda, thank you both so much for your leadership—and then helping us track down the documentation—of the community meetings held by the school in the wake of George Floyd's murder. Thank you both, also, for being the rock-star facilitators of learning that you are. HSRA's youth would not be so well-served without the two of you in their lives. Collectively, we owe a big debt of gratitude to Jon Bacal for his patience, dedication to working with young people, and kindness throughout a long editing process.

We would also like to thank Martha Diaz, Bronwen Low, Isaac Ewell, Karen Pittelman, Dicky Cluster, Adria Steinberg, and Sunanna Chand for reading early drafts of this edition and giving judicious critical feedback and warm encouragement in perfect parity. Your individual intellects and experiences, contributions to the world of hip-hop education, editing chops, and willingness to call us out on those areas of documentation that we may have missed or gotten wrong helped us produce a stronger final product. And thank you to Sophia Mathies, for your work in producing a manuscript worthy of and conforming to professional standards of publication formatting. Our appreciation to Tom Koerner, Carlie Wall, and the team at Rowman & Littlefield for working with us to bring this new edition to print and digital life.

Finally, we are humbled and honored by the words that Gloria Ladson-Billings, D Smoke, and TC provided to contextualize this edition of the book. Reading your contributions was a gift. Thank you.
—Sam, Tony, and Michael

I double-down on my love for everyone I shouted out in the acknowledgments in the first edition. Ten years have gone by, and my appreciation for each of you has only grown greater.

Love to Sunanna Tara Chand for being an extraordinary partner and person. Love to Sunanna's whole family for being such a wonderful family to me.

Appreciation to all my colleagues at the Stanford d.school, particularly the K12 Lab—Ariam Mogos, Ariel Raz, Barry Svigals, Jess Brown, Laura McBain, Louie Montoya, Marc Chun, Susie Chang, and honorary member Lisa Kay Solomon—for continuing to push my thinking on what's possible and necessary in K–12 education, and for being fun and supportive friends. Sarah Stein Greenberg, the broader d.school community, my #HipHopEd fam, the Deeper Learning network, my BIF collaborators, IDC colleagues, LaVerne Srinivasan, Elise Henson, Eileen Yang, Wendy Sauer, Courtlandt Butts, Denise Williams, Andy Calkins, Michelle Pledger, Greg Rosenbaum, Ron Reed, Ron Berger, Al Solis, Eric Shed, and Corey Scholes have all provided partnerships, places, and platforms to shape and share the ideas in this book. Thank you.

While working on this new edition, I have been working on three other books with brilliant folks who have brought a beautiful balance of patience and persistence to our collaborations: Olatunde Sobomehin, Jenn Brown, Scott Doorley, Squint, Barry Svigals, Randall Hoyt, Chris Emdin, and Isabel Huff. Thank you all.

Members of the next generation of my fam (who were not around when the first edition came out!)—Lamont, Janayah, Lalo, Julian, Harriet, Lea, and Maya—thank you for keeping me inspired.
—Sam

I would first like to thank God for his infinite patience with and enduring love for me. I also owe all that is good in me to my mother, whom I love and miss so much. She told me to shine my light on the world in service to others. My journey to do that has been through the inspiration of and collaboration with so many including all my ancestors, grandparents, mother, fathers, sisters, brothers (including fraternal), aunties, uncles, and cousins who shaped my thinking, beliefs, and culture. I also want to acknowledge all my teachers and mentors who influenced me and crossed my path at so many various intersections in my life. Special thank you to my brother David "TC" Ellis, who opened the door for me to do the work I was born to do. He continues to amaze me with his true hip-hop genius!

I would also like to mention that I owe so much knowledge that has contributed to my education vision and leadership to these superstars: Wayne Jennings, Howard Fuller, Larry Rosenstock, Ron Newell, Doug Thomas, Walter Enloe, Mary K. Boyd, Dennis Litttky, Elliot Washor, Ted Kolderie, Chanda Baker, Larry McKenzie, Chi Ellis, Bryan Rossi, and Linda Nathan (and others). Huge thanks to Charmaine Mercer and Kent McGuire of the Hewlett Foundation, Jessica Berwind of Spring Point Partners, and Justin Christy and Jackie Statum Allen of the Bush Foundation. Also to the staff and students at High School for Recording Arts and Studio 4. They are all truly special and continuously amaze me with their brilliance, creativity, and tenacity. I also owe so much of my contribution to this beautiful project of love to my brothers, Sam and Michael (and both of their better halves, Sunanna and Gaëlle). And big shout-outs to the original Hip-Hop Genius crew—Camilla, Isaac, Fanon, Jason, and TC. Also, thank you so much to Martha Diaz and Timothy David Jones for adding their own hip-hop genius to our crew. And huge love to all my peeps at High Tech High GSE, Stanford d.school, Education Evolving, Reaching at Promise Students Association, Coalition of Independent Charter Schools, Fielding International, Center for Artistry and Scholarship, and Minnesota Jazz Education. Finally, I would like to say that my greatest inspiration has been my daughter Olivia. I learn so much from her, and she is the spark that keeps me going!
—Tony

I would like to thank, of course, my parents and family for making life and all available opportunities possible. I would like to extend a special thanks to Bronwen Low, my PhD supervisor at McGill University who provided feedback on the writing included in this new edition; Sam Seidel for his mentorship, friendship, and guidance in career and professional endeavors; Tony Simmons for his ongoing mentorship, friendship, guidance, and faith in my potential and abilities; and TC for his mentorship, friendship, guidance, and understanding. Thank you to Linda Nathan as well, who has been a firm mentor, guiding hand, and example to be emulated. Without her, HSRA LA would never have happened. I would also like to thank Martha Diaz for her kindness and understanding, feedback, and guidance on the writing contained in this new edition. I would like to thank Gaëlle Janvier for being by my side throughout this process, supporting me through late nights of work and writing, and lifting me up when I needed some extra juice to get things done. Lastly, thank you to my brother, Max Lipset, who introduced me to

Acknowledgments

underground hip-hop; my mother, Kathleen Barlow, without whom absolutely nothing would be possible; and my father, David Lipset. Thank you to my younger sister, Sophia Lipset, who stands consistently on the front lines of the Movement for Black Lives and our planet. Thank you to Eoin Small—you inspire to always seek the joy of being alive. And thanks to you, the reader, for coming to this work with an open mind, an open heart, and an interest in always doing better.
—Michael

Introduction 2.0

Rest in Peace, George Floyd, and all victims of anti-Black state-sanctioned violence.

George Floyd was not just a victim. He was a creative and caring person. A hip-hop artist. A mentor. Someone who found ways to be generative and flip new opportunities out of limited resources. Were it not for the life of George Floyd and his murder at the hands of Minneapolis Police, this new edition of *Hip-Hop Genius* would not exist.

At 7:59 a.m. on May 29, 2020, I received four iMessages from Tony Simmons, now the Executive Director of the High School for Recording Arts. Tony had sent these messages to Isaac Ewell and me—the three of us close friends for the past 15 years and original members of the crew who initially coined the term "hip-hop genius."

One of the messages read: "Long day and long night. . . ." The other three were photographs of David "TC" Ellis, the founder of the High School for Recording Arts (HSRA); Big Layne Bellamy, the facilities director; and a few others standing in front of the school wearing facemasks, some holding their licensed shotguns and rifles.

Holy shit. School leaders. In front of their school. With masks on. And guns.

An unusual sight. Even in the middle of a global health crisis. Even during rapidly spreading protests of anti-Black racism sparked by the police's murder of George Floyd just a few miles from the school. Even with white agitators fomenting destruction.

Tony followed these messages with a series of videos showing footage of the school parking lot filled with smoke. Sirens wailed throughout. An individual approached the school. Before getting close, he was told to "Hold up!" so he could explain why he was on the property.

Car horns blared. Fire trucks streamed by. "No Justice, No Peace," was chanted by passing groups of protesters holding signs that read: "Black Lives Matter."

The night before, the Third Precinct of the Minneapolis Police Department had been burned down. The school next door burnt. Neighboring buildings vandalized.

The High School for Recording Arts was untouched.

At least the physical structure was untouched. The students were touched up.

Tony followed with another text message that was a flyer for an online student-led community meeting later that morning. He asked us not to share it on social media, but just with inner-circle family and friends. They didn't want it to become voyeuristic or to attract trolls, but students were hurting and seeking community; as Tony put it they needed "to express themselves knowing they have a loving community behind them."

Two hours later and two thousand miles away, my partner, Sunanna Chand and I were sitting on our couch in Oakland logging into a Google Meet video session with the High School for Recording Arts family. Students joined the call from their cell phones in bedrooms, living rooms, and cars. Some had lost their voices from shouting at protests. Others were speaking softly as they were sharing space with family members who were resting. Meanwhile, since the news of George Floyd's murder had reached Oakland, people had been in the streets protesting every night. We turned the computer volume up to its maximum setting so we could hear the students' voices over the sounds of sirens, as well as police helicopters and news helicopters, hovering outside our open windows.

Students and advisors helmed the conversation, introducing community norms such as "Everybody has a voice so please make sure you're listening and not waiting to talk." Other students introduced conversation topics, including: "With society the way it is do you feel cautious bringing Black children into this world? Should I not think this way?" and "How do we prepare our children of color to protect themselves in a world like this?"

A High School for Recording Arts advisor reflected on how his whole life he had been raised to treat the police with respect, but now felt that how he treated police did not matter—he could live by the rules, do all the right things, and still be killed. Students parsed the difference between protests and riots. Some said we should make our voices heard, but we should not destroy property. Others pointed out that there had been peaceful protests about police brutality for years that had been largely ignored, and questioned why any response was off-limits when such brutal violence had been enacted on George Floyd and the perpetrator had not yet been arrested. Poetry was shared. Tears were shed.

We stayed on the video session for over an hour. When we closed the laptop, I looked around our apartment where Sunanna and I had been quarantined for almost three months. The noise of the helicopters made it hard to think, but the voices of the students held strong in my mind. The pain, fear, outrage, and love they were expressing brought me back to protests I attended after Cornel Young Jr. was murdered by police in 2000 in Providence, Rhode Island; to the community meetings we had at AS220 Youth after members of our community were killed; to the protests I attended after Trayvon Martin and Michael Brown were killed. . . . [1]

We've seen this over and over and over. But the voices and energy of the young people reminded me how important it is not to give in to cynicism or despair. HSRA's students were at ground zero cubed: the epicenter of impact from racist violence, the coronavirus, and generations of economic disinvestment. Young people bearing the brunt of all this were speaking up and taking action. I better not be silent.

The first edition of *Hip Hop Genius* was dedicated to brilliant Black and Latinx students of mine who were murdered as teenagers. The motivation for writing the book was to share the path they and I had carved together, the path my family at High School for Recording Arts had found, too—a path honoring that brilliance and rewiring our systems so that Black, Latinx, and Indigenous young people could live, could thrive, and could be leaders of change.

A decade later, the systemic injustices outlined in the Society's Sucker Punch chapter of *Hip Hop Genius* still exist. But the morning Tony sent those pictures from the Twin Cities it felt clear that much had changed in these ten years—including a massive amount in just the past few months.

For one thing, the country had changed: On the heels of yet another devastating tragedy, this nation's populace was reckoning more publicly than perhaps ever in my lifetime with the pervasiveness of anti-Black racism. The success of ongoing activism, the pervasiveness of cell phone documentation and social media sharing, and the undeniably callous and fascist nature of the president of the country all contributed to a moment when the mainstream dialogue in this country acknowledged the brutal existence of state-sanctioned anti-Black racism.

At the same time we were in the midst of a pandemic that had almost instantaneously changed what schooling looked like globally. For decades, any of us who suggested that teaching and learning did not necessarily need to occur in 45-minute blocks 5 days a week for 180 days each year, or that it did not need to happen within the confines of a building with rows of desks and a public address system, were generally dismissed as dreamers, unrealistic in our imaginings. Now, all of a sudden, over 55 million K–12 students in the United States could not go to school buildings for the foreseeable future. At least for the time being, there wasn't much debate: Academic learning either wasn't going to happen or had to happen in radically different ways.

This was occurring at a moment when standardized approaches to teaching, learning, and testing were already on the ropes. When *Hip Hop Genius* was written and released, the national No Child Left Behind legislation was in full swing. Not only was the federal government flexing its muscles to expand standards-based accountability, local education entities and even self-proclaimed education reformers were operating as if homogenizing educational approaches and implementing more frequent and high stakes diagnostics would somehow increase equity.

By 2015, the Every Student Succeeds Act shifted authority to the state level.[2] While standardized testing is still prevalent, in recent years it has become more widely acknowledged by state education agencies, school districts, education nonprofits, and mainstream pundits and scholars that we cannot test our way to equity. It is commonly acknowledged that income and education levels of families is a strong predictor of how students will do on those tests, and that the exams privilege students whose families can afford test prep courses and materials. The coronavirus pandemic led the U.S. Education Department to waive requirements for accountability tests in 2019–2020.[3] Dozens of colleges and universities chose to waive their application requirements of standardized tests, with some, like the University of California system, announcing that they would completely phase out the use of such tests over the coming years.

As standardized approaches have become less popular, over the ten years since *Hip Hop Genius* was published, mainstream education organizations and foundations have begun celebrating approaches like "student-centered learning," "personalized learning," "learner-directed models," and "deeper learning." In other words, a burgeoning field of education reformers are trumpeting the very approaches embodied at the High School for Recording Arts and described in *Hip-Hop Genius*. Often this conversation leaves out two important facts: One, while these approaches might well be the future of education, they are also the past—groups like Big Picture Learning, EL Education, EdVisions, and High Tech High have been demonstrating that these approaches are highly effective for decades; and two, even though Black-led and Black-serving organizations have been attacked and undermined by those in power, there are still Black-led and Black-serving organizations, like the High School for Recording Arts, at the forefront of this work.

The very fact that the High School for Recording Arts has survived and thrived over these past ten years is important to recognize. In his Preface for the first edition of this book, Herb Kohl noted that many of the progressive "student-oriented" high schools founded in the 1960s were ultimately "defeated or deflated." To have weathered over two decades without being defeated, deflated, or defunded is a remarkable accomplishment worthy of note and study.

While the High School for Recording Arts serves as a particularly consistent and long-running model of such an "innovative" approach to education, it has made changes worth noting: The school has the same DNA, but—as will be shared in updates throughout this new edition—the manifestations of its genetic code have evolved in important ways over the past decade. Just in the last year, COVID-19 has forced the High School for Recording Arts to develop new approaches: How to provide culturally sustaining, personalized, project based learning, social services, and mental and emotional support for students whom society has largely forsaken *in the midst of a pandemic*.

The field of hip-hop education has also changed over the past decade. Interest, scholarship, community, and practice have all grown. This can be demonstrated through the increases in hip-hop after-and out-of-school programs, classroom teachers implementing hip-hop pedagogical approaches, principals engaging in hip-hop styles of school leadership, school founders bringing a hip-hop approach to designing new school models, new nonprofit organizations, presence at practitioner and academic conferences, and new books published. More details on all of this can be found in the new Trends in Hip-Hop Education chapter. The bottom line is that there are now far more educators, scholars, and activists constructing and spreading ideas about hip-hop pedagogy and educational models. Hip-hop education is alive.

And finally, I have changed: When I wrote *Hip Hop Genius*, I wrote about racism—I called out how institutions and society writ large were enacting violence on Black, Latinx, Indigenous, and poor students. But except in my Note from/about the Author at the very end of the book, I never addressed—or even mentioned—my whiteness. In the note at the end of the book, I explained that I had not centered my race—or anything else about myself—in the book because I felt there were enough "coming-of-rage stories" by white authors about the violence enacted on Black and Brown young people by our country's education system, and that *Hip Hop Genius* was about Black culture, a Black-led school, and ideas that were developed by a group of educators who were all Black except for me. I was a messenger who had been entrusted with the honor and responsibility of translating all that into a sequence of written words, but it was fundamentally not my story.

After 60+ speaking engagements in the few years following the publication of *Hip Hop Genius*, I stopped. As mentioned above, the field of hip-hop education was growing. When we began talking about "hip-hop genius," public dialogue on hip-hop education tended to focus on rap music as a controversial but potentially powerful way to connect with students and as content many were seeing as worthy of study in schools, but much of even the most positive public conversation presented hip-hop as a funky beat on which to "track" students. There was little to no mention of hip-hop pedagogy, school design, or leadership. I felt I had a role to play in expanding hip-hop education conversations to include these ideas. But by 2015, this had shifted. Many more were talking about hip-hop as *a way of approaching educational endeavors.* There was more oxygen and ink being given to ideas of bringing hip-hop's swagger, improvisation, and premium on realness and freshness to reimagining teaching, learning, and schooling. So I fell back.

I was hesitant to return to this text as a lone author. One of my hopes for the first edition of *Hip Hop Genius* was that it be collectively authored by members of the High School for Recording Arts community and the Hip-Hop Genius crew. While it didn't go down that way ten years ago, one of the key elements that makes this new edition possible is its coauthorship with Tony Simmons, the executive director of HSRA, and Michael Lipset, the organization's director of social impact. Throughout the new additions to the book, when we refer to "we," we are referring to Tony, Michael, and me. When we use one of our first names, it is to distinguish which coauthor we are referring to. This updated edition would not have been possible without contributions from Walter Cortina, a current student at the High School for Recording Arts; Haben Ghebregergish, Walter's advisor and a math teacher at the High School for Recording Arts; Jon Bacal, Walter's mentor; and Joey Cienian, the education program director at the High School for Recording Arts. Together, we have returned to the original text, cutting nothing, and adding new content—and through the addition of co-authors for this edition, new perspectives—to illuminate lessons from the last ten years.

In addition to phenomenal new forewords from Gloria Ladson-Billings and D Smoke, and this new introduction, this ten-year anniversary edition of *Hip-Hop Genius* features updates to every chapter in the original book. Chapter 1: Hip-Hop High, which gives readers a tour through the school's physical facility and educational model now has an update outlining ways in which the school's space and model has evolved since 2011. Chapter 2: A Day's Work, which follows one student, Lil C, through a full day of learning at High School for Recording Arts, is now updated with an account of another student, Walter Cortina, which shows what remote learning looked like for one High School for Recording Arts student during the pandemic and tells his incredible story of leading a group of young people in a battle against the state of Minnesota for access to pandemic support funds. Chapter 3: Hip-Hop Leadership, which shares stories that illuminate the leadership style of HSRA's founder, David "TC" Ellis, is now accompanied by stories and leadership lessons from Tony Simmons, who played key leadership roles from the early days of HSRA and has served as the school's executive director for the past decade.

As mentioned above, much about the systemic inequities described in the Society's Sucker Punch chapter have not changed, but we have provided some new statistics to update those included in the first edition and to illuminate some shifts that have occurred over the past decade. Chapter 5: Trends in Hip-Hop Education has an update that shares where some important strides in the field of hip-hop education have been made and where we may have yet to go as a diverse and dispersed community of theory and practice. Chapter 6: Flip-Hop Education describes what the future of the High School for Recording Arts and hip-hop education might hold, this is now updated with lessons learned from 10 more years of experimentation.

Finally, we are excited to add an entirely new chapter to this edition, Chapter 7: The Bumrush. The first edition of the book highlighted many aspects of hip-hop culture that we believed educators could learn from, such as the notions of sampling and remixing educational practices. For this edition, we have added another important hip-hop approach that educators must learn and embody: *the bumrush*. This new chapter is a call to action for the bold moves that must come next in education.

After all, when considering racism, public health crises, environmental crises, and economic crises, has there been a moment in your lifetime when creative resourcefulness in the face of limited resources was more needed?

Let's go.

NOTES

1. Lynn Curtis, interviewed by Amy Goodman, *Community Policing*, Democracy Now! March 28, 2000.

2. Patricia Troppe, Eric Isenberg, Anthony Milanowski, Roberta Garrison-Mogren, and Louis Rizzo, *The Transition to ESSA: State and District Approaches to Implementing Title I and Title II-A in 2017–18* (Washington, D.C.: U.S. Department of Education, 2020).

3. Betsy DeVos, "Key Policy Letters Signed by the Education Secretary or Deputy Secretary," U.S. Department of Education, March 20, 2020, https://www2.ed.gov/policy/gen/guid/secletter/200320.html.

PART ONE

Hip Hop Genius 1.0

Foreword 1.0

George Clinton

When I was thirteen years old, I heard a song called "Why Do Fools Fall in Love" by Frankie Lymon and the Teenagers. I had just moved to New Jersey and, barely a teenager myself, I was already working at a barbershop. I knew as soon as I heard that song that I wanted to make my living through making music. So I formed a doo-wop group and we practiced around the barbershop. Ten years later, we had our first hit single, "I Wanna Testify" and I have been traveling the universe ever since.

Just like Frankie Lymon inspired me, I have gone on to inspire others. Countless rap records have been made by sampling my songs and sounds, but it doesn't stop there. I've collaborated with some of the most talented hip-hop artists from *all over the country*—from Tupac to Too $hort, from Outkast to Wu Tang. And it isn't just about the music itself. It took a perfect storm to give birth to hip-hop and it was funk's ethos that taught hip-hop the fine art of dancing underwater without getting wet.

Because, like funk, hip-hop is not only a music, it's a way-of-life. For me, it was funk that opened doors to traveling the world, singing, writing, producing, and so many other opportunities. My musical ideas and abilities were my tickets, but funk was the passport. The same can be true for young people; through hip-hop they can discover how to transform one opportunity into the next new thing.

Whenever you hear people say, "That ain't music! That ain't no real music . . ." *That's* gonna be the new music. You can count on that being the new music. Because kids love to do what you don't want them to do. You don't like it . . . *That's what it's gonna be.* Think about it. Feedback on the guitar was noise when I was growing up. Jimi Hendrix made that sucka pleasurable!

That's what *Hip Hop Genius* is. Taking something that everyone else thought was a mistake and making it the next big sensation. Taking what you've already got in your DNA and unlocking it to make your circumstances

3

into something infinitely better. That's what I've had the chance to do. And so has David "TC" Ellis. He's done his job with the school, coming from the streets, kicking it about anything possible. Even when they try to stop his ass. And I know they've tried to stop him. But he's been doing it and he's still doing it and I'm glad to see he's still doing it.

And I'm glad to see the young people at the High School for Recording Arts doing what they do. Every day, these youngsters make the choice to be creative and collaborate in the face of the chaos around them. I know because I've been there.

I've walked through the school and felt the energy. I've been in their recording studio and watched a young man engineer as I stepped to the mic. I've rocked alongside their talented students and staff. I've known TC, the school's founder, since Prince introduced us and we recorded, performed, and appeared in a movie together!

I've seen how unique and transformational the educational model is and how hip-hop is saving lives. Through hip-hop, kids learn ways to count, sequence computers, and do the most involved tasks. Because we learn when we're interested in what we're learning.

If you can find a way to get somebody interested enough to learn, they'll do it themselves. The key is for them to learn how to learn. Not to learn tricks. To learn how to be open to learning. When you learn how to learn, *then* you're able to appreciate things.

So why aren't more people creating schools that understand and value this? When I was a teenager, I was passionate about music, but that passion had to be fed outside of school. I wish I could have gone to a high school that allowed me to focus on music and entertainment.

Every day, kids are getting struck by a desire to be something, the way I was struck by that Frankie Lymon song. The High School for Recording Arts is one of the few places I've seen that fashions itself to help those young people dive so deep into their dreams that they become their realities.

I wish everyone could visit this school. If you can't make it in person, read this book! I hope it inspires each and every one of you. I want it to spark a movement. Whether it is more schools like the High School for Recording Arts or a whole bunch of different programs coming together, I want to see a nation of talented, confident, creative young leaders rising up.

I'll see you up there!

George Clinton is the founder of Parliament, Funkadelic, P-Funk, and Mothers Hip Connection.

Foreword 1.0

Herbert Kohl

Hip-Hop Genius is an exuberant book. It tells the story of the HSRA in St. Paul, Minnesota, aka Hip-Hop High, and provides an in-depth portrait of what an effective special public high school can do to allow students, even those with the least successful school careers, to thrive.

The school is centered on the recording arts and hip-hop culture. In particular, hip-hop originated as rap-based music and dance performance in the South Bronx; hip-hop has grown into a cultural movement involving dress, entrepreneurship, and political and social activism—activism on a worldwide scale. Central to hip-hop is respect for the most creative, ingenious, and egalitarian aspects of urban African American youth culture.

Like all other cultural movements that hope to survive and grow, hip-hop culture needs to develop continuity through an education appropriate to the values it espouses. The HSRA in St. Paul is a bold and exciting attempt to build a high school rooted in this culture and based on performance, music and video production, community-based learning, the study of urban African American youth culture, and the development of performer and community-controlled businesses. It also attempts to integrate more traditional academic knowledge into its hip-hop focus. But it is resolutely centered on a music production studio, small businesses, and classes designed to analyze the role of African American teenagers in current social, political, and cultural production.

The school was developed by David "TC" Ellis who himself was a struggling student in the St. Paul public schools. According to Sam Seidel, TC "is a great school leader. This statement is true not *despite* the academic struggles he went through as a student, but *because* of them. . . . It has enabled him to understand the broad spectrum of experiences that comprise the realities for students and families at HSRA. TC has built the school to reflect and

5

make room for all of the talents and tragedies students bring through the door each day."

The brilliance of building a school around the recording arts is that the arts draw from a wide range of skills and talents. The entertainment industry employs lawyers; agents; publicists; marketing people; writers, composers, and lyricists; computer, video, and sound technicians; artists and illustrators; accountants and bookkeepers; businesspeople; producers; fundraisers; and set, costume, and rigging designers, as well as musicians and singers. The school is not for young people who want to be hip-hop artists but for students involved in a wide range of vocations who have to learn how to cooperate in order to develop, produce, and market a successful product. It is the kind of place that makes sense to many young African Americans and can lead them to complex learning and productive and profitable work.

The idea of a school for the recording arts takes the notion of having special arts, drama, music, and science high schools to a different level, with an enlarged vision of centering the school about an industry, not a particular aspect of it, such as performance.

A hip-hop school, such as HSRA, should not be mistaken for an Afro-centric school, though it is centered on certain aspects of contemporary African American and young people's culture. It is also not a school centered on black studies. It is basically an outpost for the development of hip-hop culture, for the active expression of what Sam Seidel calls Hip-Hop Genius.

The HSRA does not fit into models encouraged or mandated by No Child Left Behind or Race to the Top, but it does serve students who will not let themselves be left behind and are certainly running a race to the top, albeit on another path or maybe on a different mountain than that conceived of by politicians or educational professionals.

It is heartening to see such schools as HSRA emerging in the current educational climate. It reminds me of the sixties when, in the midst of a previous rigid-test-oriented era in public education, a number of decent schools that created more effective and student-oriented ways of educating high school students, such as Other Ways in Berkeley (where I was the director), the Group School in Cambridge, Independence High School in Newark, and the St. Paul Open School in St. Paul, were created. Ironically enough, David "TC" Ellis graduated from the St. Paul Open School.

The schools thrived for a while and then funding problems, political resistance from public school authorities, and at times just plain fatigue defeated or deflated most of them. All of these schools were willing to conform to the minimal requirements of obtaining public funding, such as some testing, legal responsibility, and evaluating and reporting their work to the school district. But they resisted attempts to rip their hearts out and become rigid, test-obsessed institutions.

Not surprisingly, HSRA is under similar pressure—as are other public high schools such as the El Puente Academy for Peace and Justice in Brooklyn. They always face the threat of being defunded since they do not fit the mold of the standards-and test-driven schools whose performance, when simplified and trivialized, can be summarized by test scores that can be used for national comparisons.

This book, in additional to making a strong case for the ideas driving HSRA, provides a powerful and vivid portrait of the workings of the school, of some of its students, and of the contents and specifics of activity at the school. It illustrates what students do, how they relate to the staff, how the curriculum is developed, and how decision making is distributed throughout all member of the school community. It also provides a history of the development of the school and its charismatic leader.

Now that HSRA and other schools that, like it, refuse to fit into a uniform model of the way high schools should work and how young people must be forced to learn are under siege, a book like *Hip-Hop Genius* is a weapon for the defense of the resilience, brilliance, and strengths of young people and for schools designed to serve them. I wish we had had such a book as a weapon for our self-defense during the struggles of the sixties. It provides evidence for the way in which diversity in schooling can overcome intractable problems of public education and should be used in defense of democratic, wider ranging schooling. The educational establishment is cynically obsessed with one-way schooling, and this book is a call for resistance and opposition through the power of the portrait it provides of what creative education looks like.

Herbert Kohl continues to teach. He is author of *36 Children, I Won't Learn from You,* and *The Discipline of Hope,* as well as other books on education.

Introduction 1.0

A TV satellite dish made of tin cans. A tattoo gun crafted out of a ballpoint pen and rubber bands. Turntables and speakers plugged into a streetlamp to power music for a block party. Cueing two records up to the same point and switching back and forth to extend dancers' favorite segments of songs. A high school dropout, turned graduate, turned drug addict, turned rapper, starting a school out of a recording studio . . .

These images exemplify *Hip-Hop Genius*—creative resourcefulness in the face of limited resources. Or as it is often said in the hip-hop community: flipping something outta nothing. In the context of a dismal national economy and an education system that abandons millions, particularly black and Latino students and students from low-and no-income families, this concept holds much-needed solutions.

The term *Hip-Hop Genius* was coined in 2005, when Isaac Ewell brought together a group of educators who were all hip-hop lovers concerned about the national dropout epidemic. Ewell had recently been hired as the director of the Black Alliance for Educational Options Small Schools Initiative.

In his work to support the formation of a network of secondary schools that provide high-quality choices for black students, Ewell had learned about a school in St. Paul, Minnesota, with an unusual model that was yielding promising results: the High School for Recording Arts (HSRA). Ewell was inspired by his first experiences at the school and invited several of us to join him on a subsequent trip.

"In HSRA I saw a school that could reach and retain the young people that few other schools wanted or knew how to serve," Ewell reflects on his first visit. Over the last six years, through his work with the Black Alliance for Educational Options, Ewell has stewarded grants to schools that provide highly structured programs for kids from the 'hood, such as the Boys' Latin of Philadelphia Charter School, where all students wear uniforms and study Latin, and many participate in extracurricular activities such as choir and a rowing team.

Boys' Latin has shown most every kind of success that can be demonstrated by a new school. But, while thrilled with the school's accomplishments,

Ewell acknowledges that these environments are not the best match for every student. "There's no one-size-fits-all solution," Ewell explains, adding that he believes he would have thrived at a school like HSRA.

"If we are serious about all kids succeeding, we really need a menu of options. Think about the cats who are really *really* struggling," Ewell pushes, "who maybe don't have anyone at home helping them get that tie on and out the door each morning? Who are having trouble figuring out how to be true to themselves and their community and at the same time be a successful and beneficial member of society?"

The young people Ewell is concerned about serving are not an anomaly in this country. Nationally, 1.23 million high school students are projected to leave school without a diploma this year.[1] Some are expelled, some more subtly encouraged to disappear, and some depart to pursue jobs, take care of children, or because school has been a painful place. These numbers are far worse for black, Latino, and Native American students; those whose families are poor; lesbian, gay, bisexual, and transgender young people; males; and those in urban schools.[2]

Although *Time* magazine hadn't yet declared on its cover that we were living in a "dropout nation," the group Ewell assembled at HSRA in 2005 already knew that our country was in a moment of crisis. He asked the six of us to consider the implications of HSRA's design in addressing the national education opportunity gap, especially as it affected young black men.

Students led us on a tour of the school, showing us the physical design and explaining how the institution functioned. At the end of the tour, one of the students, Devon Johnson, handed out business cards for his music production company and played us a few beats he had made. Impressed by the quality of Johnson's production and engineering, and always on the lookout for hot beats, I asked him if I could buy one of the instrumentals.

"No," he replied. "But we could make an arrangement whereby I'd license it to you for specific uses," he quickly added, explaining why he refused to sell his beats and pulling a two-page licensing contract from his folder. The group was blown away by Johnson's business savvy and how seamlessly it seemed to be integrated with his musical prowess.

Our hosts, HSRA's founder David "TC" Ellis and director of development Tony Simmons, described the school's origins and program design and shared stories of successes and challenges they had faced over the years. Fanon Wilkins, a professor of African American history and culture, probed the philosophical underpinnings of the school's approach and drew connections to black arts and social movements.

Having directed a community-based youth program that was an incubator for young hip-hop artists and leaders, I recognized and highlighted the possibilities that occur when students are engaged not as consumers but as creators.

Drawing on his experiences launching after-school tutoring companies, education entrepreneur Jason Green sparked a discussion of the scalability of the school's programs. Collectively we reflected on the global achievements of hip-hop culture and the devastating irony that the very demographics of young people who created it were being left behind.

Each of us had experience bringing hip-hop music and culture into our work as educators and was familiar with hip-hop-related educational approaches being implemented in various schools and programs around the country. We agreed that most of what we had done and seen was too literal and too literary. That is to say, hip-hop education had largely been viewed as classroom lessons focused on the texts of rap music.

While we had experienced and witnessed successes doing such work, we recognized its limitations: it often kept teachers in a position of authority—a peculiar position when studying something of which students often have more knowledge than their instructors; it generally occurred within traditional institutions that many young people found alienating; it privileged rap music over all other manifestations of hip-hop culture; and it often kept students in the position of consumers rather than creators of cultural products.

We also acknowledged that while we all identified hip-hop as a guiding cultural force in our lives, current students might choose to identify differently. For all of these reasons, we found ourselves drawn not just to the recording studios and overt study of hip-hop occurring at HSRA but to the more metaphorical manners in which the school embodied what we perceived to be hip-hop's essence.

In his essay "Dezyne Klass: Exploring Image-Making through the Visual Culture of Hip Hop," John Jennings, a friend of Fanon Wilkins and an associate professor of graphic design at the University of Illinois, shares his definition of hip-hop aesthetics. He suggests that due to the stark societal situations from which hip-hop emerged, it was a culture "forged in improvisation, pain, and a hope for better things."[3] Therefore, "Hip-hop was about taking nothing and making something. Its creators used what was present in their postmodern and seemingly dystopian environment and created a phenomenon."[4]

Chicagoan emcee Lupe Fiasco perfectly captures this sentiment in one line of a rap song: "I back-flipped on the mattress they slept on me on."[5] Here is a young man who feels unnoticed, who has been "slept on" by those who should have recognized his talent. Instead of shuffling off quietly, he takes an object that represents the public's doubt in him and literally flips on it, committing an act of physical agility, a staple of break dancing always sure to wow a crowd.[6]

In the 1970s, Lupe Fiasco's hip-hop predecessors in the predominantly black and Latino community of the South Bronx saw jobs disappear en masse as the area suffered from wounds inflicted by New York City's government, which had sliced through the borough to insert a highway for suburban commuters. From underfunded schools and social services to the destruction of buildings, parks, and streets for the construction of the Cross Bronx Expressway, New York City's government was, at best, neglecting and, at worst, deliberately destroying the neighborhood. Robert Caro—who wrote an exhaustive biography of Robert Moses, the urban planner responsible for the expressway—posits that Moses had a history of racist actions and intentionally sent the road through the South Bronx to damage the community, when there was a more direct route just below the neighborhood.[7]

In *Can't Stop Won't Stop: A History of the Hip-Hop Generation*, Jeff Chang breaks down the math on the exodus of jobs from the South Bronx around this time and concludes: "If blues culture had developed under the conditions of oppressive, forced labor, hip-hop culture would arise from the conditions of no work."[8] It was not a coincidence that, in the face of such racially charged economic challenges and alienation from the city's power structure, young people found the inspiration and ambition to splice wires into streetlamps, tapping the municipal grid to siphon electricity for community celebrations. Or that, in an exercise of similar bravado, young people in the same circumstances took preexisting recordings—some famous and some obscure—and manipulated them to make new music.

Artists in all genres have played and modified others' compositions; but it's another, bolder thing to chop them up and distort them by literally pulling the record backward on a turntable to make a totally different sound. In each of these instances, there's a technical innovation (converting the voltage of a streetlight to the voltage needed for speakers or wiring turntables to fade sound back and forth), but the technical know-how is only useful if you have the imagination, desire, and confidence to do something that's never been done.

As innovations emerge, societal systems respond to repress and co-opt actions that threaten the status quo. But resourceful creativity continues. Graffiti artists engaged in "reverse colonization," sneaking into train yards and reappropriating subway cars as mobile canvases.[9] They did not need representation from galleries to have their artwork seen. They painted trains and instantly had audiences all over the city. When the transit authority figured out how to clean paint and marker ink off of trains, artists sought new way to emboss their names and images. A bit of sandpaper only costs a few cents, but when scraped across glass or metal it transforms into a drawing implement that cannot be erased the way spray paint can.

At times, innovations in hip-hop culture have been sparked by tensions with laws and law enforcement. Alongside technical ability and creativity, a disregard for rules—whether on political grounds, out of necessity, out of a sense of rebellion, or out of a sense of exceptionalism—can be seen as an essential ingredient of hip-hop innovation. In some instances this has meant hip-hop heads engaging in acts that are considered illegal. Operating outside the law has come at a cost to some artists, as well as to some of those who follow in their footsteps, and others in their communities.

While *scratch tags* are an example of an illegal innovation, hip-hop artists often come up with creative solutions to regulation and repression that do not involve breaking any laws. Hip-hop DJs and producers began by using available resources, such as old records, in inventive ways to create a new style of music. But when the legal system came down on them for using pieces of other artists' music, producers responded by sampling shorter clips and distorting them, hunting down records that were not copyrighted, and using more sounds and instrumentation that they created on their own.

Whether it is metaphorical dances between artists and the legal system or the literal dances of b-boys and b-girls who lay discarded cardboard on the sidewalk to create dance floors, these types of invention do not occur *in spite of* restrictive circumstances, they occur *because* of them.[10]

"Can you teach people to be more creative?" someone once asked the philosopher Nelson Goodman. "Yes," he answered. When asked how, he replied, "Give them harder problems." Faced with racism, classism, ageism, and other forms of structural subjugation, many young people have developed the courage to break rules, the audacity to believe they can do things that have never been done, and the creativity to imagine how. This is hip-hop.

Hip-hop's music, culture, and creative resourcefulness originated in low-income, urban, predominantly black and Latino communities in the United States. While its roots extend around the world, particularly throughout the African diaspora, the sensibility, style, and spirit of hip-hop culture could only have brewed on this country's concrete.[11]

And yet hip-hop was never exclusively an urban thing, a low-income thing, a black thing, or a United States thing. Since its inception, hip-hop has touched and been touched by people from broader communities. In a matter of years, what started as a splash rippling through neighborhoods of New York City grew into tsunami-size waves rushing over continents, flowing into the biggest venues and markets in the world, and lapping up against individuals' psyches and souls.

Hip-hop is not the first cultural movement to emerge out of oppressive social conditions in the United States and rise to international popularity. Nor is it the first to combine music, dance, visual arts, and an overall aesthetic. The blues, jazz, early R&B, and funk all preceded hip-hop as art forms that emanated out of African American communities enduring the particular blend of racism and economic inequalities endemic to this country's history. Each of these musical genres was accompanied by specific styles of dance, dress, and speech—a culture. Pulling energy and influence from all of these predecessors, hip-hop has become a lasting means of understanding, existing in, and shaping the surrounding world.

A clear manifestation of this is the way in which rappers and hip-hop producers have taken their ability to lyrically and musically flip things into the business arena. Musicians from other genres have used their creativity to go from situations of extremely limited resources to tremendous wealth, but generally their creativity has been their product. They have sold their songs through preexisting systems of commerce, with businessmen—who were often white—reaping the lion's share of the profits.

In some instances, these musicians have also promoted other products, but they generally appeared as hired spokespeople, not business owners. Hip-hop artists have not just created a new kind of music; they have integrated how music is made and linked with other commodities, and altered systems of ownership and distribution in ways not previously considered possible by artists of any race.

Like all art forms that achieve popularity in this capitalist economy, hip-hop music has been co-opted and commodified by wealthy white outsiders to the culture. However, unlike any antecedents, hip-hop artists have refused to limit their creativity and swagger to their cultural products. By starting and cross-promoting their own record labels, media companies, clothing brands, lines of fragrances, and beverage companies, hip-hop stars have seamlessly enmeshed a fresh approach to the art of business into the business of art.

Hip-hop was forged in resistance to oppression, but hip-hop artists have demonstrated that the culture is no longer synonymous with struggle. Goodman may be right that "harder problems" breed creativity, but hip-hop's financial success has shown that such problems do not need to have life-or-death consequences for those involved; they can be theoretical, conceptual, strategic.

"Does the edge exist because you're poor, or does the edge exist because you're willing to challenge your reality in ways others may not?" asks hip-hop artist and activist Rha Goddess.[12] She cautions against falling into a paradigm in which struggling and starving are romanticized as prerequisites for creativity. The racism, classism, and ageism that inspired the birth of hip-hop still exist and continue to instigate innovations, but hip-hop cannot and should not be defined by desperation.

Ten years ago, if you asked a class full of fourteen-year-olds what they wanted to be when they grew up, a handful would have responded, "a rapper." Ask the question of current ninth-graders and several of those students will respond, "rapper-entrepreneurs." This melding of hip-hop art, identity, and industry led a man who grew up in the housing projects of Marcy to have clothing products at Macy's. Flipping his skills as an emcee to build his own entertainment/lifestyle conglomerate, Brooklyn-born Jay-Z returned to the mic in 2005, a year after becoming president and CEO of Def Jam Recordings, to spell it out for anyone who didn't understand: "I'm not a busi-nessman, *I'm a business*, maaan!"[13]

Although the multibillion-dollar industries that hip-hop has spawned are some of the most visible manifestations of the power and potential of hip-hop, the spirit of hip-hop is not at all limited to the realm of business. Hip-hop does not just concern itself with the content of music, culture, and commerce; its infectious mind-set and irreverent swagger rush into all aspects of society—from graphic design to community organizing to culinary arts. Hip-hop may have begun as a result of young people with limited resources figuring out how to find a power source so they could throw a party, but the same sensi-bilities have led to building the power of political parties.

Some hip-hop icons have built organizations and movements directed toward electoral engagement. Russell Simmons founded and serves as chair of the board of the Hip Hop Summit Action Network, a nonprofit organiza-tion that does a variety of community engagement and youth development work, including voter education and registration. Leading up to the 2004 elections, Sean "Diddy" Combs founded Citizen Change, a political service group that enlisted celebrities such as Mary J. Blige, Leonardo DiCaprio, and 50 Cent to encourage voting among the hip-hop generation. It's difficult to determine the precise effect of Diddy's "Vote or Die!" campaign, but 2004 saw the largest turnout of young voters in over thirty years.[14]

Jim Jones, Capone-N-Noreaga, the Beastie Boys, and many other hip-hop celebrities joined Simmons and Diddy to speak out against New York's Rockefeller drug laws. By drawing tens of thousands of people to rallies and releasing viral online videos, these artists brought much-needed public atten-tion to the organizing efforts that drug policy reform and prison reform activ-ists had been engaged in for decades against the mandatory sentencing laws. In 2009, after thirty-six years, the Rockefeller drug laws were overhauled to remove their most draconian elements.

Other groups like the Hip Hop Caucus and the League of Young Voters bring innovative organizing tactics to work with the hip-hop generation. Over the past six years, the Hip Hop Caucus has blended hip-hop culture, media, and grassroots organizing to build a 700,000-person membership base and launch national campaigns from "Green the Block" to the "Respect My Vote!" national bus tour.[15]

The League of Young Voters—which was initiated with the name "League of Hip Hop Voters"—has created a year-round, multipronged approach to voter organizing and education.[16] League chapters across the country register voters, put out voter guides to provide young voters with accessible informa-tion on all the candidates, and work to keep pressure on politicians once they are elected.

Hip-hop heads infuse the culture and sensibilities into their lives and work, no matter what they do. As a chef, author, and food-justice activist, Bryant Terry merges politics, culinary arts, and hip-hop. The section titles of his cookbook, *Vegan Soul Kitchen*, make reference to Kanye West, Outkast, and Method Man lyrics and each recipe is accompanied by a soundtrack. Leading up to the release of the book, Bryant borrowed a move from contemporary emcees. Like rappers releasing mix tapes to build hype for coming albums, Terry released free recipes over the Internet.

His publisher was concerned he was saturating the market with his material and that potential customers might not feel the need to buy the book when it came out. Terry, who had recently seen Lil Wayne's album *The Carter III* debut at number one on the charts after Wayne had flooded the streets and Internet with mix tapes, held his ground and his book is now the top-selling soul food cookbook and within the top twenty vegan cookbooks on the popular online book retailer Amazon.com.[17]

The above examples involve bringing fresh approaches to entrenched arenas. Multiple definitions of the word "fresh" apply here—*fresh* in the conventional sense of the word, meaning newly made or obtained, but also hip-hop *fresh*, which fits somewhere between "dope" and "hot" in the long list of words that hip-hop heads use to describe something favorably. And, of course, in Bryant Terry's instance, fresh has a third meaning, referring to the ingredients with which he is encouraging people to cook! What is most significant though, what makes each of these endeavors *hip-hop* beyond overt references to the culture, is the way in which their architects have pioneered new approaches to old fields.

To some, then, "Hip-Hop Genius"—the phrase that Ewell, Ellis, Simmons, Green, Wilkins, and I came up with during our 2005 meeting to describe the creative resourcefulness intrinsic to hip-hop—may sound redundant.[18] If the term "hip-hop" in and of itself implies such brilliance, why even add the word "genius"?

The English word "genius" was derived from the Latin root "gignere," meaning "to produce." It also had early ties to the Arabic word "jinn," which was used to describe individual spirits with supernatural powers. Prior to the late eighteenth century, *genius* was used to describe the magical force of an individual or a nation. In the decades leading up to the nineteenth century, European scholars began shifting the meaning of the word, using it to convey "the godlike power of invention, of creation, of making what never was before," which they used to describe the brilliant works of artists such as Homer and Michelangelo.[19]

Explaining why physicist Richard Feynman was considered the genius of his generation, biographer James Gleick concludes, "Those who tried to take Feynman's measure always came back to originality. . . . The generation coming up behind him, with the advantage of hindsight, still found nothing predictable in the paths of his thinking. He seemed perversely and dangerously bent on disregarding standard methods."[20] This explanation suggests that anything dubbed *genius* must be innovative not only in its results but also in its approach. It implies that a paradigm shift has occurred; someone has flipped or altered a deep-seated understanding of how things work.

More recently, in introducing *Black Genius: African American Solutions to African American Problems*, one of the volume's editors, Walter Mosley, returned to the early notion of *genius* as something that characterizes a populace. "We understand genius to be that quality which crystallizes the hopes and talents and character of a people," Mosley writes. "This kind of genius is something we all share. It is a presence where absence once reigned. It is the possibility for a people to look into their hearts and to see a life worth living."[21]

From supernatural abilities to collective solutions, from disregarding standard methods to the power of invention, the word *genius* carries multiple connotations. All of these meanings are relevant to the concept of Hip-Hop Genius.

Given that people have diverse, expansive, and conflicting perspectives of hip-hop, the addition of the word *genius* focuses attention on its majestic, creative, resourceful spirit. For people who view hip-hop as nothing more than a celebration of violence, sexism, homophobia, curse words, and a flagrant disregard for grammatical rules, just looking at these two phrases in conjunction with one another is a healthy exercise. Hip-Hop . . . Genius . . . Hip-Hop. Genius. HipHopGenius.

Young people who feel connected to hip-hop culture and are being slept on by society can benefit from considering the phrase *Hip-Hop Genius*. The greater the potential for their culture and actions to be accorded respect, the more self-confidence and hope can flourish.

Researchers have found that when students of color are asked to indicate their race at the beginning of a standardized test, on average they receive lower scores than control groups who are given the same test without being asked to identify their race. Social psychologists believe this stems out of a fear that their race is or may be perceived to be a disadvantage; they refer to this phenomenon as "stereotype threat."[22] In direct contrast then, the concept of Hip-Hop Genius has the potential to create *stereotype promise*.

Given that hip-hop is commonly associated with young people of color in urban environments, and given that this population has been perpetually portrayed by media outlets as "super predators,"[23] the concept of Hip-Hop Genius serves to challenge the typecasting of boys and girls in the 'hood.[24] By subverting the preconceptions of people who view inner-city children of color as criminals and charity cases, the possibility of those people acting as allies across race and class lines increases.

For those interested in dismantling systems of oppression and building a more just society, Hip-Hop Genius is an essential ingredient. As Brazilian educator Paolo Freire writes, "The oppressed can overcome the contradiction in which they are caught only when this perception enlists them in the struggle to free themselves."[25] The more intentional everyone is in honoring and cultivating young peoples' creativity and sense of empowerment, the more profound the changes young people will be able to enact both to their personal circumstances and to biased social structures.

Hip-Hop Genius holds the potential to play an important role in seeking solutions to global challenges. Our planet, as a whole, is facing a variety of situations defined by limited resources—most notably, the impending global energy crisis.

Wealthy people, companies, and countries all possess money and access to state-of-the-art equipment, but they have not necessarily cultivated the sensibilities needed to be resourceful. Identifying and honoring a form of genius that is sometimes noticed, but commonly ignored, trivialized, co-opted, and commodified, lends this raw brilliance the traction, recognition, and respect needed for it to spread like *Wild Style*.[26]

Discovery, development, and original thought are at the core of Hip-Hop Genius. This focus on artistic, intellectual, and technical innovation makes education a natural starting point when considering how to foster and support this brand of brilliance. Learning and teaching are *fundamental* to the well-being and growth of young people and our society, yet our education system abysmally fails so many.

As the statistics and stories in chapter 4 of this book demonstrate, this failure has been most egregious when it comes to the exact demographic of young people who have been at the forefront of hip-hop's creation and evolution. This is a powerful indication of the impact that the Hip-Hop Genius meme could have on the education system.

Much of hip-hop education thus far has been thought about within the context of classrooms in fairly conventional schools and out-of-school programs. Most often hip-hop is seen as a set of materials and skills that can replace the content of previous lesson plans. Instead of studying the novels of Joseph Conrad, classes study the lyrics of Joe Budden; instead of learning to write sonnets and haikus, they learn to write sixteens and hooks.

Embodying Hip-Hop Genius in an educational setting is deeper and more complex than bringing a rap song into an English class, painting a graffiti mural in a hallway, or inviting a break-dance troupe to a school assembly. It involves rethinking the very ways in which learning occurs. This is what the phrase "hip-hop pedagogy" should mean: an approach to teaching and learning that is specific to hip-hop.

But while "hip-hop pedagogy" has become an increasingly popular term in the last few years, little has been written about what might constitute the unique qualities of a hip-hop style of teaching and learning. The number of school principals who are members of the hip-hop generation is rapidly increasing, yet there has been little public dialogue about hip-hop leadership traits or the possibilities of hip-hop schools.

In many large cities, fewer than half of the black males who enter ninth grade graduate four years later. How might things change for these young men and others if schools could truly personify the spirit of Hip-Hop Genius, breaking with conventions to provide something fresh, functional, and fly? What would it look like to transform the education industrial complex in the same kinds of ways that hip-hoppers have freaked the music industry?

This book exists to bust open these conversations.

Chapter 1 introduces an innovative school, the High School for Recording Arts. Throughout its twelve years of operation in St. Paul, Minnesota, the school has avoided the limitations of traditional educational practices by blending elements of a variety of alternative educational techniques with original flavor. Through inventive and sometimes unusual approaches, the school has found unique ways to honor the brilliance of young people who have been ignored, shunned, and feared by the institutions charged with educating them. By giving readers a tour through the halls of the school and a description of the pedagogy, curriculum, and philosophy employed by the school, this chapter suggests a set of creative and promising educational practices that could be reproduced and remixed in other schools or used as inspiration for innovation in other sectors.

Because HSRA is so different from traditional schools, it can be hard to picture how the pedagogy, curriculum, and philosophy play out on a day-to-day basis. Chapter 2 follows a student through one full school day, demonstrating how the ideas described in the previous chapter manifest in the daily reality of a school community. Though it is only a description of *one* day of *one* student's experience, this chapter tethers theory to practice and provides a snapshot of how the school's philosophies, values, and methodologies affect individual students.

To understand HSRA, you have to understand how it came to exist. Chapter 3 shares stories of the school's creation and evolution by offering an intimate introduction to its founder, David "TC" Ellis. Tying stories from TC's childhood and his experiences recording with superstars such as Prince and George Clinton to challenges he has faced running the school, chapter 3 teases out unconventional yet essential qualities of TC's leadership style. From repurposing gangsta rappers' recording equipment to working with gang leaders to help squash beefs at the school, TC's trajectory holds tangible examples of the bold, unorthodox actions that exemplify Hip-Hop Genius. Without proposing that anyone should or could follow directly in TC's footsteps, these stories can provoke readers, both in and outside the field of education, to reconsider what is possible and to hustle hard.

Describing problems that plague public education in this country, chapter 4 contextualizes the struggles and successes of HSRA's students and the school itself. By presenting obstacles that HSRA has encountered in the past few years, this chapter introduces common challenges that inevitably have an impact on educators attempting to create schools that effectively serve low-and no-income students of color.

Such challenges can be especially harsh for educators who incorporate hip-hop into their practice. Yet the field of hip-hop education is growing. Chapter 5 surveys the current hip-hop education landscape, identifying how HSRA fits into several trends in the field and proposing Hip-Hop Genius as a new iteration of hip-hop education that is more radical in its approach and better positioned to fully honor the creativity and ingenuity of urban young people.

Chapter 6 suggests specific strategic possibilities for spreading the school's work and the ethos of Hip-Hop Genius. From replicating the school's design in new sites to turning the program in Minnesota into an open source laboratory for other educators and hip-hop heads to visit and learn from, this chapter explores how HSRA can be most effective in influencing ideas and infusing inspiration into the hip-hop and education communities.

There is so much potential for beauty and creation, and yet violence and destruction dominate headlines and minds. Children—full of energy and ideas—are neglected, punished because of how much melanin they have in their skin and how little money they have in their pockets. Personal greed, contempt, and contentment too often triumph over asking hard questions, striving for equality, and making meaningful change.

Society has been sleeping for too long. It's time to back-flip on that mattress.

NOTES

1. Christopher B. Swanson and Amy M. Hightower, "Diplomas Count 2008: School to College," PowerPoint slide 4, http://www.edweek.org/media/ew/dc/2008/DC08_Presentation_FINAL.pdf (accessed December 16, 2010).

2. Further statistics on the demographics of students who are not graduating from high school are provided in chapter 4.

3. John Jennings, "Dezyne Klass: Exploring Image-Making through the Visual Culture of Hip Hop," in *Design Studies: Theory and Research in Graphic Design,* ed. Audrey Bennett (New York: Princeton Architectural Press, 2006), 241.

4. Jennings, "Dezyne Klass," 242.

5. Wasalu Muhammad Jaco aka Lupe Fiasco, "Just Might Be Okay," *Lupe Fiasco's Food & Liquor,* 1st and 15th/Atlantic, 2005, compact disc.

6. I have chosen to use the term "break dancing" rather than "b-boying," which is considered by many the more authentic term for hip-hop dance. This decision was made because the inclusion of the word "dance" clarifies what I am referring to and because it does not carry the same gender privileging that "b-boying" implies.

7. Robert A. Caro, *The Power Broker: Robert Moses and the Fall of New York* (New York: Knopf, 1974).

8. Jeff Chang, *Can't Stop Won't Stop: A History of the Hip-Hop Generation* (New York: Picador, 2005), 13.

9. Chang, *Can't Stop Won't Stop,* 118.

10. B-boys and b-girls are hip-hop dancers.

11. For a more comprehensive explanation of hip-hop as black American music, see Imani Perry, *Prophets of the Hood: Politics and Poetics in Hip Hop* (Durham, N.C.: Duke University Press, 2004).

12. Rha Goddess, "Scarcity and Exploitation: The Myth and Reality of the Struggling Hip-Hop Artist," in *Total Chaos: The Art and Aesthetics of Hip-Hop,* ed. Jeff Chang (New York: Basic Civitas, 2006), 346.

13. Shawn C. Carter aka Jay-Z, "Diamonds from Sierra Leone Remix," on *Late Registration,* by Kanye West, Roc-A-Fella/Island Def Jam, 2005, compact disc.

14. Jose Antonio Vargas, "Vote or Die? Well, They Did Vote," *Washington Post,* November 9, 2004, http://www.washingtonpost.com/wp-dyn/articles/A35290–2004Nov8.html (accessed June 12, 2010).

15. For more information about the Hip Hop Caucus, see http://www.hiphopcaucus.org/ (accessed December 16, 2010).

16. The League of Young Voters has also been known as the League of Pissed-Off Voters. For more information, see http://www.theleague.com (accessed December 16, 2010).

17. Amazon.com, http://www.amazon.com/Vegan-Soul-Kitchen-Bryant-Terry/dp/0738212288 (accessed June 18, 2010).

18. The term "hip-hop" can be spelled several different ways, with and without hyphen or space and with varying capitalization. Throughout this book it will be spelled, "hip-hop" with the exception of when it appears in direct quotes, titles, and in the phrase "Hip Hop Genius."

19. James Gleick, *Genius: The Life and Science of Richard Feynman* (New York: Pantheon Books, 1992), 313.

20. Gleick, *Genius,* 323.

21. Walter Mosley, introduction, *Black Genius: African American Solutions to African American Problems,* ed. Walter Mosley et al. (New York: W. W. Norton, 1999), 12.

22. Claude M. Steele and Joshua Aronson, "Stereotype Threat and the Test Performance of Academically Successful African Americans," in *The Black-White Test Score Gap*, ed. Christopher Jencks and Meredith Phillips (Washington, D.C.: Brookings Institution Press, 1998), 401.

23. Elaine Brown, *The Condemnation of Little B* (Boston: Beacon Press, 2002), 108–11.

24. This refers to the title of John Singleton's 1991 film portraying urban youth in south central Los Angeles.

25. Paulo Freire, *Pedagogy of the Oppressed* (New York: Herder and Herder, 1971), 34.

26. This refers to the title of Charlie Ahearn's 1983 film depicting early hip-hop legends engaging in hip-hop arts. It is considered by many to be the first hip-hop motion picture.

Chapter 1

Hip-Hop High 1.0

Be a true friend to him
Before the shit put an end to him
Give a pen to him
Or lock him in a studio with a mic
'cause on the reals
It might save his life.
—The Roots

Do not train a child to learn by force or harshness; but direct them to it by what amuses their minds, so that you may be better able to discover with accuracy the peculiar bent of the genius of each.—Plato

Our goal is to get students mad enough to want more and smart enough to get it in a whole different way.—Tony Simmons

The first thing you see as you enter the High School for Recording Arts (HSRA) is a professional-quality recording studio with a red "In Session" light over the door. It's immediately clear that this studio is official: huge mixing boards, large flat-screen monitors, a glass window that reveals a microphone booth, waves of black foam on the walls, and the requisite leather sofa in the corner.

Donte Suttle, aka "Humble Child," and "Lil Layne" Bellamy are debating which combination of microphone and software is best for creating the Auto-Tune vocoder effect that T-Pain's spate of R&B hits recently brought back from obscurity.[1] Donte is seated in an ergonomic chair in front of a keyboard. He's wearing a black fitted cap and a long black T-shirt. Lil Layne is seated across from him, wearing a wave cap and baggy sweatpants. Donte and Lil Layne are studio engineers, and both of these men are graduates of the school.

The studio director, "Uncle Phil" Winden, enters and is asked his opinion on the matter. Phil is in his forties. His closely cropped hair and beard include some gray hairs and his clothes fit a bit tighter than his younger associates. A quick conversation with Uncle Phil makes two things clear: one, he has a lot of experience as a professional studio engineer; and two, he is excited to teach others how to use all the fancy equipment at their fingertips.

A stroll around the school shows that beyond the recording studios this place has some obvious differences from Central, Highland Park, Como, and the other big high schools in the Twin Cities. First of all, there are no class-rooms! There is a giant open workspace, approximately five thousand square feet divided into distinct work areas by low corrugated steel partitions, lined with counters holding computers.

In one of the five work areas, a group of twelve students is sitting in a circle of chairs discussing the book *Monster* by Walter Dean Myers. In another work area, seven students are seated at computers working quietly. There is one Latina student and one white young man. All the other students in both these groups are black.

A young woman with her hood pulled over her head has a stack of pamphlets on teen health and sexually transmitted diseases on one side of her computer and a book on website design on the other. Next to her, a young man wearing headphones is using spreadsheet software to create a rubric for how to rate emcees. Behind these two, another student is turned away from her computer, discussing her idea for a research project on the history of the WNBA with a woman in her thirties who's wearing a USB jump drive on a lanyard around her neck.

At the other end of the giant room, there is an open space that can be separated from the work areas by sliding glass garage doors. This area, which is referred to as "the blacktop," has a stage in the front and a DJ booth with a soundboard and spotlight in the back. In the middle of the space there are cafeteria tables. Six students sit on top of tables, their feet on the attached benches. They are talking and laughing. Two of them have their cell phones out and, during lulls in the conversation, they return to texting.

One sidewall of the area is covered in graffiti; students' nicknames and tags, a cartoon keyboard and musical notes, and a big "Studio 4" piece are spray-painted across the wall. Along the other side of the room, there are vending machines—one of which offers blank CDs for a dollar a piece.

In the hallways that extend off of the large room, photos line the walls, telling visual stories of students and staff traveling the world together—Africa, Guatemala, New York, Washington, D.C., and other cities across the United States. Additional photos feature an impressive list of African American celebrities visiting the school—scholar Michael Eric Dyson, actress Lynn Whitfield, jazz trombonist Delfeayo Marsalis, and rappers such as Ice Cube, Juelz Santana, and Chris "Kazi" Rolle.

Doors along each hall open onto smaller rooms containing administrative offices; multimedia workspaces; a dance studio complete with wood floors, mirrored walls, and a ballet barre; a graphic design lab; and a record label boardroom. The boardroom is decorated with clocks that show the time in major cities, a large whiteboard, and color posters of the label's album releases. One of the posters features a rap album by David "TC" Ellis, the founder of the school. Another poster advertises the release of an album by an alumnus and current employee of the school, Codie Wilson aka "Monsta Codie Indiana."

Down the hall from the boardroom, TC is standing talking to two students. He appears to be almost twenty years older than the image on the poster and he has traded in the sunglasses he was rocking in the photo for a baggy rugby shirt and a gold chain with a medallion in the shape of the African continent. Leaning up against the wall, flipping his cell phone open and shut against his leg, he is breaking down to the two young men some of the ways in which he sees students hold each other back from achieving greatness.

Without knowing anything specific about the curriculum or population, one thing is clear just from wandering the halls: HSRA is not your typical high school.

HYBRID FLAVOR

Hip-hop has never been about creating fly things from scratch. Of course, there is an irony to this statement because hip-hop disc jockeys have created so much fly music from the *scratching* of records. But the records they were scratching contained musical compositions by other artists who came before them.

DJs began selecting and repeating the most climactic segments of other musicians' recordings as part of live routines they would perform to keep partygoers dancing. The practice evolved into a set of compositional techniques that now create the backbone of the majority of hip-hop songs. By merging multiple looped samples and original instrumentation, audial pastiches are created that, in one song, can fuse musical gems from multiple genres that may have never previously intermingled.

This sort of creative collaging has long been celebrated as a quality of geniuses. In his 1767 *Essay on Original Genius*, William Duff discusses the genius's imagination as "the mind not only reflect[ing] on its own operations" but also as a faculty by which one "assembles the various ideas . . . treasured up in the repository of the memory, compounding or disjoining them at pleasure; and which, by its plastic power of inventing new associations of ideas, and of combining them with infinite variety, is enabled to present a creation of its own."[2]

In the painstaking process of combining disparate components to craft an original composition, every decision must be deliberate. Finding clips that

sound good on their own may take DJs hours of digging, but the bigger challenge is that the samples have to syncopate and sound even better together.
As more layers are added, the difficulty of aligning pieces in a harmonious
manner increases. Not only must producers balance these challenges but, in
order to be successful, they must do it in such a way that establishes their
own trademark style.

In his essay on the aesthetics of hip-hop literature, Adam Mansbach refers
to hip-hop's instinct to borrow and blend as "intellectual democracy through
collage."[3] This cut-and-paste intellectual democracy is exemplified in the
DJing of Afrika Bambaataa, who would mix Grand Funk Railroad with
the Monkees and drop a Malcolm X speech on top.[4] No matter how corny
the Monkees' reputation was, if they had a dope drum break, it was getting
played. The rule, as Mansbach points out, is that "whatever's hot is worthy of
adoption, regardless of its location or context."[5]

This tradition of sampling and reassembling is not integral just to hip-hop
music but to other aspects of the culture as well, for instance, dance. As
Nelson George points out: "What came to be labeled [breakdancing], was
actually a medley of moves adapting a number of sources—the shuffling,
sliding steps of James Brown; the dynamic, platformed dancers on Don
Cornelius's syndicated *Soul Train* television show; Michael Jackson's robotic
moves that accompanied the 1974 hit 'Dancin' Machine'; the athletic leg
whips and spins of kung fu movies—all of which were funneled through the
imagination of black New Yorkers."[6] Capoiera moves and Latin dance steps
could be added to this list, as well as other influences, large and small.

HSRA has taken this approach and implemented it in the field of education. The founders of the school do not claim to have invented the educational
and youth development practices at play within the school. Rather, they are
proud of the ways in which they have sampled, mixed, screwed, and chopped
a medley of innovative approaches to education, entrepreneurship, artistic
production, youth development, and the provision of support services.

HSRA's hybrid flavor comes from blending elements from a vast array of
sources, most notably from a several-decade-long lineage of public alternative schools that have carved out niches for themselves through negotiating
local politics, using limited funds effectively, and extreme dedication from
their staff members, students, families, and communities. These schools have
challenged conventional hierarchical power structures as well as commonly
accepted delivery methods and mandated curricula.

By engaging students as leaders and scholars, running classes democrati-
cally, introducing a wide variety of materials, building a supportive culture,
and offering students opportunities to learn in real-world contexts, many
of these alternative programs have managed to attract and retain students,

helping them to get excited about learning, earn diplomas, and prepare for life beyond high school.

If HSRA were an album, there would be extensive liner notes attributing the influences to which the school owes aspects of its unique composition. Inevitably, as there are so many elements from so many sources, some much-deserved head nods would be missed along the way, but what is crucial to understand is that there are many trajectories from which these educational solutions emerge; the genius of HSRA is the fusion.

RESPECT'S THE GAME

To explain what makes HSRA an extraordinary school, multiple concepts must be unpacked—project-based learning, advisories, authentic assessment, youth empowerment—but there is one fundamental value from which all decisions about how to run the school stem, that all students feel when they enter the school, and that troubles the traditional-minded: *The respect for the brilliance and resilience of young people—especially kids from the 'hood.* Students are not seen as problems to be solved or empty vessels waiting to be filled. They are valued as thinkers, artists, and entrepreneurs—survivors and thrivers.

There is a technical term for this value that is used in the nonprofit community: Asset-Based Community Development. This concept came about as a response to the most common way that institutions in this country treat communities of color with limited economic resources—a dehumanizing, "needs-based" presumption of deficiencies.

An increasing number of institutions are recognizing that the deficit model is the wrong approach. Some make efforts to embrace young peoples' skills and capacities but are too stuck in their old ways to move much beyond lip service. However, in the past fifteen years, the most progressive schools and youth programs have focused enormous energy on finding solutions in the strengths and talents within their communities. This trend permeates HSRA.

By requiring students to take the lead in designing their own curriculum, HSRA honors students' individual identities and capabilities. By partnering with social service agencies to provide support services, HSRA shows respect for students' fundamental rights to physical safety, health, housing, and transportation. And by creating real-world leadership opportunities, HSRA shows students the highest form of respect, the expectation that they can and should be traveling the world, representing their community, and making a difference in the lives of others.

ANOTHER LEVEL OF LEADERSHIP FOR STUDENTS

One of the strongest manifestations of the respect that students are afforded can be seen through the student-run record label and event production company, Another Level Entertainment. Through the label, students are empowered to make decisions typically assumed to be the domain of adults.

"I'm in the middle of everything," explains Buki, an HSRA senior, who is the current president of Another Level Entertainment. Before coming to HSRA, Buki attended Central High School for one semester. She didn't feel she was getting anything out of her time there and she intentionally got kicked out so that she could transfer to HSRA.

When she first arrived at HSRA, Buki wanted to be a rapper. She recalls that "after about a year and a half pursuing that dream, I realized that rapping wasn't quite my swagg." Instead, Buki discovered her passion for "helping other people handle their business."

When she's not attending courses at the local community college or working on the nonprofit she recently founded, Buki now spends much of her time making phone calls to arrange performances, facilitating meetings, and coordinating the production of an album promoting nonviolence, which is being put together by the school's Urban Music workshop.

Throughout the label's history, the students who staff Another Level Entertainment have focused on a diverse array of projects. Over the years they have collaborated with adults at the school to produce peers' albums, fulfill recording and performance contracts with businesses and government agencies who hire them to raise awareness about topics such as seat belt safety and the importance of staying in school, manage the label's finances, arrange performances, host school events, and produce a weekly radio show, the Fo-Show, on the local commercial hip-hop station.[7]

This is a unique approach to running a high school and a unique approach to running a record label. But it is especially distinctive given the cultural context of the geographic area in which the school is located. The school's education director, Paula Anderson, explains that the school "is one of the few places in Minnesota where African American culture is dominant."

The school's predominantly black student body has grown up surrounded by a predominantly white culture. Prior to attending HSRA, many students have been in schools that have little in common with their home cultures and experiences outside of school.

It can be eye-opening for students to be exposed to materials from outside their cultural contexts, but when the language, style, and subject matter they encounter in classes and other school activities is consistently foreign to them, students can become alienated. This has an adverse effect on achievement.[8]

In order to better serve students, educators must address this "cultural mismatch."[9] The multicultural tapestry of this country's current student population is incredibly complex. Bridging cultural divides is not, literally or figuratively, a black and white issue. Nor is it simply a matter of celebrating the food or customs of the many cultures from which students come. A deeper integration of young peoples' cultural experiences is needed in order for schools to be relevant to their students.

There are many ways that schools can and should engage students' cultural identities more thoroughly. Due to hip-hop's pervasive nature and the fact that it is such a wellspring of cultural cues, vocabulary, and other forms of identification, it holds great power as a source of cultural connections. Through celebrating and engaging with hip-hop, HSRA honors what is, for many students, their deepest passion.

It is extremely important to acknowledge that by no means do all young people—black, Latino, or otherwise—identify with hip-hop culture. For instance, HSRA has had students who prefer rock music and goth style. Nevertheless, hip-hop is one of HSRA students' primary cultural contexts and by incorporating a hip-hop record label into the program, HSRA sends the message, even to students who don't personally identify with hip-hop, that a spectrum of cultural and "countercultural" experiences is being recognized and engaged in the school community.

The fact that students are entrusted to run the record label, that they have access to professional quality equipment, and that this work is not relegated to one of the common diminutive categories of "after-school project" or "elective" but rather is viewed as a central piece of their academic program communicates a high prioritization of young peoples' interests and capabilities—even to students not personally passionate about hip-hop and not directly involved in Another Level Entertainment.

STUDENT VOICES ARE HEARD

HSRA's embrace of students' participation in hip-hop music and culture goes beyond the student-run record label. The school's logo has a picture of a kid in front of a microphone. His hat is turned back and he's wearing headphones.[10] Students who have consistent attendance and are in good academic standing earn an "All Access Pass," which allows them to spend free time, afternoons, weekends, and evenings in the recording studios.

Every week, students are not only allowed but encouraged to perform in a school-wide showcase, which is called a Pick Me Up.[11] In the context of school, a young person can don sunglasses and a fitted hat, grab a microphone, and spit lyrics straight from the heart, dancing across a stage followed by a spotlight, while being cheered on by fellow students and staff. This literal and figurative spotlight plays an important role in students' lives. For a host of reasons—including racism, classism, sexism, ageism, and homophobia—many students at HSRA have been ignored or told countless times, implicitly and explicitly, that their lives do not matter.

Some young people shut down as a result of such identity abuse. Others decide they will be seen and heard *one way or another*. For some, this means tireless investment in academic, athletic, entrepreneurial, or political pursuits. For others, it means acquiring luxury cars, flossy jewelry, and other accessories that will attract attention, by any means necessary. And for others, it means finding their way to the front page of the newspaper, even if it's for engaging in an act of violence or destruction. By offering opportunities to produce radio shows, CDs, and performance showcases, HSRA is providing students with creative and legal channels by which to be seen and heard.

HSRA also demonstrates respect for students by cultivating conditions that honor their lives and foster their success. For instance, like many other programs, HSRA has struggled with chronic absence and tardiness. In addition to coming up with consequences that discourage lateness, the staff and students have worked hard to understand the problem and generate innovative solutions.

One of the most fruitful changes they have instituted is to start later than almost any other high school in the country: The HSRA school day does not begin until 10 a.m. They came to this schedule shift organically through experience and dialogue, but scientific research, such as a study recently released in the *Journal of Clinical Sleep Medicine,* has since demonstrated that later school start times are actually more in line with teenagers' natural circadian rhythms. Despite the fact that data shows that later start times improve attendance and academic performance, few other schools have adjusted their schedules.[12]

The school day at HSRA also runs longer than most schools, officially ending at 4:30 p.m., with many students and staff members staying later to work on school projects, personal endeavors, and just to hang out. Given that most arrests of teenagers occur during weekday afternoons, keeping the school open during these times helps students stay productive and avoid dangerous situations.[13]

STUDYING ISSUES RELEVANT TO STUDENTS' LIVES

How can students take adults seriously if those adults don't acknowledge the challenges students face during the eighteen hours every day that they are not in school? HSRA staff members design group projects and workshops that explore societal problems, such as homelessness and violence. Through these projects and workshops, students create products—often musical compilations—that present their research and ideas in ways that can inform and inspire deeper thinking and conversation among others.

Workshops on topics such as the prison–industrial complex address the race and class conflicts that students are experiencing but have rarely been invited to discuss or analyze in school settings. HSRA staff members and students identify dynamics of oppression that are playing out within the school community and build opportunities for group study and conversation.

When Libby Harris was in her first year as an advisor at the school, she was overwhelmed by the prevalence of homophobic and misogynistic language used by students. Sick of hearing students call each other "bitch" in the halls or use "gay" to describe something they didn't like, she decided to offer a workshop on "The Power of Words" to "examine the language of ethnic, gender, and sexual orientation bias."[14] Using materials from an organization called Teaching Tolerance, Libby crafted a curriculum for a workshop.

"In most schools, I couldn't do what I'm doing in this workshop," Libby reflected after the first week, "I couldn't give out a reading with words like 'bastard' and 'pussy-whipped.'" Libby used this language to provoke students' thinking about the ways in which many words that insult men actually contain hidden insults to women. Initially her use of such language inspired some snickers and giggles, but eventually the group of students who had elected to be a part of the workshop settled into a mature discussion that touched on topics that many said they'd never discussed openly before.

When Libby says she would not have been able to lead a workshop like the Power of Words at most schools, she is speaking from experience. Prior to coming to HSRA, Libby taught at a middle school in suburban Wisconsin, which was under referendum requiring all teachers to implement the same curriculum. There was no room for doing anything different for students who had unique interests or needs. She had been reprimanded for talking with her students about global warming and suggesting it might be a cause for concern.

By contrast, at HSRA students and staff are encouraged to spend time learning about and analyzing current events. At the school's inception, the only textbook that teachers used was the daily newspaper. More recently, during the fall of 2008, as the country geared up for a historic presidential election, the entire school read President Barack Obama's *Dreams from My Father: A Story of Race and Inheritance* and discussed the book in the context of the election and the media's coverage of the candidates.

These types of workshops and activities build on the work of educators like Paulo Freire, encouraging students to peel back the many layers of their realities, ask critical questions, imagine the world they would like to live in, and consider ways in which they can take action to become the change they want to see.[15]

ALTERNATIVE APPROACHES TO ACADEMICS

If it is the music that initially attracts students to HSRA and the respect they receive that compels them to stay, it is the academic program that opens up new possibilities for their scholastic success. The key to the academic component of the school is that it too honors students' interests and intelligence.

Students are not forced through a four-year pipeline with standardized boxes to check off along the way, and the staff's role is not to lecture or issue unilateral assignments but rather to work with each student to customize her or his academic experience to maximize learning. Staff members work with each student to develop an individualized course of study that builds on that individual student's background, taps into their passions, and meets their needs as far as graduation requirements and skills necessary to pursue further education and employment.

How does something like this fit into the structure of a school? It is not possible to truly honor students' diverse interests, learning styles, strengths, and challenges if a bell is ringing every forty-five minutes and teachers are seeing more than one hundred students every day. So how do you move all students along toward graduation if every student is following a different trajectory?

FROM CARNEGIE UNITS TO MOVING UNITS

In most high schools, the only way students can graduate is by receiving course credits. The only way they can acquire these credits is by sitting in specific classes with specific titles, such as "U.S. History," for a predetermined amount of time every day for nine months.

In education lingo, the standard amount of time a student must spend in a class in order to earn credit is called a Carnegie unit, which consists of 120 hours. This system does not measure what a student knows or can do; instead, it simply counts how many minutes they spent in a classroom.

At HSRA, there are five ways that students can earn credit, all of which involve *demonstrating* what they can do as a result of what they have learned:

1. The most encouraged and popular path to earning credits is through designing and completing projects. Each project can be done as an individual or in a small group and culminates in the presentation of an original product. One common example of a student project is the

recording of an album. A student can earn Language Arts credit by authoring lyrics and liner notes; Social Studies credits by selecting and researching topics for songs on the album; Science credits by studying the physics of sound waves; and Math credits by developing a budget that calculates production and reproduction costs. In this way, a student can develop core academic skills while fulfilling her dream to not only become a rapper but actually produce an album and get it into peoples' hands. Instead of sitting back and earning Carnegie units, students are moving units, earning money and respect.

2. Through workshops. These workshops may be led by school staff members, outside instructors, alumni, or fellow students. Some regularly offered workshops include Urban Music, through which students collectively produce an album about a social issue, such as HIV prevention; The Business of Music, which offers students an introduction to the commercial and legal issues related to the music industry; and Design, which gives students a chance to develop products for real-world clients.

3. Through daily blocks of time spent in their advisories focused on math, reading, and language arts. These group-study sessions were added to the school's design in recent years in response to pressure from the Minnesota Department of Education to raise students' scores on high-stakes standardized tests. Some students and staff members feel that the daily chunks of time carved out for Concentrated Math, Quiet Reading, and Daily Language Arts are a hindrance to the individualized interest-based curriculum that lies at the heart of the academic program. Others appreciate the time set aside to ensure that all students are getting direct instruction in core academic subjects.

4. Through completing guided study packets that are structured to build skills and allow students to demonstrate their competency in specific academic areas. While advisors generally discourage students from trying to get lots of credits by completing packets, it can be an efficient way to "make up time" for students who are in their late teens or early twenties and feel the need to accelerate their journey to graduation.

5. Through Minnesota's Post-Secondary Education Option, which allows students to take college courses for free while in high school. Many states have similar programs, and increasing numbers of high school students are enrolling. Currently about fifteen HSRA students take advantage of this opportunity each year. Staff members are encouraging more students to consider this chance to get college credits and experience at no cost prior to graduation.

Through projects, workshops, academic blocks, packets, and college courses, students are expected to *show* what they know. Without a sophisticated system, it would be unfeasible for the staff of HSRA to keep track of the accomplishments of over two hundred students simultaneously engaged in their own unique blends of these methods. This would make it impossible to determine when students were qualified to graduate. To this end, HSRA has a list of "validations" that serve as the school's graduation requirements. On students' first day at the school, they are introduced to the validation system and empowered to take a lead role in keeping track of their own progress toward graduation.

Using a process pioneered by Dr. Wayne Jennings and colleagues at the St. Paul Open School, which TC attended in the late 1970s, HSRA has developed twelve "learning areas" and defined what students must produce in each area to demonstrate competence. These are the HSRA validations.

Some of HSRA's validations—such as Mathematics, Reading/Literary Analysis, and Science and Technology—are pulled directly from state standards, but they are put into language that is more accessible to students. Other validations—such as Artistic Expression and Appreciation, and Philosophical, Emotional, and/or Spiritual Awareness—emerged from school staff considering what they want all HSRA graduates to know and be able to do.

Most validations contain some state-mandated benchmarks and some school-determined criteria. For example, in the learning area of "Effective Communication," a student must pass the Minnesota Basic Standards Tests in Writing and Reading, but the student must also demonstrate "effective oral communication, which may include presentations, spoken word performances or recordings, interviews, participation in group discussions, formal oral responses, and effective day-to-day speaking."[16] In this way, HSRA blends samples of standardized assessment systems that may be used to measure students as they apply to colleges with a mix of skills that will be valuable for students in their future endeavors.

As students develop projects, select workshops, decide which guided study packets they would like to complete, and enroll in college courses, they communicate with their advisors about which validations each of these endeavors will help them achieve and how they will determine when the validations have been completed.

Advisors help students identify people who possess expertise in each learning area and can therefore serve as validators. For instance, for "Science and Technology," the validator must be a certified science instructor, while for a learning area like "Physical Education," the validator could be a boxing coach outside of the school who can verify that a student has demonstrated progress in that particular area.

The school has invested time and resources in developing *Project Excellence*, a proprietary software program designed to track each student's progress in demonstrating proficiency at the validations. Part of each student's responsibility is to document her or his progress in each learning area. Students are able to log into Project Excellence at school or from home to update their profile. Staff members can also access students' pages on Project Excellence to check on progress and correspond with students about their work.

LINES OF DESIRE

When architects and urban planners design open outdoor spaces, sometimes they delay paving paths. Landscapers seed grass everywhere and then the designers sit back and wait.

Wherever the grass is worn down from frequent foot traffic, pavement is then laid. This process of letting pedestrians dictate the paths by walking where they want to go is referred to as "lines of desire."

The style of project-based learning at HSRA functions in a similar way. Rather than educators coming with a preconceived plan for what students will study, they seed possibilities everywhere and then hang back to see where students' interests draw them. Once students have tread their individual paths, the staff members figure out how to help solidify their course ways.

There are two key manners in which the HSRA educator's work differs from the designer's in the above metaphor. While the designer is looking for a general pattern among all walkers traversing their new green, HSRA staff must find a way to support each student on her or his own journey. Also, unlike pedestrians who all walk on concrete of the same density, grade, and texture, each learner needs customized reinforcements. In this way, educators also have to be alchemists, crafting a unique blend of elements to properly support each student.

Project-based learning is a pedagogical strategy that allows young people to determine their own paths. Out of the five ways for students to complete validations at HSRA, project-based learning is the furthest from traditional pedagogies. Yet it is an educational best practice that is currently used in schools around the world.

Organizations, such as Big Picture Learning, EdVisions, and High Tech High, have been demonstrating forms of project-based learning in their international, national, and state-based networks of schools and have all served as examples for HSRA. For over twenty-two years, the Buck Institute for Education has offered extensive resources on project-based learning; worked with school districts and networks, government agencies, universities, and foundations to increase the amount of learning conducted through projects; and studied the pedagogical style's efficacy.[17]

There is a spectrum of teaching strategies that can be referred to as "project-based." Some educators play a heavy role in the design and orchestration of projects. By selecting topics, articulating what steps must occur along the way, and requesting a specific outcome, the instructor guides a group of students through a project of the instructor's own design.

At the other end of the spectrum, educators invite students to generate individual projects that the students want to design and complete. This usually starts with a general area of interest—for example, a student might be fascinated by secret societies—or with an idea of a finished product a student wishes to create—such as a website about the illuminati. From there, educators work one-on-one with students to engage in "backward planning," determining what research will need to be done, skills practiced, materials collected, and relationships cultivated, in order to complete the project at hand.

HSRA focuses on individual and group projects driven by students' passions, because it guarantees that students' schoolwork will honor their talents and skills, and align with their interests and life goals. This keeps students engaged and increases their chances of reaching their goals. For example, an alumnus of HSRA, Young Menace, confesses: "I wasn't an angel, but when music was integrated, I was motivated."

While at HSRA, Young Menace watched the industry standard for music recording change from Digital Audio Tape (DAT) to ProTools. He learned how to use each system, as well as the importance of keeping up with the latest technology. As a high school student, Young Menace had self-produced albums circulating in the Twin Cities.

"No other school would've cared or even known," Young Menace reflects on his early production achievements. He now consults on music for the MTV, Discovery, and CW networks.

Young Menace's indictment of other schools is reinforced by the example of the George Westinghouse Career and Technical Education High School in Brooklyn, where Christopher George Latore Wallace, Trevor Tahiem Smith Jr., Kimberly Denise Jones, and Shawn Corey Carter were all students within the same decade. Only Smith graduated. Despite a school that didn't recognize their potential, these four teenagers went on to become some of the biggest rap superstars ever: Notorious B.I.G., Busta Rhymes, Lil Kim, and Jay-Z. It is tragic, yet typical, that the school had no way to acknowledge and engage the brilliance of this cadre of young artists.

Student-generated projects ensure that young peoples' passions do not go ignored and unsupported. Whether a student is interested in hip-hop or hippopotamuses, project-based learning offers him the chance to explore his interests through designing and completing a project that has a purpose beyond checking off a school requirement. Because the content of their projects matter to them and because they are responsible for publicly presenting products that emerge out of their projects, students engaged in authentic project-based learning develop a level of expertise that is rare for high school students to possess.

Students at HSRA generate ideas, document their processes, and communicate with staff members by completing Project Proposal Forms for each project they initiate. The forms contain exercises to help them through the five stages of their project: Questioning, Research and Investigation, Progress Updates, Final Product and Presentation, and Reflection.

For instance, an HSRA senior, Reidun Saxerud, began with an interest in the popular Harry Potter book series by J. K. Rowling. In the Questioning stage of planning her project, Reidun used a thought-mapping diagram to turn this interest into a guiding question that she could develop a project to explore: "What makes the Harry Potter series good literature?" She also set goals for what she hoped to learn, what skills she hoped to develop, how she hoped the project would benefit others, and how she would assess herself upon completion.

In the Research and Investigation stage of her project, Reidun diagrammed and summarized the resources such as books, websites, and people that she would draw upon to complete her project. Her resource list included all of the Harry Potter books that had been released, several websites that analyzed the series, and interviews and meetings with Paula Anderson, the school's education director, who is a certified English instructor.

In the Progress Updates stage, Reidun set target dates for each of the tasks she would need to complete. Her Project Steps began with "Learning literary terms," such as allegory and personification. Reidun wanted to be able to effectively analyze and argue the books' merits. Through one of her conversations with Paula, she determined that the above terms would help her in this effort. Subsequent project steps included writing and editing drafts of what she described as a "lengthy paper" on the series.

In preparing for the Final Product and Presentation stage of her project, Reidun looked over a packet of suggestions of effective presentation methods. The packet included a checklist to help her prepare her presentation of her paper and a template of an evaluation form that attendees would use to assess the presentation. Reidun presented her ten-page, single-spaced treatise to an audience of HSRA students and staff members. She introduced her paper with the following: "When I started this project, I had the idea of writing an intermediate *Harry Potter for Dummies*-type paper, outlining at least a half-dozen characters, musing on what exactly makes this series so popular, and finally, writing one very long report on all six books (which total 3,341 pages so far, in case you ever had an itch to know). However, upon reading the fifth and sixth installments in the series, my whole grasp of *Harry Potter*, and this project, changed drastically."[18]

She went on to explain that she was so disappointed with the sixth book in the series that it changed her perspective and, while she still believed the series was good literature and anxiously awaited the final installment, her analysis of Rowling's work had shifted. Some attendees of her presentation were die-hard Harry Potter fans who agreed with her analysis, other fans disagreed, and other attendees played devil's advocate, questioning the quality of the entire series and pushing Reidun to defend the books.

Finally, in the Reflection stage Reidun looked back at the goals she had set and the validations she had hoped to complete and to assess her progress. Ultimately, in order for her to receive credit, Paula and her advisor had to sign off on each validation. Through the project, "Harry Potter and the Senior Who Needs to Graduate," Reidun received credit for state standards such as "Reading, understanding, responding to, analyzing and appreciating fiction"; "Writing with attention to audience, organization, focus and quality of ideas"; and "Applying standard English conventions while writing."

Reidun didn't read Herman Melville or J. D. Salinger while at HSRA. She loved Harry Potter, so she read J. K. Rowling.

Whether or not the Harry Potter series is of the same literary merit as *The Catcher in the Rye* is an argument best left for another book—perhaps one by Reidun—but regardless of the outcome, it is clear that through her passion for Harry Potter and the assistance of the staff at HSRA, she developed new skills, such as thinking critically, researching, dreaming up a product, developing a timeline, tracking down resources to complete the project, and presenting her work publicly. These skills and experiences will be far more crucial to her success in life than having crammed enough of *Moby Dick* to pass a quiz when she was eighteen.

Many projects are not as similar to conventional schoolwork as Reidun's paper; however, examining this particular project brings the distinguishing benefits of project-based learning into relief.

On a superficial level, Reidun wrote a paper on a book—a similar task to one she might have been given had she attended any other high school in the Twin Cities. In most of those schools, the paper would have been generated and assessed in a typical sequence: an entire cohort of students would be assigned the same book to read, they would receive the same guidelines for writing a paper, the students who completed the assignment would submit their papers to the teacher on the same date, and then wait to receive numeric or letter grades, which would most likely be the last anyone ever saw or thought about the paper.

Reidun, on the other hand, had much more control and responsibility. She could select a subject about which she was passionate. She was then able to craft a project around the specific set of skills she wanted to learn so that she could articulately defend the series and demonstrate ability in learning areas that would help her advance to graduation. And it all happened on a timeline that made sense given her other work and the nature of the project.

It may have taken Reidun a long time to read 3,341 pages and that was fine, as long as she was communicating with her advisor about her progress. If the last book in the series had been released while she was working on the project, she could have elected to extend her timeline to incorporate the final volume.

The paper Reidun generated was not just viewed in private by a teacher but vetted publicly; she had to be prepared to explain and defend her work, and it mattered because it could influence an audience of peers and elders. In the end, her assessment came from herself, her peers, and her educators. Instead of receiving a letter grade, her specific accomplishments were validated.

To live healthy and fulfilling lives, young people must graduate prepared to create, relate, and innovate. These are the types of skills that individually crafted and conducted projects build for students. Through project-based learning, students practice examining problems, thinking critically, and developing resourceful solutions—crucial skills in a world of constant change.

REAL MOTIVATION

Critically analyzing something and taking action to change it takes a lot more energy and commitment than filling out worksheets or sitting through classes. There will inevitably be setbacks, moments when students run into challenges they have never encountered before. But just because almost all of the students at HSRA have dropped out, been kicked out, or otherwise disengaged from previous schools doesn't mean that they are not capable of or should not be expected to produce work of extremely high quality.

Although it can be counterproductive to blast students with elusive expectations the moment they walk through the door, it is a mistake not to quickly challenge them with real work that matters and that will be seen and used by others. Once students feel respected and that their work matters in the real world, expectations can be ratcheted up. As teacher and education coach Ron Berger explains in his book *An Ethic of Excellence*, holding high expectations for students' work and supporting them in generating work that meets those expectations can actually *cause* their self-esteem to blossom.

Some teachers get it backward and think that if students are struggling and lack confidence, the only way to keep them engaged is by taking it easy on them. In fact, when an educator pushes a student to "make discoveries that impress their classmates, solve problems as part of the group, put together projects that are admired by others, [and] produce work of real quality, a new self-image as a proud student will emerge."[19]

Charlie Hustle is a senior at HSRA. After falling three years behind his age group at Park Center High School, Charlie left.

Charlie's primary focus when he enrolled at HSRA two years ago was to catch up on academics, so that he could graduate high school before he was in his twenties. But once he began attending, Charlie became involved in Click4Life, a partnership HSRA had formed with State Farm Insurance.

State Farm came to HSRA for assistance with a seat belt safety campaign. A few dozen students were interested in working with the insurance company to raise awareness and campaign for better public policies regarding seat belt safety. Each student found specific roles and responsibilities and received different validations for his or her participation.

Together, the crew researched issues related to seat belt use, organized a youth summit on teen driver safety, advocated at the state house for stronger laws mandating that seat belts be worn by all passengers at all times, created an album about driving safety, organized performances and events, and traveled to Philadelphia and Nashville to network with other people who shared their commitment to these issues.

Last year, the primary seat belt law that the students were advocating for was passed. And the partnership between HSRA and State Farm is still growing. Charlie and the other students involved do not have to go through HSRA staff members to interact with State Farm personnel; they call them directly to discuss products and plans. The work they do matters—to people within the school, to State Farm, and to the safety of their communities.

Several staff members noticed that Charlie liked to draw and recommended that he also join the Sweat Equity Enterprises Design workshop. Because this workshop was created in partnership with fashion designer Marc Ecko's nonprofit organization, the workshop teaches design principles through projects for actual clients, such as Ecko's own street-wear company. Students have periodic video conferences and meetings with designers, with the intention that designs from the group will be marketed and sold. This means the standards and stakes for students are high.

Charlie remembers entering the workshop: "I instantly needed to learn," he pauses to correct himself, "no, *master* Photoshop, InDesign, and Illustrator." Charlie recalls that peers joined the workshop interested in learning how to use the high-end computers and design software to customize their MySpace backgrounds, but they were quickly pulled into designing T-shirts and logos.

"I still got friends who go to normal school," Charlie says with pride, "who'll be like, 'How you do that? Where you learn that?'" In addition to the real-world nature of the projects that the Sweat Equity workshop takes on, the fancy software they have at their fingertips, and their connection to a design celebrity, Charlie attributes his rapidly developing skills and self-confidence to the way staff at HSRA interact with him. "They treat us like business partners. They treat us like adults."

As students engage in projects that matter to them and get a taste of generating high-quality products, they increasingly see value in the school as an institution. It can take some time for students to unlearn a decade of authoritarian schooling, but once students feel empowered and confident, taking on high levels of challenge becomes less intimidating and more desirable.

"Some people are skeptical about the limitations of tapping into something relevant for students to get them excited to learn," says Paula Anderson, HSRA's director of academics. But while a student's attention may initially have been sparked by music, fashion, or a social justice issue, "Once they develop personal goals and things they'd like to see change in their community, learning algebra becomes relevant, if for no other reason than just to the point of being smarter and moving forward toward their personal goals."

TO BE KNOWN

For many students, just hearing the word "teacher" evokes repulsion. Teachers have been known as authority figures charged with controlling young peoples' behavior, while assessing their intelligence and, too frequently, punishing them. One student at HSRA referred to past teachers as "resentful." Another said her teachers were "going through the motions to collect a check," and others mentioned that their teachers had been afraid of them.

Similarly, many reported that their past guidance counselors had provided little guidance. Often their caseloads were so large that they did not know students' names. Their role was to address computer glitches in class schedules and assist the fraction of students who both made it to senior year and repeatedly expressed an interest in applying to college.

And despite the mnemonic for remembering how to spell the end of the word "principal," for HSRA students, past principals have rarely been friends, or even friendly. They were just teachers who made it a step up the rude chain. Time and again, principals served as the judge and jury that exiled students from their previous schools with little due process.

HSRA does not have teachers, guidance counselors, or a principal. From orientation through graduation, these are titles that students do not hear. This is an intentional cue that the kinds of antagonistic dynamics described above will not exist at the school.

What kinds of relationships between adults and students replace the adversarial ones that too many students have come to expect in educational institutions? At HSRA, the main point of contact students have with staff is their *advisor*.

Upon enrolling at the school, each student is assigned to an advisory, which they are a part of for the duration of their tenure at the school. Students do not switch to new advisories at the end of each year. They develop an ongoing relationship with their advisor, who builds an understanding of their strengths, passions, needs, and challenges.

"She comes to my boxing matches," says one student about his advisor. "She started going to my church," says another. A third student adds that she used to be shy, but her advisor noticed this and "started making me get on stage at community meeting to announce little things like trips." At first this student felt nervous. "Now they can't shut me up!" she says with pride.

"An advisory system is the best structure to improve a school's atmosphere and culture and make an already small school feel even smaller and more personalized," explains Dennis Littky, cofounder of the Met Schools and Big Picture Learning.[20] Littky and his colleagues began using advisories in the 1970s. "In my experience, having advisories affects everything, from reducing vandalism to increasing parent participation to decreasing dropouts."[21]

Littky is a personal friend of TC, and the Met Schools were influential to TC and his team as they designed HSRA. What Littky, TC, and other educators have seen is that "Just when most adolescents are pulling away from their own families, the high school advisory and the advisor can take on some of the roles that are necessary, literally, for the kids' survival."[22]

"Being an advisor is not just a euphemism for being a teacher," explains Uncle Phil. "It's coaching [students] on a lot of things. And being there for them." When one student was hit by a car, her advisor was the first one to the hospital. When another student got locked up, his first phone call was to his advisor, and when he was released, he stopped by HSRA before he went home.

Many teachers in traditional schools see five different cohorts of students every day. Each of these classes may contain as many as thirty students and the entire schedule can change as often as midyear. This means teachers commonly work with anywhere from one hundred to three hundred students in a single year!

In such a context, how can one be expected to notice, remember, and build curriculum around Chantel's passion for singing? Whose responsibility is it to take the time to learn that Jason's family has been evicted and help him find a solution to this threat to his well-being?

Due to funding cutbacks, advisory sizes at HSRA have recently grown to as many as thirty students. To be most effective, advisories should be half that size. But even thirty is a more manageable number of students for a staff member to develop meaningful relationships with than three hundred.

Over a one- to four-year period, advisors can get to know students' passions, challenges, and idiosyncrasies. Good advisors can quickly identify an article or opportunity that would interest a particular student. They can see the difference between a student being in a funky mood because she is having a bad day and when something bigger is going wrong in her life. And they are likely to know how to defuse a situation with a student that in another context would lead to disciplinary action. They know which family members and friends to call for assistance. And they know how to get that student plugged back into an activity, as soon as she's ready.

The advantage to structuring schools in advisories goes beyond the trust that students develop with adults. Advisories also provide each student with a small group of peers within the school.

Students at HSRA spend at least eight hours each week with their advisory. They share not only academic pursuits but also triumphs and challenges from life outside of school. They give each other wake-up calls, talk each other out of fights, and throw parties for each other's graduations. Students grow close with one another, providing each other support as they work to achieve goals, calling each other out when they stray from the paths to success they have laid out for themselves, and feeling pride for one another's achievements.

In this context, lesbian, gay, bisexual, and transgender students are less prone to the harassment that is pervasive in larger, more anonymous school environments.[23] While some homophobia permeates the campus, students develop friendships in their advisories, regardless of sexual orientation. "It's not like there's no comments," advisor Kowanna Powell Anderson says, referring to a young man in her advisory who sometimes attends school in drag. "But it's never like nobody is ostracized. They all hang out. They all go to parties together. They all spend the night at the same place."

Because students attend HSRA for different durations, some students grow closer with their advisory mates than others. A student who is at the school for four years naturally has more time to bond with his or her peers than a student who arrives at HSRA at age nineteen only in need of a few credits. But students in both circumstances can have strong ties to their advisories.

Some students who come to HSRA late in their high school career have felt so alienated at past schools that advisory is the most important part of HSRA for them. Some are trying to break ties with former friends who are caught up in gangs, drugs, and prostitution, and they are actively looking to build relationships with peers on a positive path. At a maximum enrollment of 250 students, the whole school is small enough that some students look at it as "one big advisory where strong friendships develop across the school."

Ultimately, for many students and staff members, HSRA is not just a school, a recording studio, or a community. It is *a family*.

FAMILY VALUES

For a school community, being family means caring for each other through tough times. Often what students need is intense, personal, emotional support. Visitors to the school have remarked that students seem calmer in the morning and noticeably more irritable and unruly toward the end of the day. HSRA's director of development, Tony Simmons, suggests that this is because as students get closer to having to leave the safe and supportive environment of the school, they grow anxious.

Tony's statement is based on the knowledge that most HSRA students have challenging circumstances waiting for them beyond the walls of the school. Each year, approximately 30 percent have been homeless at some time within the school year. In the 2006–2007 school year, 63 percent of the students at HSRA self-reported that they were on probation or parole. Twenty percent reported having at least one child and/or being pregnant. Eight percent reported being the victim of abuse.

It is not unusual to find a student and a staff member tucked away in one of the small offices discussing a life challenge that a student is experiencing.

The culture among the school's staff—from advisors to maintenance people to administrators—is that part of working at the school, regardless of job title, is to know students well, care about them, and show it. Over the past several years, there have always been at least seven staff members (out of a total staff of approximately forty) who were HSRA graduates, with a personal understanding of the challenges that students at the school face. Several other staff members grew up having similar experiences and can relate on a personal level to the circumstances of students' lives.

HSRA also has a full-time social worker on staff to support students who are in difficult situations. Although Tabitha Wheeler is trained and licensed as a social worker, she refers to herself as a "youth advocate" to avoid the automatic distrust that many students and families have developed for anyone with the "social worker" title.

It is Tabitha's role to not only counsel students but also to hook them up with support services for additional assistance that the school cannot provide. Students in need of safe, stable housing are connected with Street Works, a local agency that helps find living arrangements for students and provides them with gift cards for food and clothing. Students struggling with drug addictions are connected to organizations such as African American Family

Services for counseling and support. Additional partnerships connect students with job opportunities, internships, sex education, and life skills.

When a student is confronted with a challenging issue, such as getting kicked out of his house, Tabitha does not just refer him to an outside agency and then move on to the next. Her experience has taught her that many young people will not feel comfortable following up with the level of persistence that it takes to get the services they need. So she begins by listening to the student's situation and presenting options.

Sometimes a student's needs require both immediate and long-term solutions. If a student comes to her with nowhere to stay that night, she is prepared with a bag of toiletries and clothing, a list of phone numbers for shelters, as well as some money for food and payphone calls.

If the student wants to seek assistance from an external agency, Tabitha and the student will rehearse calling the agency. In some cases, when students feel particularly uncomfortable or are not being treated with respect by an agency, Tabitha will get on the phone with them. And, in certain instances, she will go with a student to check out a shelter and make sure the student feels safe there or she will join their first meeting with a case manager. Verbally and through her actions, Tabitha tells students, "I'll work as hard as you do to sort out whatever's going on."

By brokering students' relationships with external agencies and providing interpersonal emotional support, the HSRA staff offers targeted, tangible assistance. The school invests a huge amount of energy in this work, and it keeps many students enrolled through tumultuous times. In the event that a student gets overwhelmed and stops attending for a while, she or he is warmly welcomed when she or he returns.

Over a fall weekend in 2008, two HSRA students were held at gunpoint. Word got to TC that they were telling people around school that they were going to retaliate, so he invited them into his office and asked them what was going on. One of them recounted the confrontation from the weekend and concluded, "When you pull heat out on me, you bodied yourself."

TC asked point-blank, "So you gonna kill him?"

"I'm not sayin' nothin,'" the young man replied, avoiding eye contact.

"You're not saying nothing, but we understand what you're saying," TC replied.

Instead of getting frightened and immediately expelling the boys or calling the police, as many schools would do, TC tried to relate to the young men and reason with them. "I've never had a gun pulled on me," he declared at one point, but then he paused and thought about it for a moment. "Well, actually I have, but that situation was different . . ."

TC brought in "Big Layne" Bellamy, a childhood friend of his, who now serves as the school's facilities manager, and Jonathan Moore, the dean of students with sixteen years of experience as a corrections officer. They each took turns expressing how much they cared about the young men and how concerned they were about the boys causing harm to others and themselves.

After over an hour of trying every rhetorical approach they could come up with, TC summed up his and his colleagues' sentiments, "We're your people. . . . Even if you fuck up, end up dead or in prison, I'm still gonna love you. But I'm gonna be like, I tried to tell the brother . . ."

Love is demonstrated by different staff members at HSRA in different ways. When a student wants a sympathetic ear, a box of tissues, or a hug, he or she goes to Tabitha's office. Offering comfort or congratulations in the form of a hug may seem commonplace, but in recent years schools across the country, including in Minnesota, have banned hugging.[24]

Many students at HSRA have histories of physical and sexual abuse, and staff members at HSRA are trained to be thoughtful about issues that may come up around physical contact, but they hug students regularly. Students do the same for staff and each other.

But some students don't want hugs. A student looking for "tough love" can go to Big Layne for a stern lecture. Even when students are upset to the point of screaming or fighting, they will often end up near a staff member who they know can help, whether "help" means getting them out of the building for a few minutes or breaking up the fight before it starts. Each day at HSRA there are examples of these sorts of organic parental and sibling-like caretaking.

Routine elements of HSRA's structure and schedule encourage healthy familial behaviors. Every day after lunch a short session called Touchback provides a time for members of the community to make announcements, share performances, and air congratulations and concerns. Weekly community meetings serve as extended opportunities for students and staff to engage in dialogues about past and upcoming issues and events. Problems are not allowed to boil beneath the surface. No matter how uncomfortable a topic, it is addressed.

Community meetings have delved into topics ranging from keeping common spaces clean to gender relations within the school to how to properly honor the life and mourn the death of a beloved staff member. All sides of issues are heard and considered.

For instance, when security guards from the nearby McDonald's approached HSRA administrators to complain about student behavior in the fast-food restaurant during lunch, they were invited to attend a community meeting. They were welcomed to present their concerns and students had the opportunity to describe their frustrations with the treatment they received from the security guards. These community dialogues can be difficult for all involved, but they can also serve to keep students and staff honest and open with each other.

Feeling like a part of a family can be a powerful antidote to the lure of gangs, which have become a path to self-destruction for far too many young geniuses. A research review on gang violence and prevention found that young people join gangs looking for love, structure, discipline, belonging, commitment, recognition, power, companionship, training, excitement, activities, a sense of self-worth, a place of acceptance, physical safety, and family traditions.[25]

Many schools offer structure, discipline, training, activities, and at least a moderate level of physical safety. Some schools also provide recognition, excitement, a sense of self-worth, and traditions. Very few schools offer belonging, commitment, power, companionship, a place of acceptance, and love.

The High School for Recording Arts creates a sense of belonging and a culture of love so powerful that some young people come to trade in their gang bandannas for "All Access" studio passes. The chance to explore musical production and other passions are a big part of the draw, but in the end, what matters most to many students is not whether they have access to beat machines and microphones, it is whether the school is theirs—whether they love and belong to it and whether it loves and belongs to them.

NOTES

1. School staff members and students are referred to by their first names and/or nicknames throughout this chapter, because that is how people refer to each other at the school.

2. William Duff, *An Essay on Original Genius* (New York: Garland, 1970), 6.

3. Adam Mansbach, "On Lit Hop," in *Total Chaos: The Art and Aesthetics of Hip-Hop*, ed. Jeff Chang (New York: Basic Civitas, 2006), 93.

4. Jeff Chang, *Can't Stop Won't Stop: A History of the Hip-Hop Generation* (New York: Picador, 2005), 97.

5. Mansbach, "On Lit Hop," 93.

6. Nelson George, *Hip Hop America* (New York: Penguin, 1998), 14–15.

7. The Fo-Show's name is a reference to Studio 4, the company that provides education management and studio services to the school. It is also a reference to the school's four guiding principles: family, community, respect, and education.

8. Etta R. Hollins, *Culture in School Learning: Revealing the Deep Meaning* (Mahwah, N.J.: Lawrence Erlbaum, 1996), 2.

9. Etta R. Hollins and Eileen I. Oliver, eds., *Pathways to Success in School: Culturally Responsive Teaching* (Mahwah, N.J.: Lawrence Erlbaum, 1999), xiii.

10. An HSRA alumnus pursuing a career as a rapper points out with pride that he is the only artist approaching record labels with such an image on his diploma.

11. The term "Pick-Me-Up" is borrowed from the Big Picture Learning school design. At Big Picture schools, Pick Me Ups do not serve as artist showcases but rather as all-school events where some type of engaging/energizing presentation occurs. For more information, see www.bigpicture.org.

12. Madison Park, "Falling Asleep in Class? Blame Biology," *CNN*, December 15, 2008, http://www.cnn.com/2008/HEALTH/12/12/sleep.teenagers.school/index.html (accessed December 16, 2010).

13. Alexander Salagaev, "Juvenile Delinquency," in *World Youth Report 2003: The Global Situation of Young People* (New York: United Nations, 2004), 201.

14. High School for Recording Arts, Course Catalog Semester 2, 2009, Version 2.1, January 2009, 8.

15. This phrase refers to the frequently referenced quote from Mahatma Gandhi: "Be the change you wish to see in the world."

16. High School for Recording Arts, "Competency-Based Graduation Plan," 6.

17. For more information on the Buck Institute for Education, see http://www.bie.org/.

18. Reidun Saxerud, "Harry Potter and the Senior Who Needs to Graduate," 1.

19. Ron Berger, *An Ethic of Excellence: Building a Culture of Craftmanship with Students* (Portsmouth, N.H.: Heinemann, 2003), 65.

20. Dennis Littky and Samantha Grabelle, *The Big Picture: Education Is Everyone's Business* (Alexandria, Va.: ASCD, 2002), 62.

21. Littky and Grabelle, *The Big Picture*, 64.

22. Littky and Grabelle, *The Big Picture*, 63.

23. Multiple studies show that approximately 90 percent of lesbian, gay, bisexual, and transgender students in this country experience harassment at school. See, for example, Elizabeth M. Diaz and Joseph G. Kosciw, "Shared Differences: The Experiences of Lesbian, Gay, Bisexual and Transgender Students of Color in Our Nation's Schools," *GLSEN* (2009): 2.

24. Mike Celizic, "Schools Jumping on the Hug Ban-Wagon," *TodayShow.com*, October 2 2007, http://www.msnbc.msn.com/id/21097673/ (accessed December 16, 2010).

25. Mary H. Lees, Mary Deen, and Louise Parker, "Research Review: Gang Violence and Prevention," Focus Adolescent Services, http://www.focusas.com/Gangs.html (accessed December 16, 2010).

Chapter 2

A Day's Work 1.0

This is my preparation to my destination
And I'm a stay committed even through the complications
I'm a stay strong an' keep my head up
I'm a give it my all until I've had enough
'Cause if I dream big I know that I can make it
This is the real me welcome to my inspiration.
—Lil C

The High School for Recording Arts (HSRA) is so unconventional that it can be hard for people who have only spent time in more traditional schools to picture how things actually flow on a daily basis.

As people who have never seen these elements in a school hear about the recording studios, the student-run record label, the hours, the trips, the advisory model, and all of the different ways that students can earn credits, a common reaction is: This all sounds amazing, but what does it actually look like day in and day out? How do students know what they are supposed to be doing, where they are supposed to be, and when? How do staff members budget their time and priorities?

The best way to illustrate the rhythm and flow of the school is to provide a snapshot of one day in the life of an HSRA student. This chapter follows Cassandra "Lil C" Sherry-Rojas, who is in her junior year.[1] When Lil C enrolled at HSRA, she had never rapped in public before. Three years later, she has won awards for her stage performances, rocked venues from local talent shows to Los Angeles, and appeared in a music video to raise money for Haitian earthquake recovery efforts that has been viewed 400,000 times.

Lil C balances her passion as an emcee with a serious approach to her academic pursuits. Some HSRA students are highly motivated when it comes to their projects and have no interest in music. Others are passionate about music but drag their feet on academic responsibilities. Although Lil C's equilibrium of the academic and musical components of HSRA's program may not be typical, it provides a rich perspective of the HSRA experience.

49

LIL C'S JOURNEY TO HSRA

In a quiet residential development called Lafayette East, seventeen-year-old Cassandra "Lil C" Sherry-Rojas is getting ready for school. She settles on a white hoody with a large silver Adidas logo, black shelltoes with white stripes, a Yankees hat with gray stripes, and red basketball shorts that hang out over the top of sagging gray jeans.

Lil C steps out the front door and walks past a row of recently constructed duplexes that look just like hers. After spending the first nine years of her life in what she described as "bad neighborhoods" in St. Paul, Lil C's mother arranged a move to a first-ring suburb so that they could enjoy a more peaceful life in a safer area.

Though South St. Paul is only ten miles from where Lil C spent her younger years, the move required her to make a cultural leap. While she'd had fun and gotten good grades in elementary school, by the time she was a freshman at South St. Paul High School, she dreaded attending.

"Man, I hated that school—they were racist! The principal wanted to kick me out for no reason," Lil C recalls. Within the first few months of her freshmen year, she was barely showing up, which further increased the antagonism she felt from school staff.

When Lil C heard about HSRA, she jumped at the chance to enroll. She now travels three hours round trip each day to attend the school.

The public Metro bus she rides does not take the highway. As it dips in and out of traffic to pick up passengers, Lil C listens to music on her MP3 player and looks out the window as tree nurseries, shopping centers, steakhouses, and soccer fields give way to the low-slung industrial, retail, and residential buildings of St. Paul. Switching buses in downtown St. Paul, Lil C rides the #16 up University Avenue, eventually hopping off at Vandalia Street and walking ten minutes to the school.

After being buzzed through the front doors of HSRA and saying "What's up?" to "Monsta Codie" Wilson, an alumnus-turned-youth-worker who now serves as school security, Lil C stops to greet "Uncle Phil" Winden, the studio director: "What up, Phil?!"

"Hey, Lil C," Phil responds from a chair positioned directly in front of the recording studio, his laptop flipped open on his lap.

"I need some studio time, bro!" Lil C tells him.

"Okay," Phil says, "come see me this afternoon. We'll see what's open."

Lil C agrees, spins, and bops across the hall ten feet to the door of her advisory.

KDA ADVISORY

While most advisories at HSRA are in the giant open room down the hall, two advisories share this thousand-square-foot space. Because the advisories share the room, they have informally merged. The two advisors, Darryl "Duke" Gibson and Kowanna Powell Anderson (whose first initials together form the name of the advisory) share the responsibility of advising the forty students who are in their collective group.

Lil C bursts in and makes a loop around the room, greeting students seated at computers that line two of the walls and others lounging on couches. Some are eating a breakfast of eggs, hash browns, and sausages provided for free by the school. Duke looks up from his computer to welcome Lil C as she approaches. Kowanna is collecting miscellaneous sheets of paper from a long rectangular table and smaller circular table that form an exclamation point on the opposite side of the room.

"Good morning, Lil C," Kowanna says as she straightens chairs around the table.

"G'morning!" Lil C shouts back.

HSRA's lead advisor, Mike Conway walks into the advisory with a new advisee who is interested in a workshop called Money Makes Money that Mike, Kowanna, and Dario Otero, the school's special education transitional advisor, offer. As Lil C chats with friends, Kowanna introduces herself to the new student and asks him about his interests.

"Cars," he says. After a bit more conversation, she gives him a packet titled "Is This Business Right for Me? A Personal Assessment Workbook," which is part of a curriculum from the Neighborhood Development Center. She asks him to use the packet to test his interest in pursuing a profession related to automobiles before coming to the next meeting of the workshop.

As Mike and the advisee leave, an alumna, Totiana Adams, comes in and wishes Kowanna a belated happy birthday. They chat for a bit and then Kowanna asks, "Okay, are we gonna do this?" Totiana raises a video camera into Kowanna's line of sight, and Kowanna says, "Oh, you're filming?!"

Totiana explains that she intends to use segments of their conversation for a play she has been working on. She has been conducting interviews to capture real women's stories, which she plans to incorporate into a performance that "speaks for the unspoken."

Lil C and other students have been hanging around the room talking, but some start to gather around to watch Kowanna's interview. She does nothing to dissuade them. One of the students warns, "Careful what you say, ten million people could see this!"

"What y'all scared of ten million people for?" asks Totiana. "I hope the whole world gets to see this play!" She returns to Kowanna, "Okay, tell me about your life growing up."

Without skipping a beat, Kowanna speaks directly to the camera, "I was raised in Chicago until I was twelve, when my family moved to Minnesota. I was the oldest of four girls and we were raised by my grandparents and my mom. I was closest to my grandfather. My mom was more like a sister, 'til I got pregnant and then our relationship bloomed and grew to more of a mother/daughter relationship."

Totiana asks about Kowanna's family's financial status while she was growing up. "I didn't think about money in Chicago, but when we moved to Minnesota I needed money, and got a job. . . . For me, money was never about material things. It was about security. I was insecure growing up—"

"What were you insecure about?" Totiana interjects.

In front of students—past and current—Kowanna exposes some of her personal insecurities. "My hair. I woulda changed my body shape—skinny girls were not 'in.'"

In talking about turning points in her life, Kowanna describes an HSRA-sponsored trip she took to Guatemala when she herself was a student at the school. Seeing people with no material possessions smiling and sharing with strangers was profound. She returned to Minnesota with a new outlook and revised priorities.

The conversation continues, touching on personal topics ranging from Kowanna's career trajectory to her marriage of ten years. Kowanna answers everything unswervingly—even the most personal questions about family and sex.

Without a bell or a formal announcement, the group has transitioned from informally greeting each other to the half hour advisory block that occurs each morning. The tone of the room has shifted, from frenetic interactions to focused attention. Duke works quietly at his desk, allowing attention in the room to rest on Kowanna. At one point during the interview, the room phone rings. A student answers in a hushed tone: "Kowanna's advisory. . . . Okay, I'll let her know."

This is an interview for an alumna's play, but Kowanna has chosen to conduct it in front of her advisees. It has become a learning moment, an opportunity to be vulnerable in front of her students. Kowanna's honesty and openness with her students adds to the atmosphere of safety in sharing that is embedded in the school's culture.

Students who have been burned repeatedly by social service agencies can be extremely reluctant to open up about even the most basic aspects of their lives, but if an adult is willing to disclose her family history and fears, students may be more willing to share and move toward healing. The fact that Kowanna has experienced some of the same challenges as many of her students and is willing to speak openly about them serves to normalize narratives that other schools and social service agencies deem dysfunctional—or won't even acknowledge.

Kowanna's candidness about her past honors hip-hop culture's emphasis on the importance of origin and identity. One of the first questions many hip-hop fans ask when hearing music by a new artist is, "Who is this?" Next question: "Where's s/he from?" A rapper's identity is a key piece of how his or her music is interpreted and judged.

Students do the same thing with their educators. It is not that an advisor has to have a particular narrative to garner respect. Sometimes commonalities between a student and advisor's background can facilitate trust and connection, but more importantly, teachers must be willing to honestly represent who they are and where they're from.

Totiana wraps up the interview with a final request: "Okay, tell 'em who you are!"

In so many ways Kowanna already has, but she obliges: "I'm Kowanna Powell, I'm thirty years old. I'm an academic advisor at HSRA and Studio Fo.' And you know what the Fo' fo': family, community, respect, and education. That's how it go down."[2]

BLOCK ONE: PROJECT WORK

Students are spread out around the advisory room. Some are seated at computers working on Project Excellence, HSRA's in-house software program designed to help students track their progress toward demonstrating competence in each of the twelve learning areas required for graduation.[3]

Two students seated next to each other have PowerPoint presentations open—one is showing the other how to add a special effect so that when slides advance they appear to fly out toward the audience before landing in place. Another student has the software program iWeb open and is adding content to her digital portfolio, while another is on MySpace listening to music on his headphones.

At the last computer, a student is flipping between celebrity gossip websites. Perhaps she intended to start working on Project Excellence or her digital portfolio and just got sucked into a juicy string of blog posts about Mo'Nique's beef with Oprah and Steven Seagal's alleged assault of Ray Charles's granddaughter. She would not be the first person, after all, to have fallen victim to the powerful distractions of the World Wide Web. Twenty minutes are STETlost—a casualty of the freedom that accompanies independent learning.

It would be easy for an observer to jump to conclusions about who's working and who's wasting time, but things are not always as they seem at project-based learning schools. In this particular instance, the young woman surfing cyber tabloids is actually conducting research for a project on rumors. The young man on MySpace may also be working, though it's possible he is procrastinating. Surface appearances can be deceptive when people are engaged in individualized projects, particularly when the canon of what is being mastered is opened up to include contemporary communication tools, current media, and other new forms of literacy.

The students who are not using computers are seated on couches and chairs. Two are reading stacks of photocopied papers; another is looking through a crate of books; the other has headphones on and his eyes closed.

It is hard to imagine what project this young man is working on—though there certainly are some projects that could necessitate such an activity. More likely he just needed a minute to chill out. Giving him the space to do that is what HSRA staff refer to as "deliberate patience."

Many of the young people enrolled at the school have a lot going on in their lives. From late-night jobs to abusive situations at home to homelessness, there are numerous reasons students may arrive at school exhausted or on edge. For some, it is the only place they can relax. So while it does not help anyone if laziness goes unaddressed, staff members temper demands that students constantly be on task with deliberate patience.

A young person cannot treat the school as a place to sleep and socialize through the week. But if a particular student needs a few minutes to recuperate, meditate, or do whatever else he needs to do to get his mind right, his advisor can give him that space. And unlike most schools where social promotion and cheating make it possible for students to sleep through classes and still pass, the longer it takes an HSRA student to get started on her work, the longer it takes her to graduate.

Deliberate patience is a deeply engrained part of HSRA's culture. When the school's founder, David "TC" Ellis, was a student at an alternative public school, he routinely crawled into a loft and slept. It was only when one day a teacher woke him and asked him if he wanted to learn how to protect his money that his passion for learning ignited. HSRA has tried to institutionalize this sort of intervention without becoming overbearing to the students who just need ten minutes to clear their heads.

Lil C is not one of those students. Like several of her advisory mates, who are spread out around the school working on projects, in workshops, or in meetings, Lil C is making moves. Her first stop is TC's office, where Tony Simmons, HSRA's director of development, is seated at a round table.

"Wassup, Tony?" Lil C says as she pops through the door.

"Lil C," Tony declares with enthusiasm, looking up from his laptop.

"Tony! Can I get those photos, bro?" Lil C asks, referring to a few dozen photographs of her that a professional photographer recently took for the cover of *City Pages*, the Twin Cities' preeminent weekly paper on local news and culture. Tony has digital versions of the photos and Lil C wants copies.

"Where's my timeline?" he says with a smile.

"Aww, man," Lil C says. "I been trying to get it done, but I just been focused on my other project."

"That's cool," Tony responds. "I'm not asking for a finished project, but you said you'd get me the timeline for getting it done. I've been telling people about it. I want to be able to share it with some people. It could help open up some opportunities for you."

"I don't even have the project proposal with me," C says.

Tony reaches in his backpack and pulls out a photocopied sheet of paper. "That's why I had you make me a copy," he tells her. "Here, go make a copy of this—no, make two copies—and put together a timeline for me. If you let this go too long, it's not gonna happen."

Lil C accepts the document from Tony, but instead of leaving to make copies, she stands at the table with him and reviews it. The project being discussed is tentatively titled "A Picture Is Worth a Thousand Words, but to a High School Student, What Is an Article Really Worth?" Her plan is to conduct research and write a response to the recent cover story in *City Pages*.

Lil C and Tony discuss the outline she crafted for the piece. The first few paragraphs will be about whether the three students featured in the article felt it was accurate. To write this, she will have to interview the other two students who were profiled alongside her in the article. The following few paragraphs will summarize audience reactions, which she will collect through additional interviews or surveys. The final paragraphs will focus on how the article affected Lil C personally.

The press frequently portrays young people, particularly urban youth of color, in a negative light. HSRA's individualized curriculum allows students to critically engage with the way the media represents them. In this case, Lil C was profiled in a cover story that cast her in a positive light while disclosing details about painful personal chapters from her past.

Regardless of how Lil C felt about the article, shouldn't she have the opportunity to respond? A great English teacher at a traditional high school might encourage something like this from a student, perhaps offering extra credit. At HSRA Lil C's critical response can be a central piece of her academic work.

Otis,[4] a student wearing a button-down shirt and sweater vest, knocks on the open door and then steps in to ask if it's all right for him to leave early because "G-Unit's manager is in town and I've gotta go meet with him." Tony tells him to check in with his advisor about this plan.

After the interruption in their conversation, Lil C changes the topic to another project of hers, one that she feels has momentum at the moment. "I'm working on a book and I need y'all to do a survey," she announces.

"If I get my timeline . . . ," Tony says, smiling again.

TC comes in, peeps the conversation, and adds his own agenda item: "We're tryna get you to take advantage of PSEO," he says to Lil C, "get you some free college credits while you in high school."[5]

"But I wanna go to McNally," Lil C says, referring to McNally Smith, a college in the Twin Cities known for its music program.

"So this is a chance to get some of your other credits out of the way and get a little bit of that college experience," TC persists.

"Can I do psychology?" she asks.

"I don't know why not," TC says. "But you need to get the ball rolling on that so that you can get in some classes for the fall and then some more next spring. You could have a nice piece of college under your belt by the time you graduate up outta here."

Lil C agrees to look into college courses and heads off to make copies of her outline and survey.

The survey is seven pages and contains about seventy-five questions, grouped in categories, such as "Profile," "Relationships," "Favorites," and "Randoms." On the back of the survey is a release form, which—in a few hundred words of legalese—authorizes Lil C to publish the information she collects. She is asking each person who takes the survey to sign a form. Discussing this issue with the school's lawyer and adding this component to the survey was part of her project.

This is one of the strengths of project-based learning: It puts students of any age in a position to develop real expertise. Lil C actually worked with a practicing lawyer to craft a permission form that meets publishing industry standards. As she pursues her interest in music, she will undoubtedly have to deal with copyright issues. This form is something she could use in future writing endeavors. But whether she ultimately settles in the entertainment industry or some other sector, she will enter her future work with a greater level of familiarity and comfort with practical legal issues than she would have if she had remained at South St. Paul High.

Lil C brings the freshly copied surveys to Tony and TC. She explains that she is writing a book on zodiac signs and wants as much original source information as she can collect. She is curious about the correlation between peoples' signs and other aspects of their identities.

"How many of these surveys are you tryna get filled out?" TC asks her.

"As many as I can right now," C responds. "I have twenty completed so far. I'm tryna get five new ones every day. I wanna get at least fifty."

"Okay, I'll fill mine out," Tony says. "But I want to see that timeline before I hand this over to you. I want to show that project to Ice Cube," Tony alludes to a visit that the rapper/film/television star made to HSRA the previous year. "I think it could lead to big things for you."

"Okay," Lil C responds. She dips back out into the hall, stopping each person passing by to ask them if they would be willing to take a survey. Some ask questions about the purpose of the survey and what it entails, most agree, and the freshly printed stack of blank surveys dwindles.

SOCIAL SKILLS WORKSHOP

No bell rings. No one screams that it is time for Block Two workshops. Dario just passes by Lil C and says, as one might to a friend, "Ay, it's time for Social Skills. You coming?" It's unclear whether he has walked by her because he happened to be passing through the hall on his way to the Another Level Entertainment board room to facilitate the workshop or because he knew C was over there and wanted to cruise by and remind her that it was time.

The school is small enough that if Dario and Tabitha Wheeler, the school's youth advocate who cofacilitates the workshop with him, decided to each walk a loop down a few halls, they could casually tap the shoulder of every student in their workshop in the span of three to four minutes.

The Social Skills workshop consists of a half-dozen students sitting around a table with Tabitha and Dario discussing life challenges and strategies for perseverance. The workshop always begins with each member—including staff—taking a card from a deck of "Tavis Smiley's Empowerment Cards for Survival Living" and discussing the significance of the words on the card to her or himself in the moment.

On this particular day, the conversation centered on one student's frustration about a project that two of her classmates had presented. The project was about violence in the Twin Cities. The presenters had included a slide that had information about the murder of this student's friend. She was frustrated by the inaccuracy of their information.

"Oh my god, I just wanted to *scream*. I really, really wanted to say something to them. It's like, where do you get your information?!" She proceeded to critique the data that they had presented about crime rates and whether they had interpreted it correctly.

The group asked clarifying questions about what she felt and why. Then they suggested some actions she could take—talk to the girls, talk with her advisor, do her own project on her friend's death.

"I don't know, I'm just glad we had group today, " the student said. "I just really needed to get this off my chest because I was, like, dying inside and I swear I wanted to take it out in some negative ways."

In a school where these kinds of dialogues aren't built into the day, this young woman might have lashed out at the two girls who presented the project or she might have bounced from school. Instead, she received empathy, suggestions, and, on the way out the door, a couple of hugs.

CONCENTRATED MATH

Lil C rolls back into the advisory room. She checks her cell phone and sits down at the long table. Leaning forward on her elbows, she talks with Fat Ellen, a young woman dressed entirely in shades of gray and black with a bus pass tucked into her tank top. There are seven students seated around the table.

One of the girls notices a colorful tattoo peeking out of the bottom of the sleeve of C's hoody. Lil C proudly shows the ink off to everyone at the table. In an elaborate design, her name is spelled out with the letter "i" replaced by a microphone. The mic cord weaves in and out through the letters, as do the lines, notes, and clefs of music notation.

Kowanna is a small woman with a big personality . . . and voice. She announces to the students spread out around the edges of the room working on computers: "Okay, y'all have to save whatever you're working on and log off now!" After giving them a few minutes to wrap up, she uses a software program on her laptop to lock down all the computer monitors, except for two where students who already have all of their math credits are working on Project Excellence.

Kowanna tells the group to continue working on the box and whisker plot graphs that they began the day before, and she asks a student to hand out the related materials. He delivers to the table a stack of four-page printouts that define and explain the graphs.

Next to it he places a stack of sheets titled "Mathematical Analysis of HSRA Absences." The sheet asks students to find the mean, mode, range, and median of absences in their advisory and then to generate a box and whisker plot, which is a graph that depicts the distribution of a set of data by marking the smallest and largest data points and dividing the space between them in a way that visually indicates the dispersion of the remaining data points.

The intention of the assignment, which was created by Mike—who, in addition to his role as lead advisor, also serves as one of the school's math facilitators—is to make a three-way connection between mathematical concepts that are useful for students to know, content that will appear on the state-mandated standardized tests, and something real that affects students' lives and the school community.

Graphing the absences of each student in their advisory (with names removed), students are able to see where they stand on the plot. By answering questions like "Was attendance even across the advisory or were a few students who were absent frequently bringing the mean down?" students and staff are able to develop better strategies to increase attendance.

Kowanna's and Duke's advisories are using the materials Mike developed and—with Mike's blessing and in the presence of one of the school's other certified math facilitators, Barbara Murphy—they have remixed the assignment, replacing the attendance data with reading progress data from the KDA advisories. Since Concentrated Math is conducted within advisories, the group is examining their own data, making it possible for students to analyze their collective and individual reading progress.

Fat Ellen starts singing "A Change Is Gonna Come" by Sam Cooke: "I was . . . bo-o-orn by the river . . ."

"In a little tent," another girl chimes in as she takes copies of the printouts.

"You just sat them on the table, I asked you to pass them out," Kowanna says to the student from whom she had requested help distributing materials. He returns to the piles, picks them up, and distributes copies to students around the room who were not seated at the table. Dreamchild is not paying attention when the papers are offered to him.

"Take a paper, Dream," Kowanna urges.

"But I just got here!" Dreamchild responds.

Another student chimes in, "That don't make no sense."

Dreamchild laughs, "I know, but I was needing an excuse!"

Everyone at the table laughs.

Kowanna cuts in, "What you was needing was a math sheet." More laughs. Dreamchild takes papers from the piles and the students' focus returns to the work in front of them.

Three of the students at the table are wearing white earbud headphones, including Lil C, who has hers in one ear. One kid's T-shirt says, "If my music is too loud, you're too old!" The boy next to Lil C, Federal, is looking at his MP3 player as much as he looks at the papers in front of him.

"Did you get 3.5?" C asks Federal, sleeve pushed up on the forearm that carries her tattoo.

"Nah, 3.9," he replies, tilting his MP3 player toward her. He has been using a built-in calculator on the device. It would be easy for Duke, Kowanna, and Mike to assume Federal was using the MP3 player to DJ for himself during Concentrated Math. They have been right near Federal working with other students but haven't said anything to him about his frequent fiddling with the gadget. Maybe he took a moment to select a track or two, but he is also building a habit of using a device he always has on him to solve problems.

Many schools—both traditional and alternative—have policies instructing teachers to confiscate such items from students without pausing to consider how they are being used or how they could be used to further the student's education. There is no doubt that the prevalence of cell phones, MP3 players, and other small electronics can be a huge distraction to students. But given that these contraptions are ubiquitous in their lives outside of school, perhaps it makes sense to help young people develop positive habits, uses, and norms around these devices in school.

Federal and Lil C continue to go back and forth about the process they are each following and the numbers that are resulting. "That's what I got the first time!" Lil C exclaims.

She goes to consult Kowanna about how to determine the median among an even set of numbers. In the course of discussing median, mode, and mean, the congestion of so many "m words" ends up confusing the matter and they both laugh as they slow down and start again. For a moment it seems they are understanding each other. Once Lil C grasps the concept of finding the mean of the two middle numbers to determine the median of the set, Kowanna encourages her: "Now all you have to do is figure out what the quartiles are and graph it."

"What do you *mean* find the quartiles, yo?!" Lil C pleads, despair rushing back into her voice. They break out laughing again and Kowanna explains.

Lil C proudly returns to Federal, who has a different number down for the median. "See, I tried to tell you, bro! I'm doing it right!" C beams.

A young man, who until this point has been reclining in a lounge chair with a Twin Cities hat pulled down over his eyes, making hand gestures as he listens to music, abruptly jumps up. Moments later he is perched on the edge of the chair leaning over the Mathematical Analysis of HSRA Absences paper, jotting down numbers. He continues, even as his peers get up and head off to lunch—the oft-elusive payoff of deliberate patience.

LUNCH AND TOUCHBACK

Unlike the cliquishness that occurs at many schools, every day different collections of students gather around the rectangular lunch tables on HSRA's "blacktop," a big space that serves as a seating and eating area, as well as a performance hall. Some students have plates of meatballs, corn, and mashed potatoes provided by the school. Others have selected salad. And others still have chosen not to grab any food.

No one has brought lunch from home, but some, including Lil C, purchase snacks from the vending machines in the cafeteria. C gets a bag of Flaming Hot Cheetos, carefully sliding her sleeves up her arms to avoid getting fluorescent orange marks on her white hoody.

On this particular day, Lil C sits down with Fat Ellen and Brooklynne. After a few minutes of eating and talking, Otis, the student who popped his head into TC's office earlier, comes over to their table with a sheet of paper containing the lineup for an upcoming artist showcase at the school. Known as a Pick Me Up, the showcase will occur on Friday at the end of the school day.[6]

This week's Pick Me Up is going to be a contest sponsored by the student-run record label, Another Level Entertainment. Otis has arranged for three music business professionals to attend as judges. Similar to reality shows such as American Idol or America's Best Dance Crew, the judges will not only rank the performers, they will also give them public feedback on their performances.

Otis shows Lil C her placement in the order of artists. As C studies the list, a discussion breaks out among the other students at the table about a recent talent show on the North Side.

"I made two stacks off that show," Otis states proudly.

"Cuz you didn't pay us!" C shouts. A conversation ensues about who at the talent show deserved to get paid and why.

"We all local artists," Brooklynne declares. "We're nobodies."

"Not me!" C says, jumping up from her seat. "I'm somebody! I was in the *City Pages*! I went to LA—"

"You might wanna ask TC how he really know me," Otis interjects. "I shook hands with the mayor."

"So? I shook the mayor's hand too—on TV!" Lil C is fired up. She's still standing, ready for the next attack on her character. The flurry of braggadocio continues and includes tales of having met Jay-Z, Diddy, and Bow Wow, and being down with Lil Wayne's record label, Young Money.

Across the blacktop, four students are gathered around a grand piano and a set of drums. One student is playing chords, while another lays down a drumbeat. The other two are taking turns freestyling.

Dario comes over to check in with Lil C and others about student profiles that he is putting together for Pick Me Up. Before the artist showcase each week, he presents profiles of a few students at the school to help everyone get to know more about each other. He checks information that he has on their profiles and makes sure that they are comfortable having him present the information on a slide in front of the whole school.

A voice comes booming out of the speakers situated at the sides of the stage on the blacktop: "Time for Touchback! Everybody go to Touchback!"

The source of the voice is Virgil Jackson Jr., better known as Mick Boulevard, who is dashing and dancing around the room with a wireless microphone. "Everybody go to Touchback!" He says over and over, beat-boxing in between.

A few dozen students who did not eat lunch in the cafeteria roll in and find seats. Several people are involved in the production of Touchback, which serves as a midday checkpoint for connecting and communicating as a community. Uncle Phil is in the sound booth. A student in a White Sox hat is filming with a digital camera.

Mick Boulevard hands the mic to a young man with a guitar strapped to his back, who announces that there will be a freestyle cipher at the beginning of the community meeting that will occur later in the afternoon. His announcement is striking because it is the first time he has spoken out loud to anyone in the school in over a week. For the last seven days, he has been communicating entirely through gestures, facial expressions, and writing. When people spoke to him, he would just smile and put a finger over his lips. At most schools, such an exercise would guarantee suspension; at HSRA this student is working on a project about his experiments with silence.

One of Lil C's advisory mates, Miss Marzetti, announces the date by which all validations must be submitted in order for students to be eligible for the next graduation. There is a graduation every month at HSRA to accommodate students who are ready to present digital portfolios that show all of their completed validations.

Dario announces an upcoming trip to the park to celebrate Earth Day. He lists some of the activities that will be available.

"Can we have jump ropes?" a student shouts out.

"I'm not opposed to jump ropes," Dario responds, lowering the mic and turning to consult with other staff members. A few seconds later he turns back: "We'll get them."

As soon as these announcements have been made, the beat for one of Mick Boulevard's songs kicks in. He jumps on stage and starts rapping. When he's done, another beat drops. Lil C lights up. She has a verse on this song. She puts down her Cheetos and jumps up to run on stage. When she spits her verse, she goes so hard that her MP3 player flies out of her hoodie.

TC is the last to speak. "You've gotta come to community meeting to get special incentive awards for testing and to hear about the prom," he stresses, before Mick Boulevard announces that Touchback is "officially over."

PROJECT PRESENTATION

Students stream out of the blacktop toward their respective advisories for Daily Language Arts. By the time Lil C enters her advisory, students are seated in a circle. She grabs a swivel chair in the middle of the circle and spins around on it.

The bulk of today's forty-five minute Daily Language Arts block in the KDA advisory room is being used for a student to present a project she has been working on. Lil C rolls her chair over toward a projection screen as Miss Marzetti's title slide comes up: "Sex, Porn and Her Industry" it says at the top, followed below by the question: "Does Sex Sell?"

Marzetti does not need to complete any validations related to this project but decided to do the research and present it because the topic is of interest to her. She walks the group through slides such as "Reasons women join the porn industry," "Correlations between careers in porn and histories of abuse/ addiction," and "Does 'sex' make a man reach for his wallet?"

At one point, she is reading a slide and gets stuck on a word. "I don't know what that word is," she announces.

"Then why'd you use it?" Kowanna asks. Her tone is not harsh and the question is not rhetorical.

"It was just something I came across in my research," Marzetti explains.

"You should have looked it up," Lil C suggests.

When Marzetti states that "Most prostitutes are drug addicts," specifically "crack heads," Kowanna presses her for the sources of her information.

Marzetti goes on to share more statistics about the pornography industry, including how much is viewed online and how much money is spent on it. She highlights statistics around child exploitation in porn, showing a clip of an Internet video of a toddler in a diaper dancing around a stripper pole. She concludes the presentation with the following warning: "Sex may sell, but you gotta remember who's watching."

Evaluation forms are passed around and all attendees, including students, advisors, the school's education director and English facilitator Paula Anderson, and a visitor, are asked to fill them out. The six questions on the form include whether the project was presented in an interesting and creative manner, and whether the presenter seemed to have a good understanding of the subject matter.

Students jot down responses indicating that they found the topic to be of high interest and appreciated Marzetti's use of media. Specific recommendations include having less information on each slide and making a bibliography available for future presentations. Kowanna collects the forms as everyone streams out of the room on the way to community meeting.

COMMUNITY MEETING

While Touchback takes place every day after lunch and serves as a brief opportunity for announcements, community meetings occur once each week and offer a more extensive occasion for schoolwide dialogue and presentations.[7]

Mick Boulevard is on stage again. This time a dude wearing a Twins hat with fuzzy earflaps joins him. Each of them has a mic, and they start the meeting by having everyone on the blacktop recite the four values of Studio 4 out loud together: family, community, respect, and education.

One mic gets passed to TeLisa "Taz" Powell, Kowanna's younger sister, who was also a student at the school before becoming a paraprofessional. Taz requests a moment of silence for Keith Turnipseed, a staff member from the school who was murdered two years earlier. A slide pops up on a big screen behind her with a picture of Keith and the phrase "In Remembrance."

For the next several minutes, the microphone is passed around as staff and students give each other "Keith Awards." Kowanna gives a shout out to the staff members who helped get dresses for girls for the upcoming prom. A student thanks Mike for his help preparing for the Minnesota Comprehensive Assessments (MCA) math test. Another student thanks staff members Darlene Leiding and Tracy Richardson for their support and adds, "My uncle, Keith. That's why I'm still here, my uncle."

The young man with the guitar strapped to his back grabs the mic and tells everyone, "I got expelled out of my last school." Whether or not it was for being silent, his statement confirms that young people with eccentricities like his are not embraced in most schools. "We spoiled here," he continues. "I wanna give a Keith award to TC. If TC didn't exist, the school wouldn't have existed and where would I be?" He is interrupted by applause. "Also, to all the staff. These teachers don't have to be here. This is the only school I know where teachers tell you they love you. And that means something."

"Big Layne" Bellamy, the school's facilities manager, gives a shout out to everyone who took the recent statewide standardized tests, "people on their game actively pursuing their goal, everyone who comes in and is respectful"—he lists the four values of Studio 4—"if you ain't on that, you ain't part of the fo', you just sit here by our good graces. So I wanna give this award to everyone who reps it here and at home."

Beyond the occasional school assemblies where an honor roll list is read off by an administrator, most schools do not create the time and space for members of the community to celebrate each other. The Keith Awards take about five minutes each week and don't require any special preparation or materials. By catching each other doing things right and honoring the memory of a beloved member of the community, they play a powerful role in creating a familial feel among the people who populate the school each day.

Next, the student hosts invite up everyone who wants to freestyle. Five boys and one girl come to the stage. A bunch of other students stand up close to the stage as the first emcee spits hard a capella with a warm echo on his voice. He's followed by the formerly silent student, who rhymes "Buddhist" and "Jewish" in a mellower flow.

Throughout the freestyles, the student hosts regulate the vibe of the emcees and the audience. When one of the rappers drops the N-word and a graphic sexual reference, one of the hosts interjects to remind him to "keep it inexplicit." A little later, some people in the crowd boo an emcee who raps too quietly. The hosts quickly remind them, "Hey, hey, no boos! Only 'ayyys' and claps!" The audience seems to get the message as the cipher ends with applause.

Two girls get up to make an announcement about a scholarship that covers full tuition for students from low-income families. "I'm going to Harvard!" Lil C shouts. "That's a law school," another student at her table says. Playful bickering ensues.

TC steps to the mic and talks about the importance of trying hard on the standardized tests that students are being asked to take. "Every one of you transfer this message to every other one of you. Dig deep down to the base-ment of your heart and bring it out through the balcony of your mind. Let's knock 'em off their feet!"

He calls the name of each student who completed a recent standardized test. Everyone claps between names. 50 Cent's song "I Get Money" comes bumping out the speakers, the music video playing on the screen behind the stage. As students' names are called, they walk up, give TC a pound, and collect a ten-dollar bill.

There are so many mandated tests it has been hard to get students to take them all, especially because most of the tests have no bearing on students' futures and many students report having had bad experiences with tests in the past. The staff members at HSRA who correspond with the state department of education about the school's annual test results have tried a number of strategies to ensure that students take the tests.

On the one hand, HSRA's staff recognizes that the tests are not authentic assessments of the knowledge and skills students develop through HSRA's program; on the other hand, they understand that the school's ability to continue offering such a program depends on the results. One way they try to encourage students to take the tests is by offering small financial incentives donated by a friend of the school.

As the "I Get Money" sample that 50 Cent's hit borrowed from Audio Two fades out, Dario, who is DJing from the sound booth pulls up "Money" by

Liza Minelli and Joel Grey. Next up is Birdman's "Money to Blow" featuring Lil Wayne. As the last students collect their cash, the community meeting turns into socializing with music in the background. Lil C goes to the vending machines with Fat Ellen. A moment later, the music is lowered.

Taz is back on the mic. "There's a paper on your tables that says 'HSRA Prom Royalty.' Fill out your nominations for king, queen, prince, and princess."

People start wiling, arguing about who deserves to be nominated. Taz asks for their attention, but side conversations have taken over. The room continues to get louder.

"Hold up!" Big Layne shouts. "Did Johnson, Henry, Arlington ever pay you to take a test?"

"Hell no!!" a student shouts.

"TC stood on this stage not twenty minutes ago and asked for your help. He tryna show you love the best way he know how." Big Layne reprimands students for acting out and implores them to improve their behavior.

Once the room has grown quiet, Taz presents a slideshow about the prom. It features pictures of past HSRA proms and information about the upcoming event.

"Girls, if you didn't already come with us for dresses and you need help finding something, come see me. Boys, come swagged out," Taz requests. "Also, if you wanna attend but can't afford it, come holla at me. And, if you don't have all the money at once, but you wanna give me five each week, Taz *will* do layaway." Free VIP tickets are available through a poster design contest and an essay writing contest, which Darryl Young, HSRA's special education facilitator, is sponsoring out of his own pocket.

In addition to the options that exist for free tickets and payment plans, the tickets are inexpensive, costing only $15 (about one quarter the amount paid by students at nearby St. Louis Park High School).[8] HSRA hosts the event at the school, keeping expenses low to make tickets as affordable as possible.

All of a sudden, the speakers boom a "student of the week" anthem produced by HSRA students. "This week, instead of student of the week," S. Michelle "Miki Starr" Martin, an advisor and the school's graphics facilitator, announces there will be a "peacekeeper of the week award," which she proceeds to present.

Throughout the meeting, internal garage doors have been pulled down to separate the blacktop from the giant open space that is home to most of HSRA's advisories. The doors are raised as the community meeting's masters of ceremonies give their final farewell to the audience. "Now go read a book!"

QUIET READING AND AFTERNOON BLOCKS

Back in the KDA advisory room, Kowanna puts out a box of books that she bought with a combination of school funds and money she raised by selling iced tea and snacks. Some students pull books out of their bags, while others pick up books that Kowanna has laid on the table. The room is rarely silent, but once things settle into a quiet murmur, Kowanna settles down at her desk with a book called *Principle-Centered Leadership* and models reading and note-taking.

Lil C reads *Blueprints*, a self-published novel about a closeted homosexual man by HSRA staff member Miki Starr Martin. After half an hour, C scoots out the door of the advisory and down the hall to the video editing room where two alumni, Jamal Aiken and the Real Young Bishop, who now works at the school as a studio facilitator, are sitting with a current student and Uncle Phil.

Lil C says, "What's up?" to everyone and then gets quickly to her agenda: She has heard that a movie called *Step Up 3* is looking for submissions for their soundtrack and she wants to send something, but she needs Bishop's help producing and engineering the song. Unfortunately, it has to be submitted this week and Bishop will not be in beyond this afternoon.

"Are there any tracks you can do without Bishop?" Phil asks.

"No," C responds matter-of-factly. And then she playfully adds, "He tells me what I'm doing wrong!"

"Maybe you could get someone to switch with you," Phil suggests, looking over the studio schedule. He comes upon the name of a student who has the studio booked for part of the afternoon but warns that "she's gonna be tough."

Lil C and Bishop move from logistics to artistics. "I have an up tempo beat," he says as he scrolls through files on the computer in front of him. Lil C spits the chorus she's been composing for the new song: "It's time to step it *UP*/Take it to the streets/I'll show you things that you can only see in 3D." She repeats it four times, on the third, Bishop starts beat-boxing the kind of beat that might sound good beneath it.

They agree that they should create something new and walk down the hall to the preproduction room. It's full of students wearing headphones and composing on MIDI keyboards and computer screens so, despite the fact that someone has the main studio booked, they head over to check it out. The student on the schedule isn't there and the two quickly settle in to work.

IN THE STUDIO

Black pen, purple grip, orange clip, gold tip. Lil C taps her colorful pen on the table. Bishop has started to program a drumbeat in ProTools. Lil C is drumming along. She does not want to write her verses until the beat is complete.

The two artists go back and forth on how the beat-in-progress fits with the hook she's written. Is it the right speed? Does it have the drive that the words convey?

While Bishop crafts the beat, C goes on a mission to find "Little Layne" Bellamy (Big Layne's son, who is also an alum-employee of the school) to see if he can engineer for her, in case she and Bishop don't have time to finish the track this afternoon.

In the hall, Lil C runs into a friend of the school and informal mentor, Susan Campion. Susan is a locally based business consultant and instructor at the Center for Business Excellence at the University of St. Thomas. The two became friendly as Susan worked closely with the students and alumni to promote the video about Haiti. Susan is at the school to meet with a recent graduate to help him on his college application. Lil C invites her to stop by the studio when she is done.

After C rejoins Bishop, several visitors pop in. Fellow alumni-turned-staff-member, Kash comes in to ask Bishop for instrumentals for a mixtape they are working on. A student named Kurtis Greenwood comes in for his studio time. C pleads with him, "Bro, please do me a huge favor. Bishop ain't fittin' to be here for the rest of the week and we need to finish this song. Please yo, I got studio time tomorrow and Friday. Can you switch with me?"

Kurtis reluctantly agrees. Uncle Phil returns to discuss more scheduling drama, but the project has momentum now. It seems that nothing is going to get them out of the studio.

C takes off her hoody, revealing a black T-shirt with a gold Adidas logo. Bishop is creating, copying, and deleting instrument tracks at a dizzying rate.

"I don't like this," Bishop says, dragging the mouse over six tracks he has just created and hitting delete.

"You're killing me, dude," C cries out, leaning back and putting her hands on her head.

"Let's look at some of the other *Step Up* joints," Bishop says, pulling open YouTube and clicking through to the lead single from the *Step Up 2* soundtrack, Missy Elliot's "Ching-a-Ling."

They begin watching the video. The song's beat includes sirens, whistles, and samples from the old school video game Donkey Kong.

"Missy's the truth," Bishop says with admiration.

"I wanna do a track with her one day," C agrees.

After watching the rest of the video, Bishop's got an idea: "See we gotta make it build. Make it cinematic." He clicks through dozens of menus of sounds, looking for a reverse cymbal clap, which he explains to C will "build anticipation."

As they talk about the structure of the song, he clicks and drags segments of tracks around the screen to reflect the changes they discuss. They agree that the song will come in hard with the hook at the beginning followed by a breakdown where the beat drops out.

"Then there'll be an intro like, 'introducing a lightweight champion with heavyweight skills . . . ,'" Bishop narrates, "then we let it build to a climax and you come in with all this energy. Make it epic like a movie!"

Lil C laughs, gives him dap, and grabs the brim of her fitted hat with both hands, pulling it off and back on her head, as Bishop turns up the audio monitors. The twenty-one tracks that make up the instrumental he has constructed are complex. Horns stutter, keys carry, double-time claps come in for the introduction and then disappear, and every eight bars there's a sample of a dude saying, "One, Two . . . One Two, Three, FOUR!"

"Oooh, I got another idea!" he shouts over the beat. "This is stadium music now—I want it to be stadium everything. I don't like the part for rapping. I wanna keep the beat simple while you rap, so it doesn't sound overproduced. I gotta make it more stadium."

As Bishop tweaks the beat, Lil C leans back in her chair and holds the sides of her head. "Man yo, man yo, if this happens . . . ," she trails off.

Susan enters, greets Lil C and Bishop, and takes a seat on the leather sofa from which she watches the two young artists at work and occasionally offers an opinion or a compliment. She pulls out her smart phone and updates her Twitter status: "Can't wait until @lilcthebaddest from HSRA takes over the world!! Making a big mark @17. Big talent in a small package."

Once in the vocal booth, Lil C bounces with the boom-boom-clap boom-boom-clap. "Turn off the lights yo!" she shouts to Bishop, who has positioned his chair directly between the two speakers. He has ProTools open on one screen in front of him and Facebook on the other.

"Remember, you gotta climax it," he says. "Start regular and then build up."

After C gets the hook, Bishop goes in and throws in baritone "step it ups" between the lines she has laid down. C jumps into his chair and engineers his recording. Each time he finishes one, C repositions the cursor and hits record on the next track, until Bishop has overdubbed his background vocals four times.

He comes out, turns the speakers up, and plays the beginning. Heads nod, hands motion, glances and smiles are exchanged.

Bishop goes back into the booth, tells Lil C to cue up another vocal track right at the end of the hook they just recorded and adds an "oooooowwwweeeeee!"

On the next track, for some reason, the sound won't record. Bishop, still inside the vocal booth, offers to come out and fix the problem. A year ago, Lil C had no idea how to use ProTools—the industry standard recording software.

Now, after scrolling through a few menus, she shouts, "I got it!" A few seconds later, the beat comes cascading out of the speakers again and Bishop freestyles the introduction they had discussed: "Ladies and gentlemen . . . boys and girls of the wooooooorld! Introducing, standing at a spiffy five three and a half . . . Liiiiiiittle C!!!"

Bishop returns to the keyboard, adds distortion to the intro, and quadruples the vocal tracks he just recorded. There are already seventeen vocal tracks and Lil C hasn't laid down her verse yet.

Checking the time, Bishop announces that he has to leave. He asks Lil C if she wants him to "bounce down" the skeleton of the song so she can write to it.

"How do you think I should come at it though?" she asks.

"Like you a dancer. It's not a swagg song," Bishop warns. "Come at it like you tryna prove yourself."

HEADING HOME

Susan offers Lil C a ride and on the way home C describes how much she's learned from Bishop: "He's taught me everything! He got me to step outta doing just one genre. Like, I made a Jerk It movement song. I sing. He's been teaching me how to engineer. And I don't do overdubs over all my lyrics now. I sound cleaner." [9]

The drive to South St. Paul only takes about twenty minutes on the highway. Lil C and Susan talk about a variety of topics, but mostly the conversation returns to music. They discuss an upcoming performance at the school and Susan tells Lil C about the CD that's playing, "Rádio Do Canibal," a compilation album featuring local and internationally known emcees over Brazilian influenced beats. [10]

The beat on track eleven slides in and locally based rapper P.O.S.'s voice bounces over it: "*Sittin,'* listenin' for a *rhythm*, tryna construct a *pattern*, pryin' apart my *habits*, dying to make it *happen* . . ." [11]

Lil C's head bops as she looks out the window at baseball diamonds and soccer fields blurring by. Little boys are taking off their cleats and climbing into minivans. It is dusk and practice is over.

NOTES

1. Students and staff members are referred to by their first names and/or nicknames throughout this chapter, because that is how people refer to each other at the school.
2. Many people refer to HSRA as "Studio 4," because when the school was founded that was the name of the recording studio that it was centered on. Studio 4 continues to be the name of the company that provides education management and studio services to the school.
3. For an introduction to HSRA's learning areas, see chapter 1 of this book.
4. Otis's last name is omitted to protect his anonymity.
5. PSEO is an acronym for Post-Secondary Education Option, which is a program that allows high school students in Minnesota to take college courses for free.
6. The term Pick Me Up is borrowed from The Big Picture Learning school design. At Big Picture schools, Pick Me Ups do not serve as artist showcases but rather as all-school events where some type of engaging/energizing presentation occurs. For more information, see www.bigpicture.org.
7. See chapter 1 for more information about community meetings at HSRA.
8. Ben Kahn, "Prom: Good Time on a Dime," *The Echo*, http://www.slpecho.com/index.php?story=194 (June 12, 2010).
9. Jerkin' is a style of dance that started a few years ago in Los Angeles, California, and has become popular across the United States.
10. BK-One with Benzilla, *Rádio Do Canibal*, Rhymesayers, 2009, compact disc.
11. Stefon Alexander aka P.O.S., "A Day's Work," *Rádio Do Canibal*, Rhymesayers, 2009, compact disc.

Chapter 3

Hip-Hop Leadership 1.0

You must know failure before success
So this is the failure I must confess
I was hanging on the street trying to deal with this
Playing the games almost got dismissed . . .
From the top to the bottom, the bottom to the top
Success is where I'm headed, there ain't no doubt
Success is something we all want
But the truth is what you need to reach that point.
    —David "TC" Ellis

The materialist doctrine that men are products of circumstances and upbringing, and that, therefore, changed men are products of other circumstances and changed upbringing, forgets that it is men that change circumstances and that the educator himself needs educating.—Karl Marx and Friedrich Engels

There are five rules. . . . The first one is to wear your flyest s**t every day. Look somebody in their eye and tell them "nope!" Be your own boss, don't take no s**t from nobody, and make the rest of it up yourself.
—Bonz Malone

David "TC" Ellis is a great school leader. This statement is true not *despite* the academic struggles he went through as a student but *because* of them.

Conquering these challenges—in combination with a range of accomplishments—has put TC in a position from which he is able to connect with the diverse set of people that one encounters when running a high school and recording studio.[1] It has enabled him to understand the broad spectrum of experiences that comprise the realities for students and families at the High School for Recording Arts (HSRA).

TC has built the school to reflect and make room for all of the talents and tragedies students bring through the door each day. From fistfights to spotlights to airplane flights, the events in TC's life and the way he has handled them have played a central role in the development of HSRA.

This chapter shares stories that illustrate TC's experiences before, during, and after starting the school. These tales reveal the genesis of the school's unique program and highlight TC's unorthodox brand of leadership.

Some of the following stories have become legends that have been passed down like a game of telephone over the past decade in the HSRA community. Details may have, over time, been rewritten or exaggerated. This is not to suggest the stories are untrue, but rather to make the point that their historical veracity is not paramount. In the long tradition of parables that are passed down to communicate morals or lessons to live by, what is most important about these stories is the values that they communicate to students, staff, and visitors of the school.

FLIP ABILITY

People actually began calling me "TC" before I started rapping. That was back when I was hustling. We grew up in St. Paul, and in the Twin Cities, if you're from Minneapolis or St. Paul, it's like a territorial beef. Still today kids get killed behind that. It isn't as much of a thing for girls to cross the line; it's mostly the guys that are beefin.'

My sister had a girlfriend who lived over in North Minneapolis and one summer they came over to our house in St. Paul for a picnic and the girl-friend's younger sister came with her. I liked the younger sister, so I ended up venturing over to Minneapolis to court her. I knew it was dangerous, but you know what a woman can do to you.

So I was over there kickin' it and I ended up at the McDonald's by her house. All these cats are comin' in there, y'know, like the real thugs, the tough dudes from the neighborhood and they're questioning who I am and where I'm from. So I hear 'em talking and they're like, "That dude's from St. Paul," "Ain't that cat from St. Paul?" And one of the dudes comes up to me and says, "Man, ain't you from St. Paul?"

And I say, "No."

So he says, "Well, where you from then?"

". . . I'm from the Twin Cities."

And he stands there for a minute and then he's like, "Oh, you 'TC,' right? You 'TC,'" and he slaps my hand.

From then on, they called me TC over North and I had a visa whereby I could handle business over there. So I became the person who could go back and forth between the Twin Cities without havin' a problem. That opened up my worth on the street, cuz I could go to Minneapolis without fear and hustle over there or if somebody had business from Minneapolis they wanted to take care of in St. Paul, I could handle that too.

This is the story of how David "TC" Ellis got his name. If not for his quick wit and ingenuity, the incident in the North Minneapolis McDonald's would likely have led to a beat down; instead, it became an urban vision quest that ended up providing TC with a moniker that signifies his ability to move across boundaries—in this case, between cities—that for many are impassable.

The same ability to think on his feet when it came to names would come in handy years later when TC was building the studio that eventually became HSRA. In the midnineties, TC was trying to assemble equipment but was running into challenges finding the funds for everything required to make it a top-notch recording studio.

Meanwhile, a younger "nephew-cousin" of his had a gangsta rap crew and they had built an impressive studio off of street hustle money. Their crew had recorded some songs and had a good underground buzz around the Twin Cities. When their album was complete, they decided they wanted to have a huge release party.

TC tried to convince them to have smaller shows first and build up to something big, but they got ahead of themselves and planned a show at one of the largest clubs in town. The show was a disaster—they got on stage way late, the sound was terrible, and a huge fight broke out. In that one night, the group combusted.

Soon after, the nephew-cousin was losing his studio space and he approached TC about providing a home for the soon-to-be orphaned equipment. TC was amped at the prospect of his studio being better amped. But there was a catch: The nephew-cousin did not want to let his crew's legacy die. The studio would have to take on the name of their gangsta rap group, "Down 4 Dirt."

"I was like, 'Well, y'know, I'm not down with no 'Down 4 Dirt' shit," TC recalls. "He was like, "Ain't there no way we can keep the '4' alive?" So I was like, 'If we can keep the equipment, we can keep the '4' alive. . . . We'll make it 'Studio 4.'

This compromise that TC crafted made it possible for him to assemble a high-quality recording studio without carrying on the negative legacy of his nephew-cousin's crew. All was good, until a few years later, when HSRA received its approval as a charter school. The event garnered local media attention and a newspaper reporter asked TC what the "4" in Studio 4 represented.

"In my head, I was like, 'Damn, it came from Down 4 Dirt,' but that was when I got blessed," TC recollects. "Y'know, it just came off the top. I was like, 'Well, that's family, respect, community, and education.'"

Surely there can be some risk and lost opportunities that come with such spontaneity. Many schools or organizations would have had a series of meetings to identify the core values of their community. Surveys would have gone out, results would have been measured and discussed, decision-making methods would have been agreed upon. In this way, they would have ensured a thorough selection process, with broad buy-in from everyone involved.

But TC didn't have time for a series of meetings. He was taking Down 4 Dirt equipment and repurposing it for something positive. At that moment, a newspaper reporter had put him on the spot and he needed a socially accept-able answer for the name of the company. He looked into his heart, pulled on the improvisational wordplay skills that he had honed as a rapper, and trusted that what came out would be right. The article was glowing and the school continued growing.

TC has never regretted making such an important decision in the spur of the moment. "It was really the perfect building block we needed at the time," he says. The staff and students instantly took to it; and to this day, family, respect, community, and education stand strong as the pillars of the HSRA community.

"I realize now that that spontaneous style was part of the school's essence. The experimentation is very important to the viability and attraction of the school. If the intent is good and the work is good. . . . Let some things come about as they may."

Beyond the name, when it came to building the recording studio that even-tually became HSRA, TC had to be resourceful. He did not have a budget, had never written a grant, and had minimal formal business experience. So he went to the richest guy he knew, Wolfie.

Wolfie was a hoodstar. He drove a souped-up Cadillac Coupe de Ville and tossed around money. But behind the flashy style, Wolfie was an extremely hard worker with a methodical attention for detail. "He was a known genius in the street for his creative hustles," TC recalls. "Everyone's passionate about something. . . . Wolfie had a paper fetish."

Wolfie loved the idea of being a part of a recording studio and began employing the work ethic and sensibilities he had honed in the street to help make the studio a reality. Wolfie's partners would give him a hard time about pouring his time and money into his newfound passion. They'd come at him like, "You're takin' a bath on that studio shit" and he'd be like, "If you wanna get cleaned up, you gotta take a bath." Being part of the studio team was Wolfie's way of moving away from street economics and into building a positive institution.

Once the studio was built, TC found ways to continue to connect Wolfie with constructive work. "The same intelligence he was known for in the street came in handy starting a school. Wolfie was great with paperwork, like orga-nizing binder books of education procedures and studying compliance regula-tions from the district. He was obsessed with playing everything strictly by the book. He'd be like, 'Look, you need to show the fire department this right here.' He was all into regulatory shit."

Wolfie also had such a thorough reputation in the street that, until leukemia claimed his life, his presence at the school rendered discipline issues virtually nonexistent. "If there was a problem, there wasn't no one in the game he couldn't reach out to and get it resolved," TC explains. "Wolfie'd come in like, 'What the fuck are you doing?' And that was the end of it. He just was not challenged."

When TC decided to start a school, he could have cut off his street affiliations. Instead he flipped those relationships into resources that helped create and run the school.

Without his nephew-cousin's equipment and Wolfie's help, TC couldn't have built the school in the literal brick-and-mortar sense. Without Wolfie's presence and sensibilities, he would not have been as successful at appealing to or working effectively with kids from the 'hood. Without his own ingenuity, he wouldn't have been able to flip Down 4 Dirt to the four pillars of Studio 4 or Wolfie's street skills and reputation into assets for a high school.

RELENTLESS HUSTLE

I was very entrepreneurial when I was in elementary school. I was into shining shoes. I had built me a shoeshine box and I would go up and down the busy street by my house, which was University Avenue, and I would literally go into bars and give guys a shine and they'd flip me a buck or two. I remember being seven or eight years old with nine or ten bucks in my pocket.

From there I advanced to selling candy. That was a big thing. We would go to this discount store, and we could buy these glossy, shiny boxes of candy, where they'd cost like a quarter a box, but we could sell 'em for a buck. So we'd buy a case of them for like four bucks and go out and sell 'em all for a dollar a box. That didn't include the other people who were just like, "I don't want no candy, but here's a dollar." We'd tell 'em we were selling candy for school or Boys Club or sum'n like that, but we were hustling. I liked that. I saw that it worked.

What do a shoe-shiner, a candy salesman, a drug dealer, an airplane pilot, a special events manager for the *Saint Paul Pioneer Press* newspaper, a juvenile corrections worker, a brakeman for the Canadian Pacific Railroad, an actor, and a signed rapper, ghostwriter, and producer all have in common?

They are all jobs TC held in the first thirty-five years of his life. The world around TC was flowing quickly. To stay afloat, he had to stay making moves. There was a period when he got pulled under by the current, struggling with a cocaine addiction, but even his path back to sobriety required determined resilience.

"The third time through rehab I got it. It was a battle for the life, believe that. It took everything in me to finally get it." Despite all of the pain and temptation, TC buckled down and studied the twelve steps. Redemption and confession were a part of the program. These concepts inspired him to riff off of his moniker and, out of the lowest moment in his life, write a rap that would change everything, launching him to higher heights than he could imagine:

> **True Confessions**
> If you listen close you about to learn a lesson
> You must know failure before success
> So this is the failure I must confess
> I was hanging on the street trying to deal with this
> Playing the games almost got dismissed
> Cocaine was the thing that I took on
> And nowhere was the place that I was going
> Now I must tell the truth I cannot lie
> I was headed for the kill, steal, destroy and die
> From the top to the bottom, the bottom to the top
> Success is where I'm headed there ain't no doubt
> Success is something that we all want
> But the truth is what you need to reach that point
> The truth is something you can't deny
> Your only defense is to tell a lie
> I had to give this message the stone cold truth
> I hope there's something in it that's there for you
> Like I said before and I'ma tell you again
> Success is something that's deep within
> So remember the truth you can't go wrong
> The flesh is weak but the spirit is strong
> I had to do this rap and I know it's right
> Cuz I did it in the name of Jesus Christ
> It's the True Confession
> Check it out for your protection
> The True Confession
> You listen close you might make a connection[2]

TC refers to "True Confessions" as "the rap that broke me free." Soon after he finished writing it, he got out of treatment and began what has now been over twenty years of sobriety.

Immediately after completing rehab, TC began tirelessly pursuing entry to the recording industry. The most obvious path was to get down with Prince and the Revolution. The superstar Prince grew up in the Twin Cities at the same time as TC. TC's sister had sung in a group with Prince and TC was friends with his bodyguards. But there was a problem: Prince didn't like rap. "Every time I'd see him, I'd confront him and ask him how he could not like rap. I didn't believe him. You're a virtuoso, how can you not like rap?" TC approached Prince on multiple occasions and requested his help getting into the music business. "His answer was consistently, 'No,' and he was getting irritated with me."

But TC could not be deterred. When Prince started working on the soundtrack for *Batman*, his guitar player, who was a friend of TC's, told TC information about the movie that he was learning from watching the dailies.

"I convinced [the guitar player] to do the music for me and I did a rap called the 'Bat Rap.' I put everything he told me was gonna be in the movie in the song and put it out before the movie came out. It was kind of expensive to get records pressed up, but I hustled. I had backers in the community and lots of people in the family pitched in because I was crazy about it. I was obsessed with making these rap records. I'd just do it any way I could get it done."

While recording the "Bat Rap," TC told Prince's guitar player about his early relationship with Prince: "Back in the day before Prince had all the bodyguards, I took up for him. One time a guy in the club who had a baby with a girl that Prince was messing with came at him pointing his finger tryna get in his ass. I got in his way and I had a lil rep in the neighborhood because I boxed Golden Gloves, so dude backed off and Prince was thankful."

The guitar player said, "Remind him, remind Prince of that!"

The next time TC saw Prince, he did.

"What, do I owe you for that?" Prince asked him, reaching for money.

"I told him, 'Nah, why don't you open the door and let me get it myself?' And he just said, 'That was then, this is now' and did his little strut away from me."

But when Prince's label, Warner Brothers, heard the Bat Rap, they were interested and asked Prince about it. Finally TC got the call, "Hey T, why don't you get your stuff and bring it out to Paisley Park?" They started cutting the album, *True Confessions*, right then.

Not only did Prince help TC negotiate a recording contract with Warner Brothers, take him on tour, and hook him up with George Clinton, Mavis Staples, Patti Labelle, and Tevin Campbell, but TC's persistent pursuit made such an impression on Prince that he wrote a part for TC in his next film, *Graffiti Bridge*. The role portrayed a character named TC chasing Prince around constantly asking to rap. At the end, TC gets his chance to perform with the New Power Generation. In the movie, this progression takes place over the course of a week; in real life, creating that opportunity took several years of relentless hustle.

CONFIDENT COLLABORATION

I had no plan on going to the Million Man March at all. I kinda got roped into it by my old mentor, Bobby Hickman. I was trying not to go, but Bobby just told me, "I'm gonna come pick you up tomorrow."

When we got to DC it was so incredible, we went to the hotel and decided not to even stay there. We went right to the National Mall and camped out. I remember in the morning when I woke up and the sun was coming up and there was just a sea of people coming in like water flowing into a lake.

We weren't probably a hundred feet away from where Farrakhan and different people were coming to speak. Farrakhan had a strong message to us to go back to our communities and do something that was healing, something that was going to be positive and supportive of our community and people in general. He really kept it all human. It wasn't all about race and being black, it was more about being a positive human being and doing something positive in whatever community you were in.

At that time, I was running a recording studio and all these kids kept hanging around my studio during the day. I'd tell them to go to school, but they'd tell me how school was wack, and that what they wanted to do was learn how to make money off making music. They wanted to learn, but just didn't have the right avenues. The march was a confirmation of what I was already thinking in my mind about what I needed to do.

The whole van ride back to St. Paul I was talking about how I wanted to start a school. Bobby kept checking me, "What you're trying to do ain't easy, it's a lot of work."

I respected Bobby and I was listening to him, but I was just blissed out. Sometimes I believe ignorance is bliss, because, honestly, if I woulda known about all the compliance issues and everything that goes along with operating a school, I probably wouldn'ta been able to do what I did. Knowing what I know now, I probably never would have started HSRA. But at that time Bobby couldn't talk me out of it. I listened to him, but I had an instinct that had been following me and I had to follow it.

Standing on the National Mall, listening to Farrakhan and looking out at the sea of Black men who had come together for the Million Man March, TC had decided to start a school for young people who shared his passion for music and his beefs with the traditional school system. He was positive that the school he envisioned should exist. He knew that he was the right person to found it, but he was also aware of his own limitations. He was proud of his vision, yet did not have too much pride to accept help.

TC had experienced the power of collaboration before he decided to start a school. Like many emcees, he was cocky and competitive, but he was also smart enough to take advice and assistance. George Clinton coached him on his cadence and delivery. Clinton's son, Treylewd, wrote rhymes for TC's album. TC was confident enough in himself not to reject these offerings of support the way many rappers do.

His openness for collaboration served TC as he entered the world of school start-up and administration. He had strong instincts when it came to what type of environment and educational experiences students needed. But when it came to following regulations, it was Wolfie who had dexterity with documents and an eye for detail.

TC also began enlisting others who could strengthen his vision and help transform it into reality. He reached out to past mentors, such as Bobby Hickman, who had run youth programs. He also reconnected with a teacher and the principal from the St. Paul Open School, the alternative high school from which he had graduated twenty years earlier.

The teacher, Joe Nathan, had become a national expert on school reform and was able to advise him and help put academic language to the ideas TC had about how he wanted to structure the school. The principal from St. Paul Open School, Dr. Wayne Jennings, had become the principal of another school nearby and was thrilled to see an old student interested in continuing the legacy of providing alternatives for students who rejected or were rejected by the mainstream.

Dr. Jennings offered to make TC's studio a satellite program from his school. The satellite status helped channel funding to TC's program, which allowed him to hire his first teacher.

While providing some dollars was important, Dr. Jennings also offered TC his perspective from fifty years in the education game. He pulled on his experience in schools and his educational research—he has hundreds of articles published—to help TC design the academic program for HSRA. Dr. Jennings's encyclopedic knowledge of educational practices presented TC with the perfect catalog of educational models from which to select and spin a unique blend of samples, creating a fresh mix designed specifically for HSRA's students.

Soon the two men began writing the charter application that would eventually incorporate the High School for Recording Arts as its own institution. At that point, Dr. Jennings began serving as superintendent of HSRA and as chair of the school's board. In these capacities, he has made it his mission to help protect HSRA from district personnel, state-level bureaucrats, foundation program officers, and teachers who are set in their ways, all of whom have tried to force the school to take on a more traditional academic program.

Dr. Jennings's status as an education OG has made it possible for him to have TC's back in these battles. If Wolfie brought street cred to the school, Dr. Jennings brought ed cred.

As HSRA grew, TC encountered other people who could help develop the school. Paula Anderson was an English teacher and an academic coordinator at an alternative learning program in the area.[3] TC met her at an Art Crawl in downtown St. Paul, and in talking with her about his vision for the school, he found that she had experience operationalizing some of the ideas he hoped to implement.

TC pursued Paula as relentlessly as he had Prince: Every time they saw each other, he asked her to work at HSRA. At first she refused, so he would pay her $50 to come by and talk to his staff about the idea of competency-based graduation plans, which had become an area of expertise for Paula through her position at the alternative learning program.

As Paula spent time at the school through her sporadic visits, she came to see it as a place that not only permitted but fostered innovation, a school where there was no box to have to think outside of.

Having hosted a punk rock radio show in college, Paula wasn't a hip-hop head, but she understood the power of music. As she grew to appreciate what a unique environment HSRA was, the Prince treatment prevailed and Paula came to work at HSRA as the academic director. With Joe Nathan and Dr. Jennings as advisors, and Paula on site, TC had crossed the "t" and dotted the "i" in "education."

When it came to the business aspects of running the studio and school, such as selecting a location, soliciting donations, or negotiating contracts, TC had a lot of confidence. Perhaps too much. His style sometimes came across as brash and aggressive.

He would show up to meetings and speak from his heart, but some people could not hear his message through his street vernacular, or else they would be put off by his baggy attire. Rather than pretend to be someone he was not, TC acknowledged his need for a CL Smooth to his Pete Rock. As long as someone had on a suit and tie, he could keep wearing his hoody and gold chain.

Tony Simmons was the perfect candidate. Tony was an entertainment lawyer TC had met through the music business. TC and Tony had hit it off at a music conference on the East Coast, but Tony had family in Minnesota, so whenever he'd come out, TC would get him to come by the school and give seminars on the business of music.

When it came time for the school's charter to be reviewed, TC was confident he knew what needed to be said. But he asked Tony to come out and help with how to say it. "I knew I was gonna offend someone and I wanted a smooth lawyer rolling with me."

"Tony is like a brother." TC describes Tony as "an extreme of another side of me. He's like the preppy, pretty boy, real smart and refined, educated type. He's not rough around the edges and I admire that." The relationship struck a perfect balance, as Tony held an equal level of respect for TC's style and quickly fell in love with the philosophy of the school.

HSRA never would have come into existence if it weren't for the absolute conviction and clarity TC felt coming out of the Million Man March. But it also wouldn't have happened if he had not been willing to reach out to and learn from his old high school principal, a white woman who'd hosted a punk rock radio show in college, and a pretty-boy lawyer from New York City.

TC relies on this team to combine all of their skills and strengths in moments when the school comes under attack. But in other instances when he has seen a need to flip the script and do something that hasn't been done before, he has had to maintain his conviction, even when his team did not see eye to eye with him. This occurred when TC was transitioning from running a for-profit recording studio to running an educational program. He wanted to continue running the studio as a for-profit company and have the school contract the studio to provide programming.

"It was kinda crazy because initially Tony, who's an attorney, my ex-wife, who's an attorney, and another guy who was the business manager told me I couldn't do that," TC recalls. "They all told me, 'It's a conflict of interest. Make up your mind, either you wanna be a for-profit company or you're gonna be a nonprofit, and really you've gotta be a nonprofit because you want to start a school.'"

But TC refused to file the papers that would dissolve the for-profit business and incorporate it as a nonprofit organization. Call it Hip Hop Genius, a premonition, or intuition, but a few weeks later, Tony came across an article in the *New York Times* about an emerging trend of for-profits and nonprofits contracting with each other. This precedent convinced the naysayers. They prepared the paperwork, and TC got his way.

"That was something I had learned from working with Prince," TC reflects. "I wanted to stand my ground. I didn't wanna give up the autonomy of having my own company."

Having a privately held business owned and operated by the recording studio within the school allows for a type of flexibility unparalleled in other schools. For instance, students can record uncensored music after hours, without it having been made on equipment owned by the school district. On the other hand, the school's nonprofit status saves taxes and enables them to apply for grants and receive donations.

TC is glad he stuck to his vision, "What we're doing is really a hybrid and it gives us an opportunity to accomplish things more efficiently."

TC likens the lessons he has learned from starting the school to the skills that students will need to be able to succeed: Always be confident. Always collaborate. Get in peoples' face and don't back down, but don't be a knucklehead either. Do it with sensitivity and style. If you're passionate about a dream, think outside the box about how to bring it into reality.

"Sometimes we gotta remember with young people to not always educate them to the reality of everything that they're trying to do, because when you do that, you make the dream impossible," TC explains. "Sometimes when they don't know all the limitations, it gives them the power to do what they want to do. All they see is the goal and they don't have enough sense not to try it. They go for it, and they make it, and that's what happened to me."

STREET CREDIBILITY

We had this one student whose father was a straight up, from the street, old school, break-it-down, hardcore pimp. He didn't have no wide-rimmed hat, but his mannerisms and his vocabulary was all the way pimpish: "Sit yo ass down, bitch. Don't get outta pocket. I'm tryna handle my business." He talked to his daughter and her mother in that manner.

One day this father showed up at the school, and he was upset because a young man who also went to the school had been over to his house while he was out of town. His daughter had actually invited the young man over and I guess they had sex or whatever, and the father found out about it and wanted to do something about it. So he came to the school to find the kid.

Two staff members had to pull him down off a table in the cafeteria area. He was up there shouting, "Where's this little muthafucka at?"

They brought him to my office, and he was snapping out. I happened to see a tattoo he had on his arm, and it was an old school gang tattoo I recognized because I had been in treatment with one of the founders of that gang. And that dude was tryna turn his life around as I was, but he was an old school OG, and still had his credibility.

So I asked the girl's father, "You know Martez?"

And he said, "You talking 'bout my son?"

I said, "Your son?"

And dude was like, "Yeah, my son's name's Martez."

So I said, "No, I mean Martez, the dude that founded the gang that you got on your tattoo."

And he said, "That's who my son's named after, of course, I know him."

He was still heated and talking about harming this young man, so I called my boy, Martez, and got him to talk to this dude. Martez squashed the whole situation real nice.

As a school leader, when it comes to dealing with gangs, it pays not to throw the baby out with the bathwater. TC's association with Martez did not mean that he endorsed Martez's gang activities. But it did mean that Martez respected him and when he needed Martez's help, TC could reach out to him.

At another school, a similar situation with an angry father could have gone a completely different way. It could have ended in violence right then and there. Or it could have led to the police being called in, which would have eroded trust and would likely have meant the girl withdrawing from the school. Instead, TC dealt with the parent on terms that were familiar to him and everyone wound up safe and feeling respected.

After that incident, TC made a point of developing relationships with the local leaders of other gangs so that everyone would understand that the school was a neutral zone for young people.

"I felt like, until I reached out and got the leaders on board, we could call the school a 'safe space,' but it wasn't truly safe," TC explains. So he connected with the United for Peace Gang Truce that was going on and let them know about the opportunity he was trying to provide for young people.

"A lot of these cats who are in gangs, or have been in gangs, are trying to do something to make their lives better, and they like to see something like what I'm doing. Once they understood what I was doing, they made it known to their kids that the school was neutral turf. Then the school was truly a sanctuary for kids."

Beyond being able to reach out to gang leaders when there are problems with students, TC also knows many students' families. "A lot of them are descendants of friends, community icons, or even distant family of mine," TC explains. "So once I get the scoop on a young person, I can usually dig around and get in touch with someone who cares about their life. 'Let me call his mother,' or . . . 'You know who takes care of him, his godfather!' And then this kid realizes, 'Damn, this cat knows my family,' and then he looks at it from a whole different way."

Connecting with students' families provides TC insight as to what is going on in students' lives and how best to reach them and work with them. And it demonstrates to students that he has credibility in their world outside of the school.

In instances where people misunderstand and think that HSRA is a regular school and can be accorded the same low level of respect that they feel toward other institutions, there is a large web of students, staff, alumni, and friends to correct that perception.

Once during a school graduation, while everyone was in the performance space at the back of the school, someone stole two of the school's three MIDI Production Centers (MPCs), which at the time were the centerpieces of the recording studio. The absence of the equipment delayed a lot of students' projects, so everybody in the school community knew that the studio was in need of some MPCs.

"One day I got a call from a student who had graduated, Shotty Boo, saying 'I heard you're looking for some MPCs.'" When TC relayed that the school's MPCs had been stolen, Shotty said, "Hell no! I'll call you right back." When he called back he said, "I think this is them." So they set up a meeting in the parking lot of a restaurant.

TC and Shotty Boo recognized the thieves as soon as they pulled up, because they had at one point been students at the school. As soon as they opened the trunk, TC pulled his truck up behind them.

"Shotty is like 300 pounds and he's all mad, like, 'How a muthafucka gonna steal some shit out the school?!' Before I could even stop him, he cold-cocked one of them. After that the other one froze up. We took the MPCs back and Shotty threw their keys over a building."

The school had their workstations back. But the more important outcome was the message that the recovery of the equipment sent. As TC put it, "Mufuckas on the street were like, 'Damn, it's hard to steal something from Studio 4 and not get found out.'"

This message has been reiterated periodically over the years. There are always new students who don't fully understand that even though it is called a school, HSRA has a different position in the community than Central, Highland Park, Como, or any other school in the area. TC has to reinforce his personal reputation and credibility as well.

Recently, Kowanna Powell Anderson, an HSRA advisor and alumna, was teasing TC, telling him he's gotten soft. "You didn't usedta take anything like that from students," she said, referring to a student who had been a bit disrespectful toward him at a community meeting.

"I'm not fighting any more students," TC replied. "If you fight 'em, you end up hiring 'em. Every student I've beefed with has ended up working here. We ain't got enough positions for me to fight any more students."

In the early days of HSRA, a young man named Codie Wilson moved from Gary, Indiana, to attend the school. Codie came from a tough background—he had witnessed and experienced gruesome abuse within his immediate family and had reacted by hurting others. By the time he was of high school age, he was rolling with gangsters and had been incarcerated several times. Throughout a three-year bid, he did not receive a single visitor.

Codie's brother had moved from Gary to St. Paul and told Codie about a new school starting in the Twin Cities that was offering young people the opportunity to record music. This appealed to Codie. He convinced his probation officer that this was a chance for him to turn his life around and he spent all his money on a bus ticket to St. Paul.

Codie quickly became one of the most dedicated students at HSRA, highly appreciative of the opportunity to get in the studio, record music, and learn about the entertainment industry. When some outsiders entered the studio and were threatening the safety of students, including Codie, he knocked one of them out.

Sometimes his tough demeanor created problems internally. At one point. he was so focused on a recording project, he had stopped working on his academic projects and had taken over the recording studio. Other students approached TC and complained that Codie was dominating the equipment and not allowing them to work on their projects.

When TC approached Codie, the interaction became volatile. TC felt that Codie was being disrespectful and asked him to leave for the day. But Codie, who had been consistently disappointed by male role models in his life, took TC's command to leave as a permanent banishment. Hurt, on his way out, Codie threatened that when he saw TC in the street he was going to beat him up.

Months later, TC ran into Codie at a gas station. Sure enough, Codie approached and swung on him. TC, who fought Golden Gloves as a teenager, exchanged jabs with Codie.

Who was getting the best of whom can only be answered by those who were there, but when the police arrived, the two men hopped in TC's car together and drove around the block. While in the car, Codie told TC that next time he ran into him, he would "put some lead" in him.

TC responded, "Look, last time you told me when we saw each other you were gonna fight me and you did. So I'm taking you seriously when you say you're gonna shoot me. So you know what that means, when you see me we're gonna have to see who can shoot the best."

Most school leaders would probably have permanently banned Codie from the school and called the police. TC did go to the police. But first he went home and got his pistol, for which he had a permit. Then he went down to the police station, let them know his life had been threatened, and that he was going to be carrying his gun in self-defense. This was written up in a Protection Order. He drove over to Codie's house and showed Codie's brother the paperwork and the gun, and let him know he would be ready if he saw Codie.

Soon after, Codie moved to Las Vegas and remained there for the next few years.

While Codie was in Las Vegas, he would call HSRA and ask people what was going on at the school and with TC, in particular. The week before Wolfie died, Codie talked to him. He told Codie, "I ain't got long and I need you to go talk to T. You need to be back in school. You need to go." Eventually Codie followed through on Wolfie's appeal and returned to the Twin Cities and got together with TC. The two spoke for several hours.

Codie reenrolled at the school and graduated. He now works at the school as a security guard and dedicated utility player, hosting weekly performance showcases, and helping on any projects that come his way. His presence as a staff member demonstrates to students that HSRA embraces street dudes as long as they're on a positive path.

Codie's journey through the school is not only an illustration of TC and HSRA's street credibility. Codie is the next generation. TC has made starting schools cool for guys from the 'hood.

"A lot of kids think if you go to your block with some education or some success, people are gonna be like, 'Nigga, this the 'hood.' *No.* The 'hood wants that." Codie spoke at Hamline University as a part of a presentation about HSRA. "When I came back and pulled out the book from [the presentation], they was *happy.*"

Codie used to want to be the toughest gangster on the street. Now he sees education as the real hustle. "It's easy to be street," Codie reflects. "Working to get you to understand something, that's hard."

Codie's dream is to start a school like HSRA in his hometown of Gary, where he says it is desperately needed. "Man, if I can do a school like this in Indiana, you know how many kids'll get diplomas? You know how much music will get made? Do you have any idea how many lives will be saved?"

Like Joe Nathan and Dr. Jennings did for TC, the leaders of HSRA will support Codie in carrying on the legacy of alternative educational innovations. There will inevitably be times when they will try to convince him to pace himself and move no more than a few steps at a time. And there will be times he'll have to look them in the eyes, tell them, "Nope," and then make the rest of it up himself. But as long as he keeps innovating, hustles hard, balances confidence and collaboration, and respects the brilliance of the students he is seeking to serve, Hip-Hop Genius will continue to thrive.

NOTES

1. School staff members and students are referred to by their first names and/or nicknames throughout this chapter because that is how people refer to each other at the school.

2. David Ellis, "True Confessions," *True Confessions,* Warner Brothers, 1991, compact disc.

3. Alternative learning programs, commonly referred to as area learning centers in St. Paul, offer alternative teaching methods and flexible hours in nontraditional learning environments.

Chapter 4

Society's Sucker Punch 1.0

The schools ain't teachin' us nothin'. . . . but how to be slaves and hard workers for white people to build up they shit, make they businesses successful, while it's exploitin' us, knowhatimsayin? And they ain't teachin' us nothin' related to solvin' our own problems . . . ain't teachin' us how to stop the police from murdering us and brutalizing us . . . how to get our rent paid. They ain't teachin' our families how to interact better with each other. . . . That's why my niggas got a problem with this shit . . . cuz it don't relate. . . . And I love education, knowhatimsayin? But if education ain't elevatin' me, then . . . it ain't takin' me where I need to go, on some bullshit, then fuck education.—Dead Prez

Urban school reform rhetoric has missed the mark. It has presumed that urban schools are broken. Urban schools are not broken; they are doing exactly what they are designed to do. This argument is not meant to excuse the academic failure in many urban schools. Instead, it is meant to shake up and radicalize the business-as-usual approach to improving urban schools by shifting the blame from the victims of an unjust system onto the fiscal, political, and ideological policies that deliberately undercut and demean urban schools.—Jeffrey M. R. Duncan-Andrade and Ernest Morrell

Unless we change the purpose of schooling from a focus on decontextualized academic learning to the explicit teaching of the knowledge and skills needed to solve complex, undefined, and value-laden problems collaboratively in a continually changing world, we will fall short of the stated goal . . . to prepare all students for leadership and success in the global economy and society.—Rona Wilensky

The same societal problems that make the High School for Recording Arts (HSRA) a deeply valued sanctuary for young people in the Twin Cities and a model of interest to educators near and far also threaten its existence. Institutional racism and classism, lack of financial resources, and a need to prepare for a rapidly changing world leave many young people desperate for respect, safety, and support. Schools like HSRA can meet these needs, but such schools are not exempt from the very same systems of oppression.

To understand the scenarios under which David "TC" Ellis started HSRA and has had to hustle to maintain it over the past twelve years, and the environmental factors that young leaders like Codie Wilson will face as they attempt to start similar programs, it is necessary to look at the fiscally, politically, and ideologically unjust policies and practices referred to in the epigraphs above.

Although by no means an exhaustive treatment of the ways in which society is stacked against young people of color, poor young people, and those in urban environments, this chapter gives a snapshot of the context in which HSRA exists. Urban public schools are hemorrhaging students and providing questionable preparation to many of those who remain.

Outlining these problems brings the significance of HSRA's work and the notion of Hip-Hop Genius into sharp relief. It also sets the stage for presenting some of the challenges that HSRA has faced in recent years. The details of these obstacles are specific to HSRA, but they exemplify the barriers that proponents of Hip-Hop Genius will inevitably run up against given the current climate around education in this country and society's seemingly timeless resistance to changes that benefit poor young people of color.

SYSTEMIC SHORTS

Excessive policing, overincarceration, and inequalities in access to health care, housing, transportation, and employment opportunities have immediate life-and-death consequences for poor children and children of color. The flaws of the education system substantially reduce the chances of any significant transformation of these dynamics. By denying young people access to the tools to analyze and alter the situations they are in, the status quo is maintained.

The alarming rate at which students are leaving high schools across this nation is a powerful indication of how severely our education system is falling short of its responsibility to prepare all young people for life beyond school. For every three high school students who graduate, one of their peers will not.[1] On average, one student will drop out of school every twenty-six seconds.[2]

As everyone who studies education knows, the statistics become even starker when race, class, gender, sexual orientation, and population density are factored into the equation. While nationally 71 percent of students who begin high school end up graduating four years later, the percentage is dramatically lower for black, Latino, and Native American students.

According to Education Week's "Diplomas Count 2008" report, which calculated data from 2005 enrollment and graduation rates, only 55 percent of black students graduated within four years of entering high school. For Latino students, the number was slightly better, at 58 percent. And for Native American students, it was the lowest, at 51 percent.[3]

When it comes to socioeconomic status, the less money people have, the less likely they are to graduate. The Urban Institute's Education Policy Center presented "A Statistical Portrait of Public High School Graduation," which included telling statistics regarding the impact of class on high school graduation. Holding other factors constant, for every 10 percent increase in the number of free and reduced lunch recipients in a district—an indicator of poverty—the graduation rate dropped by 3.8 percent.[4]

The same report found that overall males graduate at a rate 8 percent lower than their female peers.[5] And although it is difficult to find exact statistics on the graduation rates of lesbian, gay, bisexual, and transgender young people, it is estimated that almost a third leave high school without a diploma.[6]

The Urban Institute's Education Policy Center's "Statistical Portrait" shows that students in urban school districts are less likely to graduate than students in other districts. During the time period from which the report compiled data, suburban schools had a 73 percent graduation rate, while schools in "central cities" had a 58 percent graduation rate.[7]

So, black, Latino, and Native American students are less likely to graduate than white or Asian students. And poor students are less likely to graduate than middle-class or wealthy students. And this pattern continues for male students; lesbian, gay, bisexual, and transgender students; and urban students. The inequities are glaring, but *why* are so few students graduating in general?

If the number of students who were not completing high school was much smaller, perhaps an argument could be made that these students just weren't trying hard enough. But *nearly a third of all high school students are not completing high school in four years.*

When the situation is so bad that, en masse, young people are unable or unwilling to finish, it is clear that either the system itself is broken or it was never designed to work for all students in the first place. Either way, for anyone concerned about the future of this country, the numbers cited above signal an urgent call for dramatic changes to our education system.

A major part of the reason that students stop attending school is that what is occurring in their classrooms bears no relevance to their lives. One out of two high school students surveyed in a recent study by the National Research Center for Career and Technical Education reported being bored in school *every day*. One of the top two reasons they cited for their boredom was that they did not feel the material they were studying was relevant to their lives.[8]

But the disconnect between students and curriculum isn't the only aspect of education that causes attrition. It's also the way students are treated in school. A National Economic and Social Rights Initiative study of "school safety" practices in New York City found that "Because students of color are concentrated in schools with fewer resources, they receive fewer supportive interventions, such as mediation or counseling, leaving teachers with fewer options for alternatives to suspension."[9]

Despite the fact that research shows that punitive measures do not improve student behavior, "Schools with the highest percentage of African American and Latino students are also more likely to be overcrowded, to have metal detectors and police personnel, and to have higher suspension rates than less crowded schools."[10]

In case there is any ambiguity about the racial implications of what is going in with policing in the schools, the report summarizes it clearly: "It is important to highlight that African American students are suspended more often and receive more severe punishments than White students for the same infractions."[11]

Is it any wonder that young people—particularly black young people—do not want to attend institutions like these? Instead of being celebrated and supported, they are being policed and punished.

Tragically, for young people who don't graduate, the numbers sent to prison are far higher. Incarceration rates are nearly *fifty times the national average* for African Americans in their twenties and thirties who have dropped out of high school.[12] While not as stark, the incarceration rate is almost ten times higher than the national average for Latino and white men who have not graduated from high school.[13]

In the shadows of these daunting statistics, many young people strive to do their best despite the systemic barriers. Some encounter caring adults who, either informally or professionally, try to increase their chances of success. Yet too often, both the young people and the adults attempting to help them are unable to overcome the societal obstacles.

Many adults in positions of power in schools and other youth-service settings view the young people they work with in negative, deficit-oriented ways. For instance, the Texas Youth Commission has developed a "resocialization" program "to address biological factors and underlying emotional dynamics that fuel delinquent behaviors [and] to remove cognitive justifications used by youth for continued delinquency."[14] The program requires young people to admit and abandon "thinking errors" such as "feeling special."[15]

Staff from the Texas Youth Commission have been invited to train other states' employees in implementing the "resocialization" program. Across the country, deficit-oriented models like this exist and bureaucrats are paid to argue about how to help "these kids." Young peoples' strengths and talents rarely receive much more than lip service. Whether they are seen as criminals or victims, not much is expected from them.

Once institutions are established, they generally have a limited capacity to be responsive to young people. They are *institutions*, after all, with rules and procedures that, while not literally etched in stone, are certainly slow and complicated to change. Even when caring, intelligent people populate the staffs of schools and youth programs, too often young people end up passing through as numbers to be accommodated.

Despite positive individual relationships young people might have with adults they encounter, the institutional stance is that they are recipients of a service. Students might have the opportunity to pick which school elective they want to enroll in, but it is much less frequent that they are welcomed into decision-making processes that have a profound effect on their experience or the institution itself.

CHANGE RULES

Not only is it hard to change the way institutions are run, but the academic curriculum within our schools is similarly calcified. The bulk of the schools in this country still operate with what Brazilian educational theorist Paulo Freire dubbed the "banking model" of education, in which students are seen as empty vessels waiting for deposits of information.

"Implicit in the banking concept is the assumption of a dichotomy between man and the world: man is merely *in* the world, not *with* the world or with others; man is spectator, not re-creator."[16] Just as students are not included in shaping the institutions they are a part of, they are also excluded from playing a role—other than, perhaps, as a receptacle—in their own learning.

The standardized curriculum and delivery methods that are pervasive in our public schools not only risk boring young people out the door, they also fail to prepare the students who remain. Philosopher and educator John Dewey explained in 1938 that traditional schooling presents an "essentially static . . . finished product, with little regard either to the ways in which it was originally built up or to the changes that will surely occur in the future."

Dewey refers to traditional schooling as "a cultural product of societies that assumed the future would be much like the past." And yet, as early as the 1930s, he was able to point out that such traditional schooling is mistakenly "used as educational food in a society where change is the rule, not the exception."[17]

Many hip-hop artists share Dewey's disdain for the "essentially static." In the midnineties, graffiti legend Futura 2000 explained to a friend that writing on trains and walls was no longer "hip-hop." What? Graffiti was widely known as one of the four main elements of hip-hop, and trains and walls had always been the canvases of choice. And now one of its pioneers was declaring it not to be hip-hop?

It was only hip-hop before anyone else was doing it, Futura explained. So then what had hip-hop visual art become in the nineties? Getting up on the Internet, Futura had begun exploring digital tunnels where he could paint his name and iconic characters.[18] Given that this conversation occurred over a decade ago, one can only imagine what Futura might consider hip-hop art now.

The imperative for innovation is not unique to hip-hop. Four thousand years ago, the Egyptian scribe Khakheperresenb chiseled in stone: "Would I had phrases that are not known, utterances that are strange, in new language that has not been used, free from repetition, not an utterance which has grown stale."[19] The quest to be fresh is, in some sense, timeless.

But in hip-hop, the passion for originality goes beyond the "innovation-as-mandate" principle shared by other artistic and scientific movements. In suggesting guiding principles of hip-hop aesthetics in his essay "On Lit Hop," Adam Mansbach describes the "frenetic learning curve" that has driven generations of hip-hoppers: "Train pieces and rhymes and musical productions became fodder for what was to come next at the exact moment of their completion, going from innovative to passé in the blink of an eye because of the sheer intellectual force of every kid clocking and biting and scheming on how to take it one step further, chop those wild-style letter segments or that rhyme scheme or that drum loop just a little bit flyer."[20]

The premium that hip-hop places on rapid and relentless evolution makes perfect sense in a society that, as Dewey pointed out, is constantly changing. Both Dewey's concern about an educational model that fails to adapt and the relevance of hip-hop's continuous metamorphosis are ever more salient now, given the ways in which technological advances and globalization have accelerated the rate of societal change.

For the past half-century, computer engineers have kept up with Moore's law, which states that the number of transistors that can be placed on an integrated circuit doubles every two years. This explains why every time one buys a computer, camera, or MP3 player it has twice as much memory as the last time; why phones now can do more than desktop computers could do ten years ago; why today people can carry more data in their pocket than could fit in the Brooklyn Public Library a hundred years ago.

Not only is change the norm, as opposed to an exception, but *exponential change is the rule*. Where does this leave our students? If one accepts the premise that there are a finite number of jobs available, how are they going to compete for those jobs when they are not only going up against their privileged peers in this continent, but also against computers that have automated many jobs as well as millions of young people all over the world?

Even the depressingly low percentage of students who make it through the school system are in trouble. They have a diploma in hand, but what have they been prepared for?

A 2005 survey of young people who had recently graduated from public high schools found that 39 percent of those who were employed felt unprepared for their positions. Their employers made the exact same assessment, on average estimating that 39 percent of recent graduates were "unprepared for the expectations that they face in entry-level jobs." Forty-nine percent of the above graduates' unemployed peers reported that they had gaps in the skills and abilities they would need for the jobs they hoped to obtain.[21]

Attending and graduating from college may help these young people acquire jobs, but are they leaving high school prepared for the college experience? The same report cited above, which was commissioned by Achieve, Inc., asked a cohort of college students to evaluate their own level of preparation for college based on six factors. "Only 14 percent of college students feel that they are generally able to do what is expected of them in all six dimensions," the report found. Fifty-six percent of these students reported that "high school left them unprepared for the work and study habits expected in college."[22]

At the end of the Achieve report, a set of measures is suggested to better prepare students for college and employment. Ninety-seven percent of the college students surveyed felt they would be better prepared if they had more "opportunities for real-world learning and making coursework more relevant." Ninety-five percent of the employers surveyed agreed.[23]

Schools that utilize project-based learning are in a good position to offer students such opportunities. Although there are scenarios in which teachers assign projects that are contrived and irrelevant, the style of project-based learning employed by schools such as HSRA facilitates student work that is grounded in timely interests and real-world experiences.

For instance in chapter 1, the students involved in Click4Life interacted with elected officials and businesspeople on work that changed state laws and affected peoples' lives, and the students in the Sweat Equity Enterprises Design partnership interacted with professional designers to develop products that could be taken to market. In chapter 2, Lil C collaborated with a lawyer to develop a release form so that she could publish the book she was writing without facing legal consequences, and she created a song to submit for the soundtrack of a major motion picture.

The other remedies proposed at the end of the Achieve report centered on increasing standardized testing, as well as the quantity and difficulty of course work.[24] Mainstream education reform organizations, foundations, and the federal Department of Education have chosen to focus the bulk of their resources on some of the very same solutions: ratcheting up the magnitude and rigor of traditional classroom-based study, and raising the number and stakes of tests administered—these are the deposits and withdrawals of the banking model of education described by Freire.

In environments focused on course work in core academic subject areas and test results that drastically affect the futures of students, staff, and the school itself, it is difficult for schools that favor student-led learning to exist. Survival becomes even harder for such schools during financial recessions. While economic shortfalls lead to challenges for all schools, those furthest from the mainstream are often hit first and hardest.

WHEN THE CASH FLOW SLOWS

The 2009–2010 school year started with bad news for Minnesota educators. The state was looking at a multibillion-dollar deficit and the governor, Tim Pawlenty, who prides himself on being a "fiscal conservative," was determined not to raise taxes. But the state is required by law to close out every year with a balanced budget, so something had to be done with the biggest line items.

Pawlenty did not have the political capital or will to openly slash spending on education. Rather than drastically cut the state's education budget, the governor decided to hold back 27.5 percent of schools' funds until the first half of the following school year—a solution only insofar as it delayed the problem. This drove many schools to immediately take out loans in order to cover basic costs such as teachers' salaries. In turn, the schools have to use taxpayers' dollars that were intended for students to instead pay banks interest on these loans.

Charters and other small schools were affected particularly harshly because they run on lean budgets with few areas of spending that can be deferred. HSRA, which in its previous twelve years never had to borrow money, was forced to take out a line of credit. The school also had to budget conservatively and students and staff worked hard to raise additional funds, which helped close the funding gap left by the state.

Unfortunately, foundations, corporations, and other potential funders are reluctant to offer significant support to schools when those schools' main funding streams look unreliable. A corporate sponsor was considering a $5 million investment in a new facility for HSRA, but they got cold feet upon discovering that the state would be expanding the budget holdback to 30 percent for the 2010–2011 school year. They have seen that as banks tighten lending, some schools cannot secure the level of borrowing necessary to stay afloat, and they do not want to make a large gift to a school that may not be able to keep its doors open.

The financial challenges resulting from the state's budget shortfall and the governor's decisions threaten to disrupt the very DNA of HSRA's program. With fewer dollars, advisory sizes grow, hours shorten, books cannot be purchased, and trips are canceled.

NAME CALLING

When Barack Obama was campaigning for president he promised that, if elected, his administration would hold administrators, teachers, parents, and students accountable. He also promised that he would reform George W. Bush's 2001 No Child Left Behind Act, so that the government would support schools in need of improvement, rather than punishing them.

The American Recovery and Reinvestment Act (commonly known as "the stimulus plan"), signed into law in the beginning of 2009, included $90.9 billion for education, $5 billion of which came in the form of discretionary funds that the federal Department of Education chose to distribute to states on a competitive basis. Some of those funds are currently being allotted through School Improvement Grants.

Part of how the grant amounts are calculated is based on the number of "persistently low-achieving schools" in the state requesting funds. Obama was making good on his promise—schools in need of improvement would get support, an especially attractive possibility for schools in Minnesota, given the state budget issues described above.

The problem with this approach is that it rewards states for designating a larger number of schools as "low achieving." Such a designation is demoralizing to educators, students, and families. And it makes it difficult to attract community support, foundation funding, corporate partnership, and talented staff members.

In addition to the negative connotations of the terminology, being designated as "low achieving" sends schools into "corrective action." External consultants come in to assess the school and recommend improvement models. Possible recommendations include "turnaround," which entails replacing the principal and at least half the teachers; "transformation," which requires replacing the principal and reforming the curriculum; and all-out closure. Some schools may need such drastic actions. Other schools do not.

Many educators around the country have found a solution to ensure that their school will not face the consequences of being deemed "low achieving." Since the designation is made based on metrics such as test scores, attendance, and graduation rates, the quickest way to guarantee good numbers is to push out students who jeopardize the desired statistics.

A study of high-stakes accountability systems found that such methods lead "not to equitable educational possibilities for youth, but to avoidable losses of thousands of youth from our schools."[25] Principals' job security and, in some states, salary bonuses are attached to these numbers. So, rather than risk their livelihood, some find ways of getting rid of students whom they believe will not perform well.

Schools that actually try hard to keep their most troubled students or that have the gumption to go a step further and seek out young people who have been jettisoned by other schools are being penalized when the numbers are tallied. As if educating students whose lives are thick with trauma is not difficult enough, these schools end up experiencing assaults on their existence.

This is what recently happened to HSRA. In hopes of receiving federal funds through a School Improvement Grant, the Minnesota Department of Education placed HSRA on a list of "persistently low-achieving schools." The irony is that HSRA was placed on the list for doing the very thing the school proposed to do in its charter application—serve highly mobile, overage, undercredited dropouts.

Sounds crazy, right? Here's what went down: Based on federal criteria, Minnesota designated any school that had a four-year graduation rate of lower than 60 percent as a "low-achieving school." But the way the state calculates the graduation rate is based on an inelastic four-year timeline from when a student begins high school. What about the thousands of students who drop out or are kicked out of the comprehensive high schools around the city or for other reasons fall behind in their studies?

Consider a student like Josh,[26] who enrolled at HSRA in the early months of 2010, having spent four years at Gordon Parks High School, which is an "alternative learning program" in St. Paul.[27] After some staff changes at Gordon Parks, Josh says he felt "the teachers didn't believe in me, and I didn't believe in myself." So he left the school.

Determined to be the first person in his family to graduate from high school "outside of prison or a GED," Josh took it upon himself to enroll at HSRA. Despite a busy work schedule at a home for people with physical disabilities, Josh is on track to graduate in the fall of 2010 and is planning to pursue a career in counseling.

But guess what? As far as the state is concerned, Josh contributes to the percentage of students HSRA "failed" to graduate within four years, because *before he joined the school* his four-year countdown had already run out. The formula for judging the quality of an individual school by calculating students' graduation rates from the beginning of their high school experience—even if it's somewhere else—does not account for students who have switched schools during their high school career.

This is wildly unfair to students like Josh and to the educators at HSRA who work hard to serve him and his peers. It means that there is no way, based on the numbers, to distinguish between a "dropout factory" and a *dropout recovery program.*

States such as New York and California have noted this issue and taken it into account when determining which schools they consider "low achieving." A guideline from the federal government allows and suggests that an exception be made for "schools specifically designed to serve overage, undercredited students" when identifying "low-achieving schools."

Minnesota took this advice and excluded from the list alternative learning programs that did not have high enough graduate rates. But, even though 95 percent of HSRA students meet the criteria for admission to alternative learning programs, the state was unwilling to exclude HSRA due to its status as a charter school.

This is especially ironic given that many students, like Josh, actually came to HSRA after dropping out of alternative learning programs. So despite the fact that HSRA serves students that slipped through the cracks of alternative learning programs, they were not given the same immunity from the "low-achieving" albatross.

The school community was upset by the designation. While many students at HSRA are used to being stigmatized by government agencies, the insult still stung. But the primary emotional response was fear. Students worried that the school would be closed or that the staff with whom they had formed relationships would be gone.

Would this be the end to Josh's dream of being the first person in his family to graduate? This was not a hypothetical question—it was a burning concern to Josh, his mother, and the staff at HSRA.

Besides causing alarm in the school community, the "low-achieving" designation created other problems. The media picked up on it. Rather than engaging in investigative journalism about the criteria of the "low-achieving" designation, most just printed lists of the schools with the implicit assumption that whatever methodology was used to determine schools' status was sound.

This publicity was harmful to the reputations of the schools on the list. HSRA has worked hard over the years to cultivate relationships with individual and corporate donors. One can imagine the response when an executive at

LubeTech (one of HSRA's sponsors) invited a colleague to the annual HSRA fundraiser. . . . "But isn't that one of the low-achieving schools?" The school's board appealed to the state department of education to be removed from the list, but the department would not budge. So the school's leaders went to state legislators and made their case. Several of the legislators were sympathetic, but it turned out they couldn't force the Minnesota Department of Education to change anything.

"The common knowledge among schools in Minnesota is that the Department of Education is so powerful that you just can't fight them," explained Tony Simmons, HSRA's director of development. This is where school founder David "TC" Ellis's relentless hustle, confidence, and inclination for collaboration kicked in.[28]

HSRA would not roll over for the state department of education. They would fight and they would win, even if he had to do something he rarely did—put on a suit. For the next four months, Simmons and Ellis spent every day focused on this issue.

They dedicated over six hundred hours and employed multiple strategies, including frequent trips to the state capitol to engage directly with the Minnesota Department of Education; communication with and visits to the federal Department of Education; numerous conversations with state legislators, education policy experts, and lawyers; and drafting a bill amendment.

Eventually, the Minnesota Department of Education offered HSRA a waiver from the "persistently low-achieving" list. While this was undeniably a victory, it was a formidable drain of time that could have gone to supporting and improving the operations of the school.

"If it ain't one thing, it's another," TC said. "They've been trying to shut the school down since we started." From charter reviews to audits to the "adequate yearly progress" benchmarks dictated by the No Child Left Behind Act, over the years the state has threatened HSRA's existence many times. None of these threats have stopped the school from moving forward on its mission, but they have taken their toll on the community, exhausting staff time and focus, upsetting students and families, and taking the place of more meaningful measurements and assessments.

While the details of these battles may be particular, these types of skirmishes for survival are not unique to HSRA. They are indicative of the attacks that unfairly punish and distract educators who commit to a genuine *no child left behind* policy. The price that HSRA and these other schools pay for their "*by any means necessary*" approach to engaging disenfranchised students makes one thing clear: When you're on the cutting edge, sometimes you bleed.

NOTES

1. Christopher B. Swanson and Amy M. Hightower, "Diplomas Count 2008," PowerPoint Slide 4, http://www.edweek.org/media/ew/dc/2008/DC08_Presentation_FINAL.pdf (accessed December 16, 2010).

2. Swanson and Hightower, "Diplomas Count 2008," PowerPoint Slide 11.

3. Swanson and Hightower, "Diplomas Count 2008," PowerPoint Slide 11.

4. Christopher B. Swanson, "Who Graduates, Who Doesn't? A Statistical Portrait of Public High School Graduation, Class of 2001," *Urban Institute Education Policy Center,* 32, http://www.urban.org/UploadedPDF/410934_WhoGraduates.pdf (accessed December 17, 2010).

5. Swanson, "Who Graduates, Who Doesn't?" vi.

6. American Psychological Association, "Facing the school dropout dilemma" (2010): 5, http://www.apa.org/pi/families/resources/school-dropout-prevention.pdf (accessed December 17, 2010).

7. Swanson, "Who Graduates, Who Doesn't?" 28.

8. Ethan Yazzie-Mintz, "Voices of Students on Engagement: A Report on the 2006 High School Survey of Student Engagement," Center for Evaluation and Education Policy Indiana University (2006): 5, http://www.eric.ed.gov:80/PDFS/ED495758.pdf (accessed January 13, 2011).

9. Elizabeth Sullivan and Elizabeth Keeney, "Teachers Talk: School Culture, Safety and Human Rights," National Economic and Social Rights Initiative and Teachers Unite, (2008): 3, http://www.nesri.org/Teachers_Talk.pdf (accessed December 17, 2010).

10. Sullivan and Keeney, "Teachers Talk."

11. Sullivan and Keeney, "Teachers Talk."

12. Bruce Western, *Punishment and Inequality in America* (New York: Russell Sage Foundation, 2006): 18.

13. Western, "Punishment and Inequality in America," 17.

14. Texas Youth Commission, "Resocialization: The Rehabilitation Model," http://www.tyc.state.tx.us/programs/resocial.html (accessed December 17, 2010).

15. Texas Youth Commission "Family Guide to Resocialization," http://www.tyc.state.tx.us/archive/programs/familyguide/family7.html (accessed December 17, 2010).

16. Paulo Freire, *Pedagogy of the Oppressed* (New York: Herder and Herder, 1971), 62.

17. John Dewey, *Experience & Education* (New York: Collier Books, 1963), 19.

18. Sam Spitzer, in discussion with the author, 2001.

19. James Gleick, *Genius: The Life and Science of Richard Feynman* (New York: Pantheon Books, 1992), 326, attributed to Khakheperresenb, quoted in Lentricchia (1980), 318.

20. Adam Mansbach, "On Lit Hop," in *Total Chaos: The Art and Aesthetics of Hip-Hop*, ed. Jeff Chang (New York: Basic Civitas, 2006), 93–94.

21. Peter D. Hart Research Associates/Public Opinion Strategies, "Rising to the Challenge: Are High School Graduates Prepared for College and Work?" Achieve,

Inc. (2005): 3, http://www.achieve.org/files/pollreport_0.pdf (accessed January 13, 2011).

22. "Rising to the Challenge," 4.

23. "Rising to the Challenge," 13.

24. "Rising to the Challenge."

25. Linda M. McNeil, Eileen Coppola, Judy Radigan, and Julian V. Heilig, "Avoidable Losses: High-Stakes Accountability and the Dropout Crisis," *Education Policy Analysis Archives* 16(3), (2008): 2, http://epaa.asu.edu/epaa/v16n3/ (accessed December 17, 2010).

26. Josh's last name is omitted to protect his anonymity.

27. Alternative learning programs, commonly referred to as area learning centers in St. Paul, offer alternative teaching methods and flexible hours in nontraditional learning environments.

28. For a more complete description of TC Ellis's leadership qualities, see chapter 3.

Chapter 5

Trends in Hip-Hop Education 1.0

Do we realize how much power hip-hop has? The hip-hop generation can take a stand collectively and make a statement. There are a lot of people who are doing something positive, who are doing hip-hop the way it was meant to be done. They are reaching young people showing them what the world could be.—Kool Herc

For the graffiti artists, tagging walls wasn't about mimicking art school technique or being self-consciously postmodern. For the Hispanic break-ers, it wasn't about simply departing from the traditions of Latin social dancing with its rigorous turns and upright posture. For DJs, break spin-ning wasn't some departure from the norms of soul music. For all these old-schoolers it was an accidental, offhand discovery of a way to distin-guish themselves in a very direct, self-contained, and totally controllable way. They needed simple tools to make their art and they made their own decisions about what made it good.—Nelson George

Situating the High School for Recording Arts (HSRA) in multiple contexts gives the clearest picture of the school and the best perspective from which to consider the implications of Hip-Hop Genius. Whereas chapter 4 provided a societal context by discussing some of the systemic challenges faced by HSRA's students and the institution itself, this chapter focuses on the grow-ing field of hip-hop education. By profiling some of the trends in the field, this chapter locates HSRA's particular blend of hip-hop music, culture, and ingenuity.

Like any other field, hip-hop education contains a variety of value systems that manifest in a diverse set of techniques. All of the methods profiled in this chapter were developed with the intention of engaging and educating stu-dents, but some may be perceived as reductive or corny in their understand-ing of hip-hop, while others may come across as if they emerge from a deep understanding of hip-hop's intricacies. In order to place HSRA's work and the concept of Hip-Hop Genius in the vast field of education, it is necessary to consider all of these approaches.

Many experts on hip-hop education are not mentioned below—most importantly students and teachers who are engaged in hip-hop teaching and learning on a regular basis, but do not spend time writing about and publicizing their work. As happens in most arenas, a disproportionate percentage of the props end up going to academics who study and write about aspects of the work. Some innovators are lauded, while others whose contributions are just as valuable, if not more so, go unrecognized. These are the pioneers who stayed up late transcribing rap lyrics before the Internet provided tomes of such poems, who walked school hallways with karaoke machines bungee-corded to laundry carts, who slid desks to the sides of classrooms to create dance floors, and who turned cement walls of after-school centers into vertical visual playgrounds. It is because of and in honor of these groundbreakers that hip-hop education must be both defended and defined.

FROM DEFENDING TO DEFINING
HIP-HOP EDUCATION

A chart hangs on a classroom door at the state juvenile detention center in Cranston, Rhode Island. Its crooked stenciled letters inform students how many "points" they will lose for engaging in various activities. "Talking back" to the teacher costs three points; using curse words costs a student four points; *rapping costs five.* That poster-sized piece of cardstock illustrates a message: It is not that other educators don't recognize how powerful hip-hop can be—it is that they understand its potential and are scared of it.

Why are administrators and teachers afraid? Some view hip-hop as a negative influence in students' lives. As far as they are concerned, hip-hop music promotes violence, misogyny, homophobia, hypercapitalist consumption, and—to add insult to injury for the English teachers—bad grammar.

Hip-hop culture is seen as a force that competes for students' attention, which frustrates some teachers who invest time and energy attempting to engage students, only to be drowned out by cultural products that often critique the very values their schools are trying to instill.

Layers of racism, classism, and ageism also fuel some educators' negative responses to a cultural form created predominantly by black and Latino young people from low-income communities. This is likely magnified by how incredibly successful hip-hop is at engaging the very students that these same educators are unable—or, in some cases, unwilling—to reach.

In such hostile climates, it took courage for the first hip-hop educators to enter schools with boomboxes, linoleum mats, and graffiti magazines. It took tireless optimism for youth program administrators to write grants to start DJing and urban fashion design workshops.

Instructors had to justify every song they wanted to play, every guest they invited, every rhyme they allowed students to write, the way they embraced and spoke with students, the tilt of their hat and sag of their pants. They brought hip-hop culture into the classroom *despite* the systems and institutions they worked in—the potential for saving lives was too real.

For this reason and others, there has been explosive growth in the field of hip-hop education over the last several years. Hundreds of people have begun incorporating hip-hop music, culture, and sensibilities into their work as educators and education into their work as hip-hoppers. Some came up through academia, got certified as teachers, and then discovered hip-hop and the power it held in their work with young people; others were longtime hip-hop heads, who knew when they entered the profession that engaging hip-hop would be a central part of their work with students; while others found their way into classrooms through their reputations and relationships in the hip-hop community.

Regardless of how they came to it, these educators now find themselves defending the role of hip-hop music and culture. While the proliferation of hip-hop education may have chipped away at the notion that hip-hop is dangerous, there is still a battle being fought over whether it has educational merit. Cultural critic Bakari Kitwana observes: "I see hip-hop generationers who are parents, educators, artists and activists excited about the possibilities for hip-hop being used as a tool to reach students in elementary and high schools. Elite educators are concerned about the testing of such curriculum to measure its effectiveness, but hip-hop artists/educators are convinced if it helps students to connect to the material and get excited about learning, that's half the battle."[1]

A growing body of literature makes the case that hip-hop has an important, even essential, place in education. Scholars and practitioners appeal to readers from outside the hip-hop culture to "Get Hip to Hip-Hop," while hustling to assemble arguments and evidence that hip-hop is a valid literary form, a culture worthy of academic attention, and an effective instructional tool.[2]

In his essay "The Culture of Hip-Hop," sociology professor and prolific author on race and culture Michael Eric Dyson argues that rap music is rich with literary traditions and historical information.

"Rap expresses the ongoing preoccupation with literacy and orality that has characterized African-American communities since the inception of legally coerced illiteracy during slavery," Dyson explains. "Rap artists explore grammatical creativity, verbal wizardry, and linguistic innovation in refining the art of oral communication."

Dyson writes about how "rap has retrieved historic black ideas, movements, and figures" and posits that "this renewed historicism permits young blacks to discern links between the past and their own present circumstances, using the past as a fertile source of social reflection, cultural creation, and political resistance."[3]

"Regarding twenty-first century urban public school classroom instruction, what is more culturally responsive than Hip Hop?" asks education doctoral student Keisha Green in the Hip-Hop Association's *Hip-Hop Education Guidebook*. Green goes on to relate personal experiences as a high school English instructor in New York City, in an effort to demonstrate how "culturally responsive teaching and learning practices significantly enhance student academic achievement and overall engagement, particularly among black and brown students."[4]

Green explains how, in her class, hip-hop served as a "bridge between [students'] lived experiences, prior knowledge, and academic literacy." By designing a curriculum that related and compared the writings of Langston Hughes and Lorraine Hansberry to contemporary rap lyrics, Green "hooked" her students, "who, as a result willingly participated in classroom discussions and responded to the readings through essays that were written passionately and skillfully."[5]

As Green's example illustrates, much of hip-hop education thus far has been thought about within the context of classrooms in relatively conventional schools and out-of-school programs. Even more specifically, most often, hip-hop education has meant the study, analysis, and creation of texts—generally rap lyrics, videos, or films. This prioritization of the textual components of hip-hop—over the visual or physical elements—reflect society's privileging of cultural products that are easily monetized, such as CDs, DVDs, and MP3s, as well as schools' obsession with literary skills over all other forms of intelligence.

As the field has grown, practitioners and scholars have begun to document a variety of creative approaches to integrating hip-hop and education. Out of this wide range of methods, some overlapping trends have emerged, including using hip-hop as bait to get students in through the door of the classroom, studying hip-hop art as content, looking to hip-hop as fertile grounds for social justice education, and engaging hip-hop texts to investigate issues of identity with students.

USING HIP-HOP: THE PEANUT BUTTER AND THE PILL

Dogs hate pills. So, when a dog falls ill, how do you get it to take its medicine? One trick is to dip a spoon into a jar of peanut butter and then bury the pill in the lump of sweet saltiness. The dog will then lick at the spoon until all the peanut butter, and the pill, is swallowed.

The motivation of many educators who have turned to hip-hop is not to delve into the intrinsic values and lessons that the culture holds. Instead, teachers attempt to use hip-hop music and culture as peanut butter to get students to swallow pills—playing a rap song at the beginning of a class about poetry, while only making cursory efforts to find—or better yet, to ask students to find—connections between the song and the lesson.

There is no doubt that an opportunity to engage with hip-hop art can be a motivating factor for many students. HSRA has found that granting "All Access" passes to the school's recording studios on a weekly basis contingent upon each student's attendance and completion of tasks on their learning plan improves students' performance. But this is only one strand of the complex web of ways in which HSRA builds around hip-hop culture. There are inherent risks when schools use hip-hop as peanut butter and nothing more.

Just check out the language here: *Using* hip-hop. This is often the first instinct educators have when they begin to consider hip-hop's efficacy. A teacher uses Tupac (or fill in the rapper of choice) to try to lure students into studying Shakespeare (or fill in the traditionally valued writer of choice). It is not that such activities cannot be effective; it is that there are a number of unsafe assumptions that go into such a move.

One assumption is that students will relate to Tupac's music. Just because a student is a sixteen-year-old black male who lives in an urban community doesn't mean he listens to rap music. And, just because a student listens to rap music, does not mean she likes *all* rap music. Students of different ages from different areas of the country listen to different artists. For some students, 'Pac is not going to be peanut butter.

The final, potentially most harmful assumption is that students are like dogs that adults have the right to trick into swallowing something. There are times when students may resist doing certain things that are good for them, but the solution must be much more dynamic and authentic than bribing them using the Tupac–Shakespeare bump and switch.

HIP-HOP AS CONNECTION, CONTENT, AND CONDUIT

Some educators have combined the immediate interest hip-hop music can evoke with comparative and critical analysis of literary arts. California's 2007 Teacher of the Year Alan Lawrence Sitomer and the executive director of Urban Word NYC Michael Cirelli published *Hip-Hop Poetry and the Classics*, a book that provides teachers with lesson plans and worksheets that build on hip-hop's appeal to interest young people in "classic poetry," and on classic poetry's esteem to validate hip-hop's literary merits.[6]

The standards-aligned curriculum is intended to excite students about the complex meaning, power, and beauty of the written and spoken word while also aiming to teach them literary devices and analytical skills. These skills prepare students for success on standardized tests and, more importantly, they enrich students' experiences engaging with cultural products and media, as students develop new methods of interpretation and analysis.

Although these sorts of curricula can be extremely useful for English teachers overwhelmed by trying to build engaging lessons into state standards, there can be a problematic value judgment built in—generally by the authors of the standards and not the hip-hop educators—that what all students really need to read is "the classics." This is a manifestation of the commonly held belief in a canon of content—written almost entirely by white men who are no longer living—that all students need to know. The enforcement of such beliefs can alienate students, deny educators the freedom to be creative, prevent students from being exposed to many excellent texts, and perpetuate racism, classism, sexism, and other systems of hate.

In *Hip-Hop Poetry and the Classics*, Sitomer and Cirelli challenge this sort of hegemony, overtly calling existing power structures into question by inviting students to analyze lyrics from songs such as Public Enemy's "Fight the Power" and Tupac's "Me against the World." As their book demonstrates, hip-hop can be more than bait.

Rapper Gabriel "Asheru" Benn and his colleague Rick Henning have developed a catalog of "culturally relevant teaching materials" based on rap lyrics.[7] Their company, Educational Lyrics, creates National Reading Standards–aligned student workbooks, teachers' guides, and assessments that aim to improve student literacy without tying into canonical texts.[8] Each workbook focuses on one rap song, such as "The Ghetto" by Rakim or "Bridging the Gap" by Nas and his father Olu Dara, and provides more than sixty reading and writing activities stemming from the text.

Rather than referring to songs and lyrics by established rap artists, some teachers and students have organically developed raps, dances, and multimedia productions to communicate concepts that students are expected to learn and remember. In search of hip-hop materials that engage students, provide rich learning opportunities, and carry standards-aligned information and ideas, others have turned to a growing industry of nonprofits and companies who create CDs and complementary workbooks, offering them online with downloadable purchase orders for school administrators' convenience.

The website Mathraps.com advertises CDs by the Rappin' Mathematician, who on one volume kicks rhymes about a wide range of topics, including

"Geometric Shapes, Math Vocabulary, Saying NO to Drugs, . . . Parts of a Circle [and] Not Believing Everything on TV."[9] Other companies, such as Rhythm Rhyme Results and Flocabulary offer an array of textbooks and accompanying CDs on language arts, social studies, math, and science.[10]

Unlike the Rappin' Mathematician and Flocabulary, Smart Shorties, a subsidiary of the Scholastic publishing company, engages students in the *production* of songs and videos that teach mathematical concepts.[11] With the guidance of an experienced teacher and a pop music producer, a small group of students craft catchy lyrics and set them to the most popular rap beats of the moment. These songs are then sold to schools, where students are encouraged to memorize their peers' creations through repetition of the lyrics and choreographing dances to the songs.

A pilot study conducted by the company found that 67 percent of Smart Shorties' participants in Washington, D.C., improved their test scores.[12] The point here is not that test scores are an accurate measurement of a program's efficacy, but rather that these approaches are being marketed and measured as tools for success within established educational systems.

Similar to the Smart Shorties model, HSRA students compose original beats and lyrics to build their own mathematical knowledge while creating songs to help others learn as well. Mike Conway, one of HSRA's math facilitators, partners with Phil Winden, the school's studio director to engage students in learning math and music production skills in tandem.

As students compose beats in software programs such as ProTools and Logic, they see visual representations of sound waves. By drawing connections between the sound waves and trigonometric concepts, Mike equips students to read the visual information on their screens. This provides young producers with another source of information when making beats.

One group of students produced a half-hour radio show on the "Music of Math" that aired on the Twin Cities' commercial hip-hop station, KTTB-FM, 96.3.[13] They employed mathematical concepts, such as amplitude, frequency, and phase shift, to construct beats for songs about those very concepts.

Between playing original songs like "A Story of SOCATOA" and "Speaking Statistically," students talked about the connections between math and music; and one student, "Ruby P.," demonstrated the concepts of amplitude, frequency, and phase shift through an improvisational beat-boxing routine.

Other groups of HSRA students have produced songs to teach younger learners math rules, replacing mnemonics like "Please Excuse My Dear Aunt Sally" with hip new ways to remember the order of operations. The tutoring company, Rocket Learning, has commissioned HSRA students to develop such songs. Students and staff are now considering starting their own business producing educational music.

While some of the songs that HSRA students record integrate academic subjects, HSRA provides ample opportunities for students to teach and learn the art of hip-hop lyricism and music production as an end in itself. Like their counterparts at HSRA, other educators across the country also teach hip-hop skills for the sake of deepening students' understanding, appreciation, and mastery of the art forms. This most commonly happens in the context of out-of-school programs or school electives.

Rather than inviting kids to record songs for the purpose of helping them learn math or any other traditional school subject, these educators have put together lessons that teach students how to write rhymes, freestyle, DJ, make beats, breakdance, draw and paint graffiti pieces, design apparel, and build other skills related to hip-hop culture. In these instances, the creation of hip-hop art is itself *the* subject of study.

THE THIRD HALF

Even when teachers have the freedom to move outside the realm of standards and classics to introduce hip-hop texts and techniques on their own merits, the focus is often more on *what* is being learned than *how* learning is happen. Lesson plans that teach hip-hop skills can be highly appealing to students, as can lessons that involve analyzing popular texts, but—unless approached creatively—both kinds of lessons are more innovative in content than pedagogy.

Asking a whole class to watch a video that they find exciting and then break into groups to discuss the subject matter can be a cool, engaging, and even transformative thing for a teacher to do. But it is a classroom exercise. It is not necessarily flipping dominant educational practices.

If Kitwana is correct that getting students connected to school and excited about learning is "half the battle," the other half, which is equally important, is what to do once they're connected. A central piece of this second half is the development of literacy and numeracy skills, as described above as well as in examples from HSRA that appear in previous chapters, such as Reidun's paper defending Harry Potter and Lil C's book on astrology. Ensuring that young people develop proficiency with words and numbers is key to ensuring that they are able to live fulfilling lives.

But *how* will they acquire those skills and what other abilities and sensibilities might they develop? Once they are drawn in, will hip-hop music and culture be engaged through teaching methods that mimic the "essentially static" styles criticized by John Dewey? Or does hip-hop hold new pedagogical possibilities?

Some educators and scholars are working with students to identify approaches to teaching and learning that are unique to hip-hop. In these ways and more, hip-hop's potential to reshape educational practices may be an equally important *third half* of Kitwana's equation.

HIP-HOP EDUCATION AS
SOCIAL JUSTICE EDUCATION

The Hip-Hop Association's *Hip-Hop Education Guidebook* is arguably the most comprehensive hip-hop education text available.[14] In addition to providing lesson plans and worksheets that would fit into the trends explored above, the guidebook provides a theoretical framework for what hip-hop education should entail.

One of the authors and creators of the guidebook, Marcella Runell Hall, explores hip-hop's place in social justice education, arguing that "All hip-hop education should be grounded and contextualized in the belief that our society is characterized by oppression, which includes but is not limited to racism, classism and sexism."[15] In this context, Paulo Freire, Gloria Ladson-Billings, and Sonia Nieto are invoked, and the case is made for a shift toward social justice education, which Runell Hall describes as an "interdisciplinary, comprehensive" extension of critical pedagogy.[16]

In his essay "We Can Relate: Hip-Hop Culture, Critical Pedagogy, and the Secondary Classroom," education professor David Stovall describes several social studies lessons he facilitated in which the critical analysis of rap lyrics sparked group discussions about topics relevant to students' lives.[17] For instance, Stovall recounts linking Talib Kweli's rap remake of the song "Four Women" by Nina Simone to Howard Zinn's *Peoples' History of the United States* to initiate a conversation about historical accuracy. The class looked at the portrayals of slavery in the texts and discussed how they differed from the historical narratives generally disseminated in schools. They were asked to consider how schools promoted deception and "What would be included in a curriculum that challenged dishonesty?"[18]

A media education nonprofit, Just Think, has created a curriculum called "Flipping the Script" that answers this question by providing educators with tools to provoke students to think critically about the messages propagated by hip-hop artists and companies that associate themselves with hip-hop culture. Lesson plans delve into topics such as the ways companies covertly advertise products through hip-hop songs and the ways that hip-hop magazines and videos affect young peoples' views on sexuality and body image.

Many of Just Think's lesson plans not only have students analyze existing hip-hop texts but also ask them to create their own songs or videos. In this way, curriculums such as Flipping the Script invite students to critique systems of oppression and then develop their own alternative cultural products that subvert these systems.

Over the course of their tenure at HSRA, many students engage in a similar process of critical analysis and cultural production through Urban Music workshops facilitated by Darryl Young, a special education facilitator, and Phil Winden, the school's studio director. Urban Music teaches participants how to use audio production skills to make an impact on issues that affect their lives and communities.

Past Urban Music groups have produced compilation albums on topics ranging from homelessness to HIV awareness. These professional quality, mass-produced albums are distributed to audience members of all ages with targeted recipient groups depending upon the issue addressed.

The songs on each compilation represent research the students have conducted and offer multiple viewpoints on the topic, as well as their personal experiences and perspectives. These songs serve as words of inspiration and sometimes warning for their peers while also giving outsiders a glimpse at some of the challenges they face.

Urban Music carries on the hip-hop tradition of critically addressing social injustices. Although hip-hop has always included party music, it has also always told stories of experiences that were not being represented in mainstream media. Urban Music continues this legacy, teaching students how to make their songs sound good but also instilling a level of consciousness and responsibility around the message of their music.

If hip-hop education is not limited to using hip-hop culture to entice students or engaging hip-hop music as content to study for the purpose of teaching academic skills, but instead is a continuation of the traditions of popular education and critical pedagogy, then it can be a movement toward liberation. This offers students the chance to become architects of a more just destiny for themselves and their world—and it is fundamentally empowering.

As Freire states, "In order for the oppressed to be able to wage the struggle for their liberation, they must perceive the reality of oppression not as a closed world, from which there is no exit, but as a limiting situation which they can transform."[19] The work Runell-Hall, Stovall, Flipping the Script, HSRA, and others are doing to make this happen using hip-hop texts and culture is crucial to breaking systems of violence and oppression.

IDENTITY EXPLORATION

Critically examining hip-hop texts and other media holds the promise of preparing students to be conscious consumers and creators of cultural products. But education professor Greg Dimitriadis encourages educators to let go of the "notions of control and competence that often gird . . . discussions about media literacy."[20]

Dimitriadis outlines two common problematic assumptions among media literacy educators: the first being that educators "need to teach young people to protect themselves from the pernicious effects of media," and the second being that there should be a predetermined "end point of school knowledge in mind."[21] By making these assumptions, Dimitriadis argues, educators miss important opportunities to understand young peoples' lives in more nuanced ways and overlook valuable information that could help them reconsider their own roles as teachers and thinkers.

Dimitriadis spent four years conducting one-on-one interviews and focus groups with an "almost wholly black and poor population" of young people at a community center in a small Midwestern city to develop an understanding of how they interpreted and experienced hip-hop texts (which included songs, videos, and films) in their lives.[22] In his book *Performing Identity/Performing Culture: Hip-Hop as Text, Pedagogy and Lived Practice*, Dimitriadis offers an ethnographic treatment of these conversations and explores the dynamic manner in which hip-hop texts interplay with each other and with young peoples' experiences to carry out an important function in formulating knowledge and identity.

Dimitriadis points out that much media literacy work—both in and outside the hip-hop genre—treats individual texts in isolation. It does not take full account of the ways in which young people actually experience and interpret texts: in conjunction with many other texts, in relation to other people, and as influenced by their environment.

Building on Dimitriadis' foundation, education professor Marc Lamont Hill's book, *Beats, Rhymes, and Classroom Life: Hip-Hop Pedagogy and the Politics of Identity*, explores engagements of hip-hop texts in a classroom setting. Hill's book offers a participant-researcher's anthropological perspective of teaching a yearlong course called Hip-Hop Lit at an evening program for students "who do not fit comfortably within the day school environment."[23]

Hill is not only concerned with the impact that introducing hip-hop texts can have on students' academic engagement and literacy but also on the effects that studying such texts—and, in particular, studying them in a formal schooling context—can have on their identity. In turn, Hill also looks at the ways in which students' presentations and transformations of their identities affect relationships within the classroom.

Although the stated goals of Hill's Hip-Hop Lit course revolved around literary interpretation, analysis, and criticism, Hill structured much of the class around students' personal stories. By asking them to journal about how the song lyrics they studied related to their lives and inviting them to share their responses with the group, Hill engaged the class in a process he describes as "wounded healing," whereby students "shared their stories in ways that provided a form of release and relief for themselves and others."[24]

Eliciting such personal disclosure was intended not only to be therapeutic but also to offer students a way to critically engage with specific texts as well as dominant narratives. Hill argues that "these practices not only defy a priori analyses, but also radically challenge sanctioned formations of knowledge and produce new categories of meaning."[25]

Many English and social studies teachers invite students to explore their identities through journaling and sharing stories with each other. The lyrics selected by Hill and his students provided them with entry points, content, and frames of analysis. As students developed dexterity relating to the texts, they practiced critical thinking, literary analysis, and the exploration and articulation of self-awareness.

At HSRA, self-awareness is explored, sanctioned forms of knowledge are challenged, and new categories of meaning are produced through students' creation of their own music and texts. Some students at the school choose to explicitly analyze other artists' compositions, some organically refer to previous works in their own creations, and some staff members bring song lyrics into workshops to be discussed, but the main way in which students experience release and relief, and present and explore their identities, is through assuming the role of artist and author.

There is an empowering and generative quality to such practices, as they avoid the preordained, teacher-determined end point about which Dimitriadis cautions. But there are also risks that come with encouraging such personal engagement with and creation of texts. Hill relays a story in which he introduces song lyrics about abortion and pushes a female student to share her analysis. Eventually, he realizes that she does not want to discuss the text because of her personal experience with abortion, but by the time he figures this out, she is upset and ends up disappearing from school for seven days.

"By linking the curriculum to the lived realities of the students, particularly those from marginalized groups, we position ourselves to hear stories of pain . . . that are often difficult to hear and even more difficult to tell," Hill warns.[26]

While the disconnect that students commonly feel between their identities and their academic experiences is in many ways a barrier to engagement and academic success, there is a new set of risks and responsibilities once students feel their identities are bound up in their schoolwork. This is true whether students are analyzing and reflecting on texts by others or creating their own works of art.

In the final section of his book, Hill discusses possible meanings of "hip-hop pedagogies": "In addition to using hip-hop as a scaffold for teaching traditional skills, educators must also draw from the alternative forms of knowledge and new categories of meaning that are produced through a pedagogical engagement with hip-hop culture. . . . [For instance,] How could the notion of a 'hip-hop cipher,' which marks the democratic ethos of hip-hop culture, allow us to reimagine classroom participation?"[27] These are the sorts of questions that must now be contemplated. Hill limits his query to locating "new sites of educational possibility within hip-hop based-classrooms," but it is time to go further.[28] It is time to call into question not only what happens within classrooms but also whether classrooms are needed at all.

This is the Hip-Hop Genius approach to education. No structure or convention should be viewed as unchangeable. As HSRA demonstrates, entire institutions can be reimagined and reconfigured. From promising new possibilities to explore within the context of classrooms to a fresh examination of the overall structure of schooling, the time has come to approach the field of hip-hop education in a more holistic light.

NOTES

1. Bakari Kitwana, as quoted in Paul Farber, "Hip Hop High," originally in *Philadelphia Weekly*, www.iahhe.org/HipHopHigh.pdf (accessed December 17, 2010).

2. Edward DeJesus, *Makin' It: The Hip-Hop Guide to True Survival* (Gaithersburg, Md.: Youth Development and Research Fund, 2003), 7.

3. Michael Eric Dyson, *The Michael Eric Dyson Reader* (New York: Basic Civitas, 2004), 408–10.

4. Keisha Green, "Check It: Reflections on Hip-Hop & Education," in *The Hip-Hop Education Guidebook*, Vol. 1, ed. Tatiana Forero Puerta, Marcella Runell, and Martha Diaz (New York: Hip-Hop Association, 2007), 20.

5. Green, "Check It," 21.

6. Michael Cirelli and Alan Lawrence Sitomer, *Hip-Hop Poetry and the Classics for the Classroom* (Beverly Hills, Calif.: Milk Mug, 2004).

7. Educational Lyrics, "About Educational Lyrics," http://edlyrics.com/about-h-e-l-p/about-educational-lyrics/ (accessed December 17, 2010).

8. Educational Lyrics, "What is H.E.L.P.?," http://edlyrics.com/about-h-e-l-p/what-is-h-e-l-p/ (accessed January 13, 2011).

9. The Rappin' Mathematician, "The Rappin' Mathematician Volume 1," http://mathraps.com/volume_1.htm (accessed February 18, 2009).

10. Rhythm Rhyme Results, http://www.educationalrap.com/ (accessed December 17, 2010); and Flocabulary, http://www.flocabulary.com (accessed December 17, 2010).

11. Smart Shorties, www.smartshorties.com (accessed December 17, 2010).

12. Scholastic, "Musical Math," http://www2.scholastic.com/browse/article.jsp?id=3750328 (accessed December 17, 2010).

13. To hear the "Music of Math" radio program, which aired on KTTB-FM, 96.3, Minneapolis/St. Paul on June 8, 2008, visit http://www.thefoshow.com/2008/06/09/the-fo-show-episode-37-math-of-music/ (accessed December 17, 2010).

14. Puerta, Runell, and Diaz, *The Hip-Hop Education Guidebook.*

15. Marcella Runell, "The Organic Connection between Hip-Hop and Social Justice Education," in *The Hip-Hop Education Guidebook,* 60.

16. Marcella Runell Hall, in discussion with the author, October 2009.

17. David Stovall, "We Can Relate: Hip-Hop Culture, Critical Pedagogy, and the Secondary Classroom," *Urban Education* 41, no. 6 (2006): 585.

18. Stovall, "We Can Relate," 596–97.

19. Paulo Freire, *Pedagogy of the Oppressed* (New York: Herder and Herder, 1971), 34.

20. Greg Dimitriadis, *Performing Identity/Performing Culture: Hip-Hop as Text, Pedagogy, and Lived Practice* (New York: Peter Lang, 2009), 159.

21. Dimitriadis, *Performing Identity/Performing Culture.*

22. Dimitriadis, *Performing Identity/Performing Culture,* 3.

23. Marc Lamont Hill, *Beats, Rhymes, and Classroom Life: Hip-Hop Pedagogy and the Politics of Identity* (New York: Teachers College Press, 2009), 15.

24. Hill, *Beats, Rhymes, and Classroom Life,* 65.

25. Hill, *Beats, Rhymes, and Classroom Life,* 121.

26. Hill, *Beats, Rhymes, and Classroom Life,* 96.

27. Hill, *Beats, Rhymes, and Classroom Life,* 124.

28. Hill, *Beats, Rhymes, and Classroom Life.*

Chapter 6

Flip-Hop Education

More overtly than ever, the nature of genius . . . has become an issue bound up with the economic fortunes of nations. Amid the vast modern network of universities, corporate laboratories, and national science foundations has arisen an awareness that the best financed and best organized of research enterprises have not learned to engender, perhaps not even to recognize, world-turning originality.—James Gleick

The possibilities are numerous once we decide to act and not react.
—George Bernard Shaw

So what is the future of Hip-Hop Genius? Will the ideas and practices that have been brewing at the High School for Recording Arts (HSRA) over the past decade penetrate the education mainstream? These questions must be considered on multiple fronts.

On the theoretical tip: Will hip-hop education practitioners and scholars continue to focus primarily on what occurs inside classrooms in traditionally structured schools or will the conversation expand to imagining new kinds of educational programs and leadership?

And on a practical level: Can HSRA continue to offer such an unconventional diploma-granting program in an age of increasing standardization and decreasing state education budgets? If so, will it always be a small anomaly in St. Paul, Minnesota, or will its sphere of influence grow?

This chapter explores a few of the ways that HSRA might play a direct role in spreading Hip-Hop Genius sensibilities throughout the field of education and beyond. Beginning by describing the interest the leaders of HSRA have in expanding the school's impact, the chapter goes on to weigh the merits and challenges of attempting to replicate the school in other locations, consider the possibility of establishing the existing program as a lab school to accommodate and acculturate visitors, and highlight the school's potential as a source of inspiration. The chapter concludes by contemplating the broader implications of Hip-Hop Genius and suggesting the benefits such a concept could have outside the purview of the education system.

INCREASING IMPACT

Despite the challenges that HSRA has faced locally as described in chapter 4, the school's successes have been lauded around the country and internationally. Staff and students have presented in settings from open houses to Oxford, and the school has been featured in several articles and short films.

HSRA is one of twenty-four "mentor schools" for the Coalition of Essential Schools, a national network of six hundred small schools that strive to be "personalized, equitable and intellectually challenging."[1] HSRA's role as a mentor school has involved hosting visitors and leading sessions at national conferences.

HSRA has also been a model school for the EdVisions network. EdVisions is an education development organization based in Minnesota. In 2000, EdVisions received a grant from the Bill & Melinda Gates Foundation to develop a cohort of small, project-based schools.

In developing their network, EdVisions embraced HSRA as one of their schools. EdVisions has several successful schools to show visitors, but HSRA demonstrates the success of EdVisions's design principles with urban students of color. When EdVisions has needed to demonstrate the potential of its model for this population, they have brought visitors to HSRA.

In the last decade, educators, nonprofit administrators, and foundation program officers have invested significant time and money in exploring the possibility of replicating successful school designs. Organizations like EdVisions, Big Picture Learning, Communities in Schools, Diploma Plus, Gateway to College, Knowledge Is Power Program (commonly known as KIPP), Street Schools Network, and YouthBuild USA have launched national replication projects. Others, such as the Association for the Advancement of Mexican Americans, Good Shepherd Services, Green Dot Public Schools, High Tech High, and the See Forever Foundation have embarked on regional or local replication efforts.

The leaders at HSRA have decided to explore this possibility as well. A large part of the reason they became interested in expanding their work is the demand they have had for it. In addition to guests who come through EdVisions and the Coalition of Essential Schools, educators from around the country visit to learn from the school. Others invite HSRA's founder David "TC" Ellis and director of development Tony Simmons to speak to and coach school staffs and consult in the development of new schools and programs.

While HSRA is proud to be a part of these networks, the school's leaders feel that over the years they have developed their own unique brand of school. What's more, they believe the design they have developed could make the difference between dropping out and success for many more young people across the country. The question the leadership of HSRA has been asking themselves is, how can they most effectively share and spread what they have built in St. Paul?

REPLICATING A SCHOOL'S DESIGN

In 2007, Dr. Jennifer Murphy, the program director of Centinela Media Arts Academy in southwestern Los Angeles County, California, learned about HSRA and felt such a program would be the perfect direction for her urban media arts school. Dr. Murphy worked with Ellis and Simmons to structure an agreement through which Studio 4, the education management and studio services company that provides the programmatic backbone for HSRA, would branch out to work with Centinela Media Arts Academy to transform it into the High School for Recording Arts Los Angeles (HSRA LA).

Studio 4 provided materials and coaching for the Centinela Media Arts Academy staff. Ellis and Simmons personally traveled to Los Angeles many times to work with the school's leadership. HSRA Minnesota's studio director, Phil Winden, moved to Los Angeles to build the school's recording studio and to develop the music-engineering program.

The physical layout of the school was arranged to reproduce elements of HSRA Minnesota's design. There was a large open workspace divided with half walls into advisory areas. Posters of the HSRA validations and principles were hung about the room, as were graffiti-style murals. The media lab upstairs was lined with computers stocked with music production and graphic design software. And, of course, there was a state-of-the-art recording studio.

The school's program also followed HSRA Minnesota's design. Students were grouped in advisories and learned through projects and workshops; credits were awarded based on validations; students earned All Access passes, which granted them entry to the school's recording studio; on Wednesdays they held community meetings and on Fridays they had Pick Me Ups.[2]

The first year of the Media Arts Academy/Studio 4 partnership was promising. Students demonstrated their appreciation for the program through consistent attendance and the passion with which they spoke about the school. "[In traditional schools] people looked at me like a low-life gangster," a student named Giovanna Zepeda said. "When I got to Media Arts Academy, they looked at me different, they looked at me like I was somebody. . . . This is the only place we can be ourselves and express ourselves."[3]

There would not be a chance to find out how successful the program could become. A bureaucratic technicality placed the school's future in jeopardy.

The school's charter application renewal date was listed differently in two documents. Murphy was basing her understanding on language in the school's charter, which indicated that there was another year before the charter would have to be renewed. The Centinela Valley Union School District was going by a different date, which they had specified in their resolution to approve the charter. While most districts send notice to schools a year before their charter expires, the Centinela Valley district did not provide any warning or notification to the school until after this expiration date had passed.[4]

There was speculation among charter school advocates that the technicality which threatened the school's future might have been politically and economically motivated. The Centinela Valley district serves as the authorizer for charter schools (though Media Arts was the only one they had ever approved), but the district is also in direct competition with charters for students—and the funding that follows them.

While one would hope that everyone would have students' best interests at heart, some speculated that the district wanted to close Centinela Media Arts Academy to have access to the funding that was allotted to the students who attended the school. Others questioned whether the school board was prejudiced against Centinela Media Arts Academy because of the school's newfound allegiance to hip-hop culture.

As all this was going down in Southern California, a group of educators a thousand miles north in Portland, Oregon, reached out to Studio 4 to ask for help starting an HSRA-style program for local teenagers. Through a consulting contract, Studio 4 provided technical assistance and materials to the Portland educators as they wrote the application for a charter school. In December of 2009, the Portland School Board unanimously approved the school's charter application, and the school opened in the fall of 2011.

Throughout the replication efforts in Los Angeles and Portland, Studio 4 has also been working to open a school in New York City. The leaders of HSRA believe that, as the birthplace of hip-hop, New York is the perfect place for a hip-hop high school.

Simmons is a native New Yorker, and since he moved to Minnesota to work with the school, he has dreamed of bringing HSRA's unique design back to his hometown. HSRA has received planning grants for a New York City school from the Black Alliance for Educational Options Small Schools Project and the New York City Center for Charter School Excellence, and has convened a planning team on the ground in New York.

The e-mails and calls requesting HSRA's style of education continue. In 2009, HSRA got word from a team of educators in Atlanta who had already applied for a charter to open a high school based on the HSRA design.

Educators who run two successful schools in Baton Rouge have expressed interest in bringing the design to their area.

Replication is an extremely challenging undertaking, but its potential impact makes it tempting. Any school that HSRA helps to open would be able to serve a few hundred students every year, providing them with an educational experience and path to graduation that otherwise would not have been available. For students who have been kicked out or have slid out of all other available options, this could be their only chance at receiving a high school diploma.

Though in the current funding climate and standards-based culture, it would be extremely difficult to support a network of multiple schools like HSRA, if it came to a point where there were a handful of HSRA-style schools spread out around the country that were showing significant signs of success in student retention and achievement, it is possible more would follow. Not enough programs have triumphant track records serving young people who have dropped out and been pushed out of other schools. To the extent that HSRA establishes itself as a proven and replicable design, many more communities could request similar programs.

A small thriving network of schools would put HSRA in a better position to influence national dialogues in both education and hip-hop circles. While successfully developing and running one school for over a decade is significant, demonstrating a distinctive school design's efficacy at a larger scale attracts more attention and inspires different levels of conversations. It compels educational theorists to contemplate the effectiveness of the schools' approach. It pushes funders who are committed to reducing the opportunity gap to consider supporting the development of such programs. It challenges heads from within the hip-hop industry and its fan base to reimagine what it means to *be hip-hop*, and it provokes a reconsideration of the power that the music and culture possess.

Successful replication of the HSRA design would have the potential to have a ripple effect on education. If schools can carry out a high-quality implementation of HSRA's school design and principles, the effect will be broader than just the students they are able to serve. Other schools in their geographic areas can be influenced by their successes and may try implementing elements of the school's design.

Whatever proven successes the HSRA schools can boast will help create political cover for nearby schools to follow in their footsteps in the celebration of hip-hop culture and young peoples' intelligence and abilities, and in the areas of project-based learning, performance-based assessment, and culturally relevant instruction.

The other ripple of influence that a national network of HSRA schools could have would come from the schools' graduates. Having experienced racism, classism, and a range of other structural shorts, many of these young people have had an inside perspective on society's worst problems.

By the time they emerge from HSRA with diplomas, graduates have had the chance to identify and pursue their own passions, they have been responsible for the production of professional-quality products, and they have tasted the powerful positive impact they can have on the world. This boost in skills, self-confidence, and hope, combined with intimate knowledge of society's shortcomings, is powerful.

Some alumni will go on to pursue careers in music like Young Menace, who, as mentioned in chapter 1, produces for several television networks, and Beatnick who—along with his partner K-Salaam—has produced tracks for reggae, dancehall, R&B, and hip-hop artists, such as Buju Banton, Dead Prez, Sizzla, Talib Kweli, Trey Songz, and Young Buck.

Other alumni will make an impact in the field of education. Like the many alum-employees mentioned in earlier chapters, future graduates may work for HSRA or other schools like it. And, as Codie Wilson expressed an interest in doing in chapter 3, some will endeavor to start their own schools or youth programs.

Still others will carry these attributes to other industries, taking the spark of inspiration from attending a school so different from the traditional paradigm and running with it. The more HSRA schools there are around the country, the more graduates will bring this unique blend of self-confidence, skills, and inspiration to external communities. This could be the most powerful impact of replicating HSRA's model.

But maybe none of this will happen through bringing HSRA-style schools to more cities. Replication is a grueling endeavor—one that, if educators are not careful, can pull them away from what they do best: running a great school. It demands immense capacity.

For every day that Ellis, Simmons, and Winden were in Los Angeles, Portland, Atlanta, or New York City, they were not in St. Paul. HSRA has twelve strong years to build on, so it will not fall apart if some of its leaders are away from time to time, but even the best schools are fragile. Removing leaders—or just distracting them—can take a toll.

There is also a danger, whenever a school's design is replicated, that the original model can be copied too literally. A solution that works in one community doesn't necessarily work in another.

This is why High Tech High founder Larry Rosenstock keeps a definition of the word "model" on a scrap of paper stuck to his computer monitor: "Model: a non-functioning replica." Over the years, Rosenstock, who has led a few different approaches to replicating High Tech High's school design—which he intentionally no longer refers to as a "model"—has come to understand that schools are living organisms. Given the right set of conditions, they can spawn new, highly successful sibling schools, but they cannot be cloned.

A large part of HSRA's success is the swagger and agility with which Ellis and his colleagues govern the school. If there is a good idea—like starting the school day at 10 a.m.—even if it is unconventional, they will try it. But what about a school leader who is running HSRA Gotham? What if she has an idea for how to change the program? Can she go ahead and make that change or would it then no longer be an HSRA school?

It would be in the Hip-Hop Genius ethos to allow extreme flexibility for change. But what if she made another substantive change? And then another? Eventually the school might look nothing like HSRA. Students might wear uniforms and sit in rows in traditional classes. There might no longer be recording studios. Everything that makes HSRA unique might be gone.

This metamorphosis may sound unlikely—why would someone go to the trouble to start a new school based on an existing school's design, only to change it so dramatically? Yet this has happened to other alternative schools that have tried to replicate.

In fact, the myriad forces that tug schools toward conventional practices can be overwhelming. Even after decades of experience in the field and possessing celebrity education reformer status, Dennis Littky and Elliot Washor felt the powerful pull toward the traditional when they began the Big Picture network of schools. In response to these pressures, in their early years they sported T-shirts emblazoned with the mantra "No Backsliding."

The backslide can happen for many reasons. Sometimes the inspirational leader who has a passion for the alternative design leaves (or is ousted). Other times, new school leaders like the *ideas* of the design in theory, but later they discover that they do not like what these ideas look like in *practice*.

School districts can put tremendous pressure on school leaders to move their designs toward the middle—that is, away from the most edgy and innovative. Or, in some cases, everyone supports the design, but school staff members just don't have the experience, training, or instincts needed to implement it.

For all of the reasons stated above, the balance between maintaining fidelity to essential elements of a school's design and allowing leaders the flexibility to riff on the design is a tricky one. HSRA is in an experimental phase. The school's leaders are testing approaches to replication and trying different levels of involvement in schools that are fashioning themselves in HSRA's image. They may decide to be highly proactive in the replication of HSRA or they may opt for a different approach to creating influence.

AN OPEN SOURCE LAB SCHOOL

Another way HSRA's leaders could pursue sharing their successes with the world would be to focus on their flagship school. Rather than spending energy helping people in other cities launch hip-hop high schools, they could focus all of their efforts on advancing and articulating the program in St. Paul. Running one phenomenal program could ultimately be their most effective avenue of influence.

If HSRA's leaders double down on innovating within the context of one small school that is already up and running, they will be able to tighten elements of the program and continue the types of creative interventions for which they are known. Further, they could focus on developing materials that document their innovative educational methods, and they could prepare their students, staff, and facility to host visitors on a regular basis.

This approach would allow them to build and share expertise in a different manner. It would also serve as inspiration to all who are attracted to what they are doing and it would bolster their reputation, thereby amplifying their voice in national dialogues.

Other schools have taken this approach. After ten years of outstanding results helping middle and high school students become the first members of their families to attend college, the University Park Campus School in Worcester, Massachusetts, partnered with Jobs for the Future and Clark University to open the University Park Campus School Institute for Student Success.

Seven times throughout the school year, the institute offers a two-and-a-half-day training for school developers and leaders. Attendees are exposed to the University Park Campus School's culture and program design through immersion in the regular activities of the school. Participants have the chance to observe classes, talk with students, meet the principal, and attend leadership and instructional workshops. They then participate in guided opportunities to process and debrief their experiences.

Similarly, Good Shepherd Services in New York City has been developing and enacting a strategy to share their successes. Good Shepherd Services operates a "Learning Lab" out of the South Brooklyn Community High School. About twenty visitors each month have the chance to receive a tour from a current student at the school, observe classes, listen to an overview of the school's design, receive materials, and debrief their experiences. Good Shepherd Services has codified their best practices in a 115-page manual, which they offer for free on their website.[5]

While University Park and Good Shepherd Services built training opportunities around successful schools, the Eagle Rock School and Professional

Development Center in Estes Park, Colorado, was, from its founding in 1991, deliberately intended to be both a school for young people who had "not experienced success in traditional academic programs" *and* a professional development center for aspiring and established educators.[6]

People are invited to visit the school through a wide variety of options, including tours, residencies, fellowships, student teaching, and research residencies. Eagle Rock's students and staff also travel to present at conferences and to assist in school reform efforts. Two books and a DVD about Eagle Rock provide additional opportunities for the public to learn about the school.

Like University Park, Good Shepherd Services, and Eagle Rock, HSRA could focus its efforts on develop programming and materials to share with people who visit their school and website. Rather than attempting to manage a replication process, the school's leaders could instead concentrate on making their school as excellent as possible in every area, and then create channels for others to borrow, adapt, sample, and remix elements of their design.

SERVING AS AN INSPIRATIONAL BURST

HSRA's existence is improbable. Who would have thought that the art and style of poor teenagers in New York City several decades ago would be the basis for a school in Minnesota? And when David Ellis dropped out of high school and was messing with drugs, who would have predicted that he would found such a program? The fact that the school has continued to persevere, grow, and gain momentum for over a decade only adds to its power as a beacon for people who have held little hope for public education.

Hearing Ellis speak about the genesis of the school can inspire people to think differently about what is possible in the field of education. Talking with students about the difference attending HSRA has made in their lives can do the same. The bold and unconventional approach the school has taken to helping students learn, graduate, and succeed beyond high school can replenish people's gusto for thinking and acting outside the box.

This sort of inspirational burst may be HSRA's most effective tool in changing the experiences for students in large public schools. It is unlikely that the administration of such schools would approach HSRA with a desire to adopt the school's design. It's hard to imagine how they would even implement the HSRA model at such a large scale. But individual teachers or administrators could still find inspiration in the radical approach that HSRA has taken as an institution.

Also, hip-hop artists and fans who hear Ellis's story could become inspired to enter the field of education. The fact that Ellis was not formally trained as an educator yet has managed to do so much in the field might inspire others to try similar endeavors in the education space or in other social sectors. Ellis's story could have a similar effect for people who don't identify with hip-hop but relate to his struggles as a young man with the education system, drugs, and finding a productive role in society.

HSRA's innovative spirit inspires people beyond the field of education. Susan Campion, a business consultant and instructor at the Center for Business Excellence at the University of St. Thomas, recently presented about HSRA at a Global Leadership Conference in Prague.

Campion's workshop, entitled "Beats, Rhymes and Breakthrough Ideas: Lessons in Innovation from Hip Hop High," drew messages for businesspeople from the work of the students and staff of HSRA. Others outside of the education field have and will continue to learn from and be inspired by HSRA's innovative and entrepreneurial spirit and actions.

After all, HSRA's existence and practices exemplify exactly what our education system and our planet need right now: creative and audacious solutions to massive problems. The current secretary of education, Arne Duncan, recognizes this need and uses the term "innovation" frequently. His department has recently launched a $650-million Investing in Innovation Fund.

In order to apply, programs must have "demonstrated success in significantly increasing student academic achievement for all groups of students."[7] In other words, the fund will support organizations that have successfully run a program for long enough that they have had time to measure its effectiveness—undoubtedly great work to sponsor, but perhaps not a true boost to innovation.[8]

A more direct investment in innovation would be awarding grants to programs that were setting out to try new things; initiatives that had not demonstrated success yet but were good ideas with good people behind them. There would have to be a built-in tolerance for the unknown, for failure—or, at least, for unexpected results. This would be a risky move for the federal government to make, but it would encourage dramatic and profound discoveries, as opposed to incremental change.

Regardless of federal support, real innovation will occur in the education sector.

Consider the hip-hop industry. Major record labels keep serving up the same formula: misogynist, hypercapitalist, super-gangster lyrics over beats by the producer du jour. But there are increasingly large amounts of good, genre-boundary-defying music being made. It is just being released on independent labels, more likely to be sold on the Internet than at the record store. This is not to belittle the challenges faced by independent artists. Rather, it is to point out that there are always channels, literal and figurative, through which cutting-edge music can be heard. HSRA's songs and stories of success can provide voices of inspiration—theme music for the changes to come.

THE FUTURE OF EDUCATION

Blending multiple elements, flipping their original uses and meanings, and creating some newness—education must continue in the spirit of hybridization and innovation exemplified by hip-hop. Evolving manifestations of social justice education, media literacy, and identity development are crucial parts of this, but there are countless additional opportunities to reconsider educational experiences at every level, from individual interactions to the very structure of the institutions in which those interactions take place. Traditional schooling and even many iterations of hip-hop education are not designed to fully honor and engage students' brilliance in all the diverse and sometimes contradictory ways it can occur.

Whether students are weaving clever wordplay into their writing, blinging out the rims of their bike with tin foil, or starting up a natural soda business, educators must encourage, extend, and learn from students' ingenuity and resourcefulness. This cannot happen in a reality confined by rows of desks, textbooks, lockers, and bells that ring every forty-five minutes—even if during those periods the desks are pulled into circles and the textbooks are replaced with the hippest hip-hop workbooks.

When hip-hop educators began bringing hip-hop texts into schools, most did not have much power or validation. They were visiting artists, teachers' assistants, student teachers, and new teachers. They did not have a body of scholarly work supporting their efforts. But times have changed.

There are annual conferences about hip-hop education. Research studies have been conducted and books have been written. New York University has launched a Hip Hop Education Center for Research, Evaluation, and Professional Development. And, perhaps most importantly, many hip-hop educators have gained power within their schools.

Teachers' assistants have become teachers, and teachers have become principals. Others have moved from the schoolhouse to district-level employment, education nonprofit organizations, and academia. College students writing essays about hip-hop for undergraduate education courses have become tenured faculty members. This means that, collectively, hip-hop educators are in a position to consider different, bolder levels of hip-hop education.

The time has come to follow HSRA's lead in breaking the elements of schools into pieces, reconfiguring and reassembling them, just as a hip-hop producer patches together segments of songs to construct a new musical composition. Most good hip-hop beats don't consist of samples from just one song. Similarly, as HSRA has demonstrated, a hip-hop school can pull from a diverse array of sources, fading between techniques, and occasionally speeding one up or pulling it backward to concoct something no one previously knew was possible.

"Struggle breeds creativity," graffiti legend Doze says, articulating a belief shared by many in the hip-hop community and beyond. "We've got it good in America, so maybe that's why hip-hop is so fucked up, 'cause we got it so *good* now."[9]

Doze's statement about hip-hop could apply to the education system or to the nation more generally. This country's ethos of abundance has led to some lazy habits. But there are urgent battles afoot. Needs for ingenuity now come in other forms: the energy crisis, unemployment, keeping communities safe without incarcerating millions of people, keeping our country safe without fighting wars.

Underlying all of these challenges is the need to improve the education system, which despite millions of intelligent, caring people dedicating their lives to it, is losing far too many students and failing to prepare many others for the struggles ahead.

Whether you view it as music, a movement, or a mind-set, it would be unfair to expect hip-hop to solve any of the problems listed above. Yet it would be a mistake to ignore its resourceful reflexes: creativity, collage, collaboration.

Had the New York City Sanitation Department been more diligent about trash collection in low-income neighborhoods, breakdance moves like the windmill and the head spin might never have been invented. But because in the 1970s countless families chose to replace their linoleum floors from the previous decades, and because all of this linoleum was left in the trash along with copious amounts of cardboard, b-boys and b-girls discovered a new surface to dance on, and invented new moves to maximize its potential.[10]

Parents' trash was children's treasure. The city's neglect was irresponsible, but in its negligence young geniuses sweated out possibility.

There are too many problems to solve, yet our society is dancing around so many wasted resources. What refuse could we be dancing *on*? And what are the new moves? Whether hip-hop continues to be a dominant cultural force or fades, the instincts, ingenuity, and swagger must continue—in honor of all of the geniuses who have come before, for all of the geniuses to be.

NOTES

1. Coalition of Essential Schools, "About the Coalition of Essential Schools," http://www.essentialschools.org/items (accessed December 17, 2010).

2. See chapters 1 and 2 for descriptions of community meetings and Pick Me Ups.

3. Mitchell Landsberg, "Hip Hop High Loses Its Charter," *Los Angeles Times*, July 10, 2008, http://articles.latimes.com/2008/jul/10/local/me-hiphop10 (accessed December 17, 2010).

4. Ibid., http://articles.latimes.com/2008/jul/10/local/me-hiphop10/2.

5. The Good Shepherd Services manual can be found at: http://www.goodshepherds.org/programs/community/transfer-schools/replication.html (accessed December 17, 2010).

6. Eagle Rock School and Professional Development Center, "Quick Facts," http://www.eaglerockschool.org/about_us/quick_facts.asp (accessed December 17, 2010).

7. U.S. Department of Education, "Investing in Innovation Fund (I3) Eligibility Criteria," *Ed.gov*, http://www2.ed.gov/programs/innovation/eligibility.html (accessed December 17, 2010).

8. There is a bottom level of grants in the Investing in Innovation Fund for "Development grants," which require less preexisting proof of success, but Duncan makes clear in the U.S. Department of Education's press release "Secretary Duncan Releases Application for $650 Million to Support Innovation" on March 8, 2010: "This fund awards three different grants to programs at three different stages of development that all share one thing in common—evidence of success." The press release can be found at *Ed.gov*, http://www2.ed.gov/news/pressreleases/2010/03/03082010.html (accessed December 17, 2010).

9. Jeff Chang, "Codes and the B-Boy's Stigmata: An Interview with Doze," in *Total Chaos: The Art and Aesthetics of Hip-Hop*, ed. Jeff Chang (New York: Basic Civitas, 2006), 319.

10. Danny Hoch, "Toward a Hip-Hop Aesthetic: A Manifesto for the Hip-Hop Arts Movement," in Chang, *Total Chaos*, 353.

Author's Note 1.0

One day in 2004, a crew of out-of-towners rolled into the converted garage that housed the youth program I directed on the south side of Providence, Rhode Island. The small group of teenage and adult visitors was from the Midwest and, while in the area to attend a conference, had been told to check out our program—the AS220 Broad Street Studio.

Youth staff members gave them a tour of our hip-hop recording studio; showed them the murals, photographs, magazines, and apparel being produced; and explained our mission to serve as an incubator for young artists and leaders, especially those in and transitioning out of juvenile prison, group homes, and foster care.

Our guests told us a bit about the school they came from, which sounded very similar to our organization, except that they had figured out how to infuse a diploma-granting academic curriculum.

I didn't learn more about their school until a few years later, when I began working for the Alternative High School Initiative, a national network of organizations replicating innovative schools.1 One of my responsibilities was to make site visits to schools that were members of the initiative.

Our midwestern visitors' school, the High School for Recording Arts (HSRA), was one of the first that I saw. On that trip I found a community that was merging the creative youth empowerment work that we engaged in at AS220 Broad Street Studio with an academic program reflective of best practices in alternative education.

I was struck by HSRA. It was unlike anything I had ever seen. A group of us in Providence had struggled to build a space where young people could be themselves, rep their cultures, broadcast their voices, and have agency in the governance of the program. And I had attended, worked in, and visited schools that engaged students through alternative methods.

But I had never seen a place that did both, especially—though by no means exclusively—for black students. What captivated me about HSRA was that not only did the culture and atmosphere mirror students' interests, identities, and instincts, but so did the curriculum.

Since that first visit, I have engaged with the school in several capacities. I have worked on coordinating a national conference that featured a visit to the school; attended events with HSRA students and staff in Atlanta, Los Angeles, New York, New Jersey, Philadelphia, and San Francisco; brokered relationships between the school and national youth programs; facilitated professional development workshops for staff members; and spoken publicly about the school at events across the country.

When the leaders of the school and I agreed that I would write this book, I moved to Minnesota, lived in Minneapolis for a year and a half, and spent more than one hundred hours in the school, observing and engaging with students and staff.

This is not an objective study. I came to this project a proponent of the ideas and a friend of the people discussed herein. I also came with the agenda of identifying and explaining the elements of Hip-Hop Genius as they are operationalized in an existing institution. To this end, I did not describe everything about HSRA the way I might have if I had set out to write a portrait of a school. I focused on highlighting aspects of the school's program that I believed would push public dialogue about the possibilities that lie waiting in the intersections of hip-hop and education.

That said, I have made every effort to be precise in my descriptions, claims, and conclusions. My goal is not to place the subjects on a pedestal from which they cannot move, morph, or grow. Rather, I hope that by dedicating these pages to describing HSRA's history and programs and defining Hip-Hop Genius, I can advance conversations that will ultimately bring greater attention, including both accolades and constructive criticism, to the school and the concept.

Since this book is about the powerful potential of merging hip-hop and education, I wrote it in a hybrid language. I hope my hip-hop family is patient with any words that are specific to the education genre and that my fellow educators hang in with the hip-hop slang and quotes that are woven throughout. In some ways, the words and concepts with which we are least familiar offer the greatest opportunities for learning.

I intentionally have written very little about myself in the preceding chapters. In these final few pages, I intend to share a bit of who I am, my relationship to hip-hop education and the High School for Recording Arts, what motivated me to write a book about Hip-Hop Genius, and my choices regarding narrative style.

This book emerged from a collective effort. As explained in the introduction, the concept of Hip-Hop Genius was generated in fellowship with several other educators. Similarly, many of the ideas presented in the preceding pages were developed through our communal conversations.

When I began writing, I was not sure whether I would ultimately be the sole author, so it made sense to compose in the third person. Even once it became clear that I would complete the manuscript alone, I decided not to insert myself as a character beyond the introduction both for the practical reasons described above and for the ideological reasons that follow.

On a conceptual level, Hip-Hop Genius has become a mantra for us, and for a growing group of educators who have joined us. We have become an informal think tank with the goals of advancing the ideas described in this book and housing resources to enable the development of schools and organizations that support the brilliance of young people.

Rather than establishing a stringent set of criteria for Hip-Hop Genius schools or educational practices, the intention is to engender global dialogue about the importance of recognizing and supporting resourceful ingenuity, particularly in students who have been scapegoated by society.

Our hope is that by codifying these concepts and serving as a repository for relevant resources, we can inspire individuals who, whether formally trained as educators or not, have the potential to bring empowering experiences to populations of young people who have been treated as burdens, liabilities, and criminals. With the right spark and support, these young people can become change agents—leaders in positive systemic change, by whatever means are most transformative.

No formal think tank or organization is needed. The spirit of Hip-Hop Genius can be embodied and built upon anywhere.

Hopefully this book can be a part of the process. The intention is not to over-romanticize a complex culture or encourage uncritical duplication of a particular institution but rather to inspire resourcefulness and innovation in education and all walks of life. Because this book has a social justice agenda that comes from this collective vision, it did not feel accurate or effective to present it as "Sam's story."

As I corresponded with agents about the idea for this book, I was asked more than once if it could be written in a Jonathan Kozol-esque style. I was told that if I built a dramatic narrative around my experiences at the school it could be "best-seller material."

When done well, a white author's moral outrage—brightened with an appropriate ratio of rays of hope—can indeed become a best-seller. But as the only white member of the Hip-Hop Genius collective, I felt uncomfortable inserting myself as a protagonist. This book exists to push conversations about how to creatively change systems and I did not want to occlude the discussion of these ideas with my own moral coming-of-rage story.

Of course, even in absence of personal anecdotes, this book is still informed by my experiences and perspectives. I am not an impartial researcher who dispassionately selected hip-hop education as a subject of study.

I was raised by educators, studied education history and policy, was certified as a teacher, and have worked with young people my entire career. Growing up in an urban environment in the 1980s and 1990s, hip-hop was cemented as an integral part of my cultural identity long before I ever heard the term "cultural identity." And for years, I have taught hip-hop workshops in elementary, middle schools, high schools, and juvenile prisons.

Whenever I facilitate hip-hop workshops with groups of young people, I like to begin by asking their names and what music they're currently feeling. When they list their favorite artists, I often ask, "Why?"

Almost inevitably, the exact phrase "Because he's real" will be at the top of the list. While beat selection, rhymes, and flow—and increasingly, advertising and cross-branding—all influence which rappers people prefer, another critical piece is who listeners believe an artist to be—in other words, the artist's identity.

Of course, many rappers understand this and, in an effort to please, craft back-stories that are more faithful to the popular "Get Rich or Die Tryin'" narrative than to their own realities.2 Others shine off the strength of their own personal truth, like a young Common Sense telling listeners that he did not grow up poor and that he worried about his own drinking, when those were far from common things to say.3 Either way, the point remains: People want to know who's behind the curtain, and this information affects their interpretation and reception of the product.

When it comes to writing on hip-hop education, heads want to know: Is this cat who's writing a book about hip-hop education *hip-hop*? Does he understand the history and the elements of the culture? *Does he live it?* Can he rhyme, b-boy, DJ, or write graffiti? Or does he just talk about it? All of these concerns can be wrapped into one simple three-word question: *Is he real?*

My first instinct could be to respond to such questions as if someone just disrespected me in a freestyle battle. But I want to put my hip-hop bravado in check and tell you how real and not-real I am, so that you have a sense of where I am coming from and so that ambiguities and speculations don't cloud your interpretations of this book.

Despite trying hard as a seven-year-old, I was a terrible b-boy, graffiti artist, DJ, and emcee. I gave up the dancing first—pretty much as soon as I started (I had rhythm and coordination—just not both at once!). I continued to mess with graffiti through my middle school skateboard phase and into my teenage years (mostly just as a lookout for my far-more-talented friends).

As a freshman in high school, I inherited two record players and a mixer and made a lot of mixtapes. Throughout college, I DJed parties, co-hosted a hip-hop radio show, and co-directed the hip-hop department at the station. I've never been a skilled turntablist, but I have always enjoyed selecting music that moves the crowd—on the dance floor and emotionally.

My love of emceeing began in the middle of the 1980s with my brothers and a tape recorder. First, we rapped along with Melle Mel to "The Message" and the "Beat Street Breakdown." Then we recorded our first track, "The Ewok Rap."

In high school, I began freestyling and fell in love with the fast-paced improvisational creativity it demanded. After graduating I began recording a lot more and occasionally performing locally. A compilation that I had a song on sold some copies in France, but that was the height of my fame. I never put any energy into making a career out of making music. It just was and is something I love to do.

Much of my successful teaching and work with young people has been based around hip-hop music. This was not an intentional choice I made at the beginning of my career as an educator. It is something that emerged naturally. I love to rap and talk about hip-hop music, and so do a lot of students. Others enjoy listening, critiquing, and making beats.

When teaching social studies, students and I have analyzed the commentary in relevant rap songs. When teaching language arts, we have looked at the compositional techniques and poetic devices at play in rap music. When helping young people stay out of prison, the opportunity to record and perform has served as a motivating factor.

For students in prison or feeling trapped in their environs, freestyling and writing rhymes can be a powerful channel for self-expression, the exploration of fantasies, and the development of societal critiques. As poet Jimmy Santiago Baca who taught himself to read and write in prison explains, "Through language I was free. I could respond, escape, indulge; embrace or reject earth or the cosmos. I was launched on an endless journey without boundaries or rules, in which I could salvage the floating fragments of my past, or be born anew in the spontaneous ignition of understanding some heretofore concealed aspect of myself."4

Over the years, students have expressed similar sentiments, and Baca's description resonates with my own relationship to the act of selecting and arranging words.

One of the most effective elements in my interactions with young people has been my willingness to do this spontaneously. The rawness and unpredictability of a teacher or youth program director freestyling grabs and hold students' attention. It demonstrates a willingness to be vulnerable in front of them.

At its essence, freestyling works when an emcee taps into her or his soul and lets it flow out in rhyme. Though I rarely freestyle these days, for many years composing free associations aloud in front of students allowed me to get closer to answering the perennial questions about my realness.

In addition to how deeply immersed one is in hip-hop culture, another issue of authenticity arises around whether an emcee or author has really experienced the harsh urban realities that they are rapping or, in this case, writing about. Like Common Sense, I did not grow up poor. My parents made living wages as teachers and eventually transitioned into work in higher education and nonprofit organizations. There was not a bunch of surplus money hanging around, but there was never a lack of food on the table.

There was, however, a lot of other privilege flowing through my upbringing. My grandfather was a doctor. His financial success allowed us to spend summers on Cape Cod. All four of the adults in the house I grew up in were college educated. Three are published authors. Two are bilingual.

I grew up in North Cambridge, Massachusetts, a racially and socioeconomically diverse urban environment. I lived a few blocks from low-income housing towers, which featured prominently in the view from my bedroom window and in my childhood understanding of the universe in which I existed.

As a kid, I saw how poverty affected families. So, even though he intended it in a derogatory way, when Jay-Z rapped to Nas, "You ain't live it, you witnessed it from your folks' pad," it resonated with me.5

I didn't live it. It wasn't me walking down the street with the ghetto blaster on my shoulder bumping the hottest new songs. It wasn't me getting harassed by the cops or stabbed at Popeye's. But on warm nights I would press my face against the screen window of my third-story room to see if I could find the sources of the music, shouting, and occasional gunshots, and the next day on the bus to my alternative public school I'd hear stories about what went down.

I have continued to live in similar neighborhoods and when I got too old to attend diverse urban alternative schools, I began working at them. Through each of these experiences, I have been one of the most privileged members of these communities.

I am a white, heterosexual man with a degree from an Ivy League institution. While I do not come from the wealthiest family or an Aryan background (as a Jew, I have a heritage of persecution, despite the current ruling class's embrace of my garbanzo complexion), I have pounds of privilege and access that are systematically denied to the groups of young people who created the culture and are enrolled in the school that comprise the major focal points of this book.

Some of those young people will undoubtedly write books that better address the topics touched upon in this volume. I humbly offer this as an interim text. My beliefs, ideas, weaknesses, fears, sense of humor, and passion are, of course, present throughout. I am proud of these qualities as they help illuminate new understandings and I apologize for the moments in which they cloud the brilliant subject matter.

NOTES

1. The Alternative High School Initiative is now known as the Association for High School Innovation (AHSI).

2. "Get Rich or Die Tryin'" is the name of 50 Cent's debut album and also a mantra for some members of the hip-hop generation (as well as capitalists of all ages).

3. Lonnie Rashied Lynn Jr., aka Common Sense, "Rich Man vs. Poor Man," *Resurrection*, Relativity Records, 1994, compact disc.

4. Jimmy Santiago Baca, "Coming into Language," in *Doing Time: 25 Years of Prison Writing*, ed. Bell Gale Chevigny (New York: Arcade, 2000), 103.

5. Shawn C. Carter, "Takeover," *The Blueprint*, Roc-A-Fella/Def Jam, 2001, compact disc.

PART TWO

Hip-Hop Genius 2.0

Chapter 7

Hip-Hop High 2.0

Walking into the High School for Recording Arts (HSRA) today, much of what you see is quite similar to the picture painted in the first edition of this book. Students' and staff members' clothing isn't as baggy, flip phones and MP3 players have been traded in for smartphones, and the vending machine no longer sells blank CDs, but fundamentally the school continues to match the description written 10 years ago. Like any hip-hop production, its creators continue to reconfigure elements to keep it fresh and responsive to today's—and tomorrow's—audience. The following pages hold a few of the most significant developments that have occurred in the past decade—from a relocation to a new facility to learning opportunities more overtly directed at issues of social justice to more robust post-secondary programming and culturally responsive student support systems.

SPACE IS THE PLACE

A few years after the 2011 *Hip Hop Genius* came out, HSRA moved on from its building at 550 Vandalia, which is the space described in detail at the beginning of the previous chapter. HSRA spent formative years in that retrofitted old warehouse, situated in an industrial park with a neighboring recycling plant, radiator repair shop, and reptile store—a location that embodied the philosophy of flipping something outta nothing. In 2016, the school moved to a more spacious, high profile, centralized St. Paul location.

The new building sits prominently on a new light rail line on University Avenue West, occupying the grounds of what used to be the historic St. Paul Prom Ballroom, which hosted parties, famous jazz musicians, and cultural moments of the St. Paul community of yesterday. The school is now writing the next chapter to the spirit of joyous gathering, fun, and creative expression that once lived in this physical space.

Most recently a Bally's Fitness Center equipped with a full NCAA-regulation sized gym and a small pool, the space is three times larger than the school's former location. This has allowed HSRA to add over 100 students to its enrollment. Today, the school serves 350 students ages 14–21 and has expanded its staff to accommodate this growth.

The school now also offers an expanded athletics program. Students have entered the state sports league in volleyball and basketball. Other opportunities for kinesthetic education are available as well, such as morning basketball leagues, fitness workshops, and an expanded dance studio with community connections to local groups such as the Ananya Dance Theatre.

RECORDING HE(ARTS)

The identity of the school remains centered on the recording arts, and this identity and the high quality studio facilities continue to attract and ground students. With multiple individual recording booths, a live performance room, a beat-making lab, and two professional studios, HSRA's students have unparalleled opportunities to express their musical talents, build their careers, blow off steam with therapeutic sessions in the booth, or have fun jamming out on the drums or guitar with a student band in the afternoon. This space is a curative chapel and a magic ingredient for many students who find an authentic connection of expression that helps them embrace the broader HSRA program. HSRA still houses the continually developing student radio show "4 Tha Air," formerly known as "The Fo-Show," which can be heard on local radio stations weekly. The school also still operates its student record label called Another Level Records and its Business of Music program. They have grown to become the internship and workforce development hubs of the school providing students with paid, for-credit internship opportunities on and off campus that did not previously exist.

With support from the local nonprofit Rock the Cause Records, HSRA's Business of Music program now also offers a Business of *Media* component in collaboration with the school's Visual Inclusion Program (VIP). VIP is a multimedia art program based on a reverse inclusion special education model. Students with Individualized Education Programs (IEPs) become the student peer leaders in video/photography/editing group projects. The VIP students help their peers develop their abilities to produce social media content related to their artistic careers. These programs together help young people understand how to protect, promote, monetize, publicize and distribute their art and music. The student-led Visual Inclusion Program collaborates with the rest of the school's creative spaces as students learn photography, graphic design, video editing, and project management to help other artists showcase their work.

Recently, an HSRA student named Smiley sought support from Business of Music Facilitator Scott Herold when her cover to Alicia Keys' song, "Unthinkable," went viral. Smiley needed help navigating the results of her success. Scott immediately taught Smiley how to monetize the video she had posted online of her cover and soon it had hundreds of thousands views. The video has continued to spread—at the time of this book's publishing Smiley's cover had over 15 million views.[1]

Smiley's success covering "Unthinkable" highlights the amazing rewards students experience, as well as the potential accompanying risks. In the wake of her shine, a local news media outlet contacted Smiley to share her story. In the process, the young artist noted how much money she'd made from the project. The news outlet published that impressive figure. The school immediately took action to get the outlet to redact that information from the story for fear of such news bringing danger to Smiley and her family.[2] As Biggie said, "mo' money mo' problems."[3] The more seasoned staff at HSRA had seen this truism play out too many times and swung into action to help Smiley forgo as many of those problems as possible before they became obstacles to her success.

Many other HSRA students and graduates have seen success within the music industry over the last decade. To share a few examples, Steven Franks has produced a number of top ten songs for major recording artists like Arianna Grande, BLACKPINK, and Justin Bieber; TryBishop (referred to in the first edition of this book as The Real Young Bishop) has signed to a major record label and written, engineered, and produced for artists such as Akon, Kanye West, Snoop Dogg, and gospel superstar Lecrae; Christopher Chrishan Dotson, better known by his stage name, Prince Chrishan, is now Grammy-nominated and writes in-house for Atlantic Records; and Nimic Revenue signed to Def Jam Records and has produced music included in the NFL Madden 21 soundtrack.

One of the greatest recording arts accolades for HSRA came in 2017 when, in collaboration with the Grammy Award-winning vocal and instrumental ensemble, Sounds of Blackness, a group of HSRA students were nominated for the prestigious NAACP Image Award for their song, "Royalty." This song was written as part of a grant project to promote a healthy view of Black identity. Focused on African American culture, the chorus melodically rang, "Royalty, you are Royalty, I got a message from above, you ain't no thug you're Royalty. Brother you're a king, sister you're a queen, children of the dream, I got a message from above you ain't no thug you're Royalty." In their bid for the prestigious NAACP Award, the song came up against such stiff competition as Common, Bruno Mars, and other superstar artists.[4]

Ultimately, the group responsible for the song's magic lost the award to none other than Beyoncé.

While HSRA's rep for supporting students to and through recording arts-related moments like those described above has continued to grow, the school has also been ramping up its capacity to support students through creative career paths in a variety of fields adjacent to the recording arts. In the Visual Art Lab, for example, students experiment with graffiti, fashion design, painting, drawing, sneaker design and customization, and 3-D sculpture. Students often bring their creative work to a maker space in the new facility known as the Design Zone, which builds on some of the best practices in maker education that have been developing and rising to greater prominence over the past ten years. Here, students can be certified in power tool safety and usage, work with traditional materials in construction and the finishing trades, integrate electronics into their work, and tinker towards wherever their interests lead. The design zone teaches design thinking abilities such as critique, ideation, iteration, prototyping, and testing. These art, design, and maker education experiences provide students with opportunities to earn integrated math and science validations.

GROWING FAMILY'S VALUES

The wraparound services HSRA has historically prioritized have expanded from the "youth advocacy" described in the first edition. The school's licensed social worker described in the original Hip-Hop High chapter, Tabitha Wheeler, has been joined by a team that provides young people with the therapy, housing, food, clothes, shelter, job opportunities, college counseling, and other resources they need. She was also named Minnesota Social Worker of the Year in 2020. The school now has a full-time therapist from the Wilder Foundation, an expanded social work team, a housing specialist, and deeper connections with a variety of community partners so that students receive necessary resources as soon as they enroll and for as long as they require. Through the ingenuity of its team members, robust service offerings, and important community partnerships, HSRA provides as many services as possible to help hold its students.

The school has also made some changes in recognition of the large number of students facing housing instability: 40 percent of students at HSRA could be considered houseless or highly mobile on average over the years. The school is in the planning stages of building on-campus housing through a project called the Twin Cities Youth Village. This housing-first approach would offer students a stable living situation so that they can attend school, graduate, and achieve without the obstacle of unstable housing. To envision this project, the school is working with Fielding International, the same architecture firm that designed the school's first two buildings.

As the school's grown, so has its abilities to document its work in representative ways. At HSRA, almost none of the students have been at the school for four years. Measured by traditional four year graduation rate standards, the school would be considered a failure. But, the school's one-year graduation rate—i.e., the number of students eligible for graduation at the beginning of a school year who then actually go on to graduate by the end of that same year—stood at 89% in 2019, which met or surpassed most schools serving similar student populations.[5] The school uses this data to advocate for its students in ways that support the school's ability to continue providing state-of-the-art facilities and educational best practices.

TAKING IT HIGHER (ED)

Recently, HSRA has extended its programming in the post-secondary realm. In the first edition of this book, there were descriptions of students being encouraged to take and receive credit for college classes as part of a Post Secondary Enrollment Options program. That program continues to enable students to get to know the excitement and challenges of college coursework and earn credits toward an associates or bachelors degree for free, while receiving support from the HSRA community. In 2019, the school launched a new post-secondary diploma- and certification-granting institution licensed by the Minnesota Office of Higher Education called Diverse Media Institute (DMI). DMI was created to offer a way for HSRA's students to continue their learning in the areas of music production and the business of music without the high cost of post-secondary, for-profit recording arts colleges and institutions. These institutions have placed HSRA and other young people in financial debt and usually do not have the cultural competency of HSRA. DMI has made a commitment to providing free tuition to any graduate of HSRA through scholarships and financial aid. DMI trains students for jobs in the recording industry while attending the program so that they gain the skills and build the relationships for meaningful employment upon graduation.

Students are certified in audio/visual technology through the AVIXA CTS (Certified Technology Specialist) training, and audio engineering and production through the AVID ProTools curriculum. Over the course of this 900-hour program, students achieve professional certifications in these fields.

DMI is housed on-campus at HSRA and supports HSRA alumni as well as members of the broader community who have graduated high school. The co-location with HSRA reduces the overhead of the program and increases the likelihood of longevity in a city that has seen both of its major post-secondary recording arts programs fold due to budgetary constraints in recent years.

SAME MISSION, NEW VISION

Unlike many schools that experience mission drift over the years, HSRA has never stopped reaching out to and enrolling out-of-school youth. Now, ten years since the first publication of this book and over twenty years since the school's opening, HSRA's student population still overwhelmingly consists of reengaged students. The school's growth is an indication of the traditional education system's failure to successfully engage and graduate all of its students. At the same time, given the underpinning word-of-mouth that drives much of the new enrollment, the school's growth also stands as a testament to the school's high quality and unique offerings.

HSRA has fashioned a new vision statement and established four primary pillars that frame the school's work. The vision statement, understood to be ever-evolving, reads:

High School for Recording Arts is defined by its commitment to find and nurture the genius and creativity of every student despite any life challenges or system-driven setbacks. Our school is built around the recognition that every learner has:

- Special talents and strengths
- Passionate interests
- Impactful experiences
- Unique perspectives

At HSRA, each student's unique experiences are matched with appropriate supports and connections to enhance that learner's potential.

We believe the key to meaningful learning lies in the authentic acknowledgment of each learner's unique abilities and experiences. We encourage each learner's journey to explore and affirm meaning in their lives using creative learning opportunities and strategies. This leads to their active participation in the learning process.

HSRA/Studio 4 focuses on developing a learner's ability to see the importance of living and sharpening their talents and abilities so that they may develop self-efficacy, contribute to a better space and place for them to prosper, grow, create, and be a change agent in their community.

This effort leads to our learners becoming positive contributors to their communities, productive and enterprising workers, engaged citizens, and lifelong learners.

This vision statement is important in making a declaration of the innate abilities that HSRA's students possess. This is a vision statement about human worth and dignity. Out of the vision statement came four pillars that define the design principles of HSRA. They are:

- Asset-based
- Wraparound services
- Innovative practices
- Social justice lens

While these design principles guide the work of HSRA staff, they also describe the way students work and the way the school engages the surrounding community. The student-produced documentary *Rondo: Beyond the Pavement* illustrates how these four pillars show up in student work. In this project, the school collaborated with the local Public Broadcasting System, filmmakers from the Rondo neighborhood in St. Paul, and elders from the community to produce an award-winning documentary on a historically Black neighborhood that was forever changed by discriminatory public policies.

Just as the construction of the Cross Bronx Expressway—and the destructive toll this took on Black and Latinx neighborhoods in the South Bronx—plays an important role in the origin story of hip-hop, much of the housing and businesses occupied by the Black community of the Rondo neighborhood was demolished in the 1950s and 1960s to make way for the construction of I-94. The student-produced documentary tells the story of this historic neighborhood, which at one point housed half the city's Black population.[7]

Rondo: Beyond the Pavement has been seen around the world, showcased in seven different film festivals, and was an official selection at the 2019 InJustice for All Film Festival International, the 2019 International Social Change Film Festival, the 2019 San Francisco Black Film Festival, the Indie Short Fest at the Los Angeles International Film Festival, and can be streamed on Amazon Prime Video.[8] The film showcases the school's social justice lens and demonstrates how that pillar is supported by the school's foundational pillars: students could not have completed the project without having been seen as capable of taking on responsibility, without the support of HSRA's wraparound services, and without the innovative educational practices that allowed this project to fit into the context of a diploma-granting high school.

ADVISORY THRIVES

In the first edition of this book, "advisory" was described as an asset-based youth development approach that puts building strong relationships with young people and their families as a top priority for the school. Advisors still help students develop personal learning plans rooted in their interests, needs, learning styles, and creative curiosities, and which include the supports needed to overcome any obstacles that block students' paths to achieving their goals. Advisors are still their advisees' daily alarm clocks, cheerleaders, coaches, and mediators; focused on seeing each student exactly as they show up with a goal of helping them to plan, goal-set, and do the work to get to where they want to be.

However, HSRA's advisories are also no longer led by the school's content instructors. HSRA has taken a new approach to staffing in the last ten years—hiring advisors from a variety of experiences, backgrounds, and specialties, many of whom graduated from the school or grew up in the same community as the school's students. In Minnesota, where only 5% of teachers are people of color, allowing space for more positions that do not require teacher licensure means making more room for those positions to be filled by qualified people who represent the student population along the lines of race and ethnicity.[9] The advisory system, therefore, gets to focus on relationship-building, project management, social-emotional learning, and the maintenance of school culture. The role of the advisor has become, as Joey Cienian, the Director of Education Programming, says, "To bring an asset-based, authentic, care-based approach to starting a conversation with a young person about their goals, needs, and living situation. HSRA calls each student—returning and new—and asks, 'How are you? What are you doing? What do you need? Are you struggling with housing? Anything? Need a gift card? Food?' Then the advisor empathizes. There are a lot of students who engage because of this opportunity to relate."

R.I.P. BIG FLOYD

As mentioned in the introduction to this edition, 2020 brought an added slew of challenges felt acutely by the educators and community of HSRA after COVID-19 ravaged the world and George Floyd was murdered less than eight miles from the school's campus. The protests that resulted from the heinous suffocation of Floyd and Black communities across Minneapolis under the knee of the Minneapolis Police Department led to the destruction of property as activists attempted to make statements that would be heard in the highest offices of the country and provocateurs set out to create danger and sow divisiveness. As storefronts erupted in flames mere feet from the front doors of HSRA in St. Paul, Minnesota, those charged with protecting the school from destruction stood out front. On their faces and in their raised fists rested a clear message of solidarity with the community. Included in this group were alumni of the school who voluntarily showed up to stand watch, vowing to keep the sacred space of HSRA safe. In their minds and hearts rested a vigilance necessary to protect the building from anyone who might have tried to make HSRA a target. Luckily, the schoolhouse made it through those smoky nights unscathed, thanks to those who camped out day and night on campus and to the reputation of the school in the community as a place to be preserved.

In addition to protecting the schoolhouse, the school served its students and staff through these traumatic events, which included the added presence of tanks, soldiers, helicopters, and the National Guard. In what has become a legendary community meeting facilitated by HSRA advisor Tiki Blackmore, students and staff aired their grievances, processed their trauma in real time, and made plans to support the ongoing movement for the preservation and protection of Black Lives. Educators from across the world, including Isaac Ewell, Fanon Wilkins, Lawrence Patrick III, Ashanti Branch, Courtlandt Butts, Corey Scholes, Louie Montoya, Jess Brown, Christopher Emdin, Charmaine Mercer, and Dr. Bronwen Low tuned in to witness and lend support to the work of a culturally sustaining institution navigating its way through one of the tensest moments of racial injustice in American history and amid the worst pandemic of the last century.

SUSTAINING EACH OTHER THROUGH COVID-19

When the pandemic struck, HSRA found itself better positioned to handle the challenges of the moment than many schools. To be responsive to the high mobility of its student population, HSRA already hosted most learning experiences in-person *and* online. Many workshops and sessions were already recorded and shared through digital platforms for students who were not able to physically attend school at a certain time. The online availability of learning had, before the pandemic, mostly been accessed on-campus when students who had missed a session or two returned. Once the pandemic began, students accessed these remote options from their homes. HSRA provided computers, tablets, and Wi-Fi hotspots to every student that needed them.

Most important to maintaining relations and connection with the students during Covid was the work of the school's community-based and community-connected Student Support team. Already central to the school's functioning, this team became the glue that kept the HSRA student community together through the roughest time of Covid. Ray Womack, Director of Student Support, became responsible for delivering mobile devices and hotspots, as well as coats, jackets, food, and other essentials for students without housing and basic necessities. What was clearly the most important aspect of what the student support team did was *to be seen in the community where the students lived.* With masks on and practicing social distancing, they showed the students that they weren't forgotten and that they were still loved. The student support team listened to them, continued to mentor and mediate conflicts like they always did, both inside of the school as well on the blocks in which the students (and the support team members themselves) lived.

Dan Frey, the director of student engagement, and his team did daily audits of student enrollment to ensure each student still completed a viable personal learning plan. Utilizing online, hands-on, and in-building targeted support, Dan's team ensured that students received the support they needed to access the school's many offerings. When Dan identified a student who hadn't been in touch or hadn't completed a piece of the learning plan, he would enlist the appropriate departments to step in, including the Student Support team. In response, Ray's team might take forms to a student or find a student and identify what was missing for them to complete the process, reporting back to the school throughout.

To support project-based learning while learning could not take place within the school building, HSRA also secured grant funds from Teach for America and the VELA Foundation to buy materials that would support students in remote, hands-on project engagement. These projects included augmented and virtual reality learning opportunities; Polaroid cameras for photo/visual creations; materials to construct biomes, design clothes, compete in virtual sports tournaments; and, of course, recording equipment to make music. Through these projects, core content instructors designed learning opportunities for credit accrual in the areas of Science, Technology, Engineering, Arts, and Math (STEAM), Physical Education, and Humanities. These projects included the work of Walter Cortina at the state level to win the rights of unemployed young people (described in greater detail in the new addition to chapter 2: A Day's Work). They also included creative projects, like the HSRA feature song with the Sounds of Blackness called "Sick and Tired of Being Sick and Tired." This song served as the follow-up to the NAACP Image-Award nominated collaboration "Royalty" with the same group and represented the community's fatigue in response to George Floyd's killing.

The school plans to maintain a fully blended option, with greater supports for students in need of technology to engage. Much of what can be learned through HSRA's navigation of COVID-19 serves as perennial lessons about culturally sustaining responses to crisis intervention. The practices HSRA developed before the pandemic enabled the school to continue to serve its young people with the most complex sets of needs during challenging times. In turn, the practices HSRA developed through the pandemic enable the school to better serve its communities' young people with the most complex sets of needs into the future.

No matter what circumstances the future holds, the school will continue to be defined by students' sense of love, belonging, and ownership. This will continue to shine as will the staff's commitment to learning and evolving alongside the students.

Special thanks to Joey Cienian for helping deeply with this chapter.

NOTES

1. DGainz, "Smiley—Unthinkable," YouTube, October, 11, 2019, https://www.youtube.com/watch?v=0jZuXh1Jb8Q

2. Adrienne Broaddus, "Teen Gets 22 Million Hits on Viral Video, Captures Attention of Major Record Label," News Center Maine, November 11, 2019, https://www.newscentermaine.com/article/news/local/breaking-the-news/teen-earns-100k-from-viral-video-captures-attention-of-major-record-label/89-5f7336ba-6337-4605-a1fb-d447e75f686a.

3. The Notorious B.I.G., "Mo Money Mo Problems." Recorded 1996 at Arista Records. YouTube video, 5:47.

4. WCCO—CBS Minnesota, "St. Paul Students to Face Off with Beyoncé for NAACP Image Award," YouTube, January, 19, 2017, https://www.youtube.com/watch?v=fHKyhc_XTOc.

5. Andrew O. Moore, *Reengagement: Bringing Students Back to America's Schools* (Lanham, Md.: Rowman & Littlefield, 2016).

6. Designs for Learning. "Charter School Annual Report 2019–20." hsra.org. May 31, 2021. http://hsra.org/_REPLICATION_EXCLUDES/Uploads/Resource-Center/201920_HSRA_Annual_Report.pdf.

7. Maury Glover, "How I-94 Ripped Apart the Rondo Neighborhood and One Group's Plan to Help Restore It," Fox 9 KMSP, February 15, 2021, https://www.fox9.com/news/how-i-94-ripped-apart-the-rondo-neighborhood-and-one-groups-plan-to-help-restore-it.

8. *Rondo: Beyond the Pavement*, directed by Bianca Rhodes and Georgia Fort (2018; St. Paul, Minnesota: Saint Paul Almanac, St. Paul Neighborhood Network, High School for Recording Arts, 2018).

9. Wilder Research and Professional Educator Licensing and Standards Board, 2019 Biennial Minnesota Teacher Supply and Demand (St. Paul, Minnesota: Wilder Research, 2019).

Chapter 8

A Day's Work 2.0

Despite the passage of time, Lil C's experiences as described in the previous chapter still paint an accurate picture of what a day at the High School for Recording Arts (HSRA) might look like for a student. Students still design their own learning plans and engage in learning experiences through a combination of scheduled activities and spontaneous interactions throughout the day. HSRA is still designed to catch and amplify learning where and when it happens.

To capture how HSRA has continued to deliver on such learning opportunities, even during the COVID-19 pandemic, in this edition we offer a portrait of a current HSRA student, Walter Cortina. While the "A Day's Work" chapter in the first edition of this book presented Lil C's experiences by following her through one complete day, this description of Walter's learning takes a different tack, instead illustrating his learning at HSRA through an in-depth description of a powerful, real-world project he engaged in during the pandemic. This update shows how HSRA's systems, structures, and staff have supported and responded to Walter's learning to ensure he receives the credit (and recognition) he deserves for his work. In this section, Walter and his young colleagues engage in the legal pursuit of CARES Act compensation for unemployed youth through the development of an organization called Bridgemakers.

Given the flexible nature of HSRA, its multimodal approach to documenting and accrediting learning, and the school's commitment to respond to Walter's interests in the context of a pandemic, his interactions with his advisor look and feel different than those of Lil C. Walter's story is an example of what distance learning can look like for students who aren't doing it within the very limited context of on-screen instruction. What Walter was able to do with the support of his HSRA community offers a new and powerful example of hip-hop genius.

WALTER'S REAL-WORLD HIGH SCHOOL LEARNING

Throughout his junior and senior years, Walter has worked closely with HSRA staff to ensure that his passion for activism and leadership is a core part of his graduation plan. Walter and his HSRA team were able to accomplish this goal through HSRA's validation system described in the Hip-Hop High chapter, which encourages students to seek out valuable learning experiences and provides a structure for translating that learning into concrete high school academic credit. Despite attending only a few classes and activities that resemble traditional school, Walter is on track to graduate.

Similar to Lil C and many other HSRA students, Walter's frequent one-on-ones with his Advisor and Math Teacher, Maureen Foss; HSRA Content Advisor, Haben Ghebregergish; and HSRA's Director of Education Programming, Joey Cienian, have helped him receive validation for his real-world demonstrations of learning and skill growth. To do so, Walter's HSRA team reviewed the legislative testimony, presentations, agendas, budgets, grant proposals, video recordings of meetings, and other materials Walter has prepared. These learning artifacts are a critical part of HSRA's validation process and, though only some of them were identified with Maureen and Haben as necessary at the outset of the project, all of them became part of his demonstrations of learning.

In addition to these artifacts, Walter also drafted reflections on what he had learned and, with the help of HSRA's validation guide, he identified the competencies that he developed through his experiences. Some of those include effective communication, collaboration, entrepreneurship, positive relationships with mentors, and analysis of inequity and prejudicial systems. Walter also secured a "community validator" letter from a mentor, Jon Bacal, who spoke to the quality, depth, and impact of the work Walter had done. This is why Walter is continuing to collect more community validation letters from prominent individuals with whom he has worked, including former Mayor of Minneapolis and CEO of the Minneapolis Foundation, R.T. Rybak. Letters of validation from community members and mentors, as well as artifacts from students' experiences and work, factor into the school's consideration of which validations to recognize and what credit to attribute to the work.

The validation system at HSRA is more than a protocol that gives students credit for activities outside of the traditional classroom context. Rather, it is something that facilitates a critical dialogue about learning and honors the experiences that are meaningful for students, experiences that may have been ignored in traditional educational settings. Take, for example, this conversation between Walter and Haben after he and his peers released their first one-pager describing the youth leadership nonprofit they cofounded, Bridgemakers, in April of 2020:

Haben: Walter, what?! This is such a strong vision for your organization. The language is clear, precise, and I feel your passion, man. Well done!

Walter: Haha, thank you so much. I really wanted to create an organization that was for the youth, by the youth.

Haben: How did you make this? It really gets the message across. . . . I'm impressed!

Walter: With a loooot of editing, and I also got good feedback. It was honestly one of the hardest things I've ever written, but it's also one of the best.

Haben: The hardest things are often the most rewarding, I find. What did you learn from writing this?

Walter: I learned how to present my ideas clearly and how to seek advice from others. I learned how to tell my story, too. . . . Oh yeah, I also got a better understanding of what I wanted Bridgemakers to be about.

Haben: Exactly. Writing is often about clarifying our own thinking, and that's what you did. And what makes it even more meaningful is that by articulating your ideas so well, you're going to have a huge impact on your community. There's no doubt that you'll be able to get some grants with this. It's not just a paper you turn in for a grade. It's a living document.

Indeed, Walter's one-pager for Bridgemakers went through multiple edits in the last year. The newest version ties the purpose of the organization to the most important issues of today, stating that "George Floyd's murder and its aftermath provides fresh evidence that our nation's fraying social fabric and institutions are struggling to serve youth of color." The conversation between Haben and Walter highlights the ways in which learning outside of the classroom can be as rigorous—if not more—than that which happens inside the classroom. Teachers who want to provide an education that is relevant for students might start by talking to students about what they're already doing. Relevance doesn't sacrifice rigor. Conversations with students may sow the seed for a learning experience that is even more engaging and rich than what a teacher might imagine for them.

"Two of the things I appreciate most about HSRA are its flexible academic support system and my regular sessions with Tabitha," Walter reflects, shouting out HSRA's Student Advocate, Tabitha Wheeler. Tabitha, named Minnesota's School Social Worker of the Year in 2020, has supported Walter's mental health throughout his time at the school, most significantly helping him cope with the murder of his best friend in August of 2020. After graduation, he plans to continue leading Bridgemakers to help youth reimagine and revitalize communities to break out of oppressive cycles that keep them from achieving greatness. Walter says his ultimate goal in life is to never see anyone else go through the same struggles he went through.

BUILDING BRIDGE(MAKER)S

In his prior high school, Walter had started a student-led "Changemakers" team—a predecessor to Bridgemakers—that advocated for school improvement and innovation. When he learned that HSRA had long been offering students the passion-based, experiential, and relationship-based practices for which he and the Changemakers had been advocating, Walter decided to check the school out. He went for a tour, which allowed him to ask questions of students, teachers, and administrators. After another visit and having taken the time to consider HSRA as an option, he made the decision to leave his old school behind and enroll at HSRA.

Walter brought his passion for student voice to HSRA even before the new school year started. With the support of HSRA's leadership and coaching from his advisor Haben, Walter and Lincoln Bacal, a fellow Changemaker from Walter's prior school, launched a "TC Changemakers" team with students from each of their schools. Walter met with interested HSRA students over the summer of 2019 and organized a two-day team-building retreat to plan activities. In January 2020, Walter decided to expand the Changemakers group he and Lincoln had formed into Bridgemakers—a paid, mentored experience to provide intensive coaching and support for young activists of color. The 17-year-old junior soon pitched two funders on his idea. As a result, Bridgemakers secured two $10,000 pledges. This provided Walter with a chance to turn his and Bridgemakers' mission into a living reality: to amplify the stories and mentor the leadership of youth to reimagine and revitalize Minnesota communities through the power of passion, purpose, and relationships that break cycles of miseducation, poverty, violence, and addiction.

When the pandemic and subsequent shutdown hit, Walter lost his job at a local car wash. For the first time since his mother had been deported to Mexico three years earlier, he had no source of income; no way of helping to cover the rent for his aunt, who had opened her home to him but due to her own illness could not pay the rent; no way to pay for meals or other living expenses; and no way to help out his mother and baby brother in Mexico. He had to put his plans for Bridgemakers on hold. After a few very anxious weeks, he saw in his crisis an opportunity to put his organizing skills to work: Walter and his friend Lincoln Bacal discovered that they and other

out-of-work Minnesota high school students weren't eligible for unemployment benefits due to a state law that had been passed in 1939 banning otherwise eligible high school students from access to benefits. While other states
had a similar law at one point in time, almost every state except Minnesota
had since rescinded those laws.

THE CULMINATION

It was 11:00 a.m. on April 11, 2020. Walter welcomed a group of peers in
their late teens and early twenties to their first video conference together. The
meeting was the culmination of three years of student activism and months
of careful planning. Walter opened the call by sharing his personal story and
his plans and hopes for the future. Each participant then presented their own
personal stories and struggles with the passions that had brought them to this
conversation about addressing unemployment caused by COVID-19.

The team discussed a documentary about civil rights hero John Lewis,
who had died two weeks earlier, and the lessons his life offered for their road
ahead. Most immediately, they agreed that in the next three months their key
priorities were: to engage Minnesota youth in the campaign Walter and other
students had launched to convince state leaders to give out-of-work high
school students access to unemployment benefits on the same basis as other
workers, to encourage and support youth voter registration, and to organize
forums for youth to develop and share perspectives on key policies like reimagining education.

Through their work together, the young people shared their stories of unemployment as a result of the pandemic. One young woman started them off:

> Hello, I'm Omariasha Houston and I go to [HSRA] and I'm in the 11th grade. I
> was working at Appetite for Change and they had to close down. Some people
> don't have support systems and they gotta feed theirself and clothe theirself.
> Unemployment benefits will help our family with food. You know how we go
> to school and we have breakfast and we have lunch. Now we have to eat all of
> our food at home. And our bills, you know, it's just added on.

After her, another young man named Kojak shared his story. "I'm 20 years
old. My job was not deemed an essential job so that establishment had to
close. I'm unable to apply for Covid benefits because I'm a high school student even though I'm 20 years old. But I still have to support myself." Then
it was Walter's turn:

Hello, I'm Walter Cortina Martinez. I live on the Northside of Minneapolis, I'm also an 11th grader at the High school for Recording Arts. My mom got deported when I was 13 and ever since then I've been on my own. Ever since the age of 14 I've been working and I've been sending a lot of money back to my mom and my little brother that lives with her. My mom can't work because she's been diagnosed with breast cancer. I also support myself.

The weight of these stories, though normally felt as a heavy load, began to lighten and lift as each shared a look of recognition across the virtual platform. The young people slowly began to recognize a shared experience in each other. The need was clear, the path was not. While each story built, from one to the next, a sense of release as well as a sense of urgency, the last two stories lit a particularly furious fire inside the group:

My name is Carlos Jimenez. I was unable to get the Covid relief fund because my parents are immigrants. I'm also a cancer patient. I suffer chronic leukemia and I have to take oral chemotherapy every day to stay well and stay alive. To take this medication I have to go to the pharmacy every single day. I have to take my car to get there because I can't take public transportation since I'm immuno-compromised. In order to take my car I have to be able to afford gas. Because I can't work, I can't do that and I can't afford my medication.

Silence, and some tears. Then came Ezra's story:

I'm Ezra Augustine. I'm unable to access Covid-19 because my parents are undocumented. I'm also a transgender person of color, I have to pay out of pocket for my hormone replacement therapy because I do not have insurance and I have no income to, you know, pay for that. I'm also an at-risk person and that makes it really hard for me to get a job.

By the end of the meeting, those present vowed to continue working on behalf of unemployed young people like themselves for whom access to Covid unemployment benefits might mean the difference between life and death. It was this meeting that launched their most successful initiative to date and that would eventually win every young person in Minnesota facing unemployment as a result of the pandemic access to unemployment benefits. But how did Walter and his comrades get from this meeting to their historic victory? And, how did HSRA help this group of young changemakers get there?

On May 8, the *Pioneer Press* daily newspaper published an opinion piece by Walter asking the State to reverse its benefit denial.[1] "We've lost our jobs. Many of us high school students need benefits to get through this," it read. Four days later, local news station KARE11-TV ran a story on Walter's fight for benefits.[2] These two were the first of 54 total media features on the youth-led campaign over the next eight months, seen by hundreds of thousands of readers/viewers, including stories in the *Star Tribune* (five separate articles), the *New York Times,* and *Teen Vogue.*

Walter and his team began to organize a student-led campaign for access to benefits. Like Walter, many of Minnesota's 20,000+ newly out-of-work high school students depended on their work income to cover core household expenses, and yet Minnesota now seemed to be the only state denying them access to either regular state unemployment benefits or the federal pandemic unemployment help that had just been approved in the $2.2 trillion CARES Act.[3] At the end of May, Walter received a call from Youthprise, a national foundation eager to promote youth engagement in the 2020 elections. Youthprise was seeking high-impact, youth-led civic projects. Two weeks later, the Bridgemakers proposal was one of only six "Civic Spring" projects selected out of 147 applications nationwide to receive a $90,000 grant from Youthprise.[4] By the end of 2020, Walter and his team had raised a total of $124,000 from four funders. Over the next two months, with the support of a coalition of allies, Walter and his colleagues made steady progress toward reversing the state's policy denying students benefits. They converted their testimonies into short videos and social media posts on Facebook and Instagram and, with the support of HSRA advisors, organized several online "Town Meetings" to share student stories and engage more young people. The young leaders started meeting with an aide to Minnesota governor Tim Walz; his employment commissioner Steve Grove; and key legislators and legislative aides of both parties, including two meetings with Minnesota Senate president Jeremy Miller. The young leaders drafted emails and made outreach plans in collaboration with HSRA advisors Haben and Maureen as well as Bridgemakers mentor Jon Bacal, Lincoln's father. On May 15, 2020, after consulting with one of the nation's top unemployment benefits experts, Walter wrote the governor a four-page letter explaining point by point how the state's policy was unjust. Walter copied top state officials and legislative leaders on the emailed letter. Within hours, the governor's aide called Walter, pledging the governor's support for overturning the 1939 state law.[5]

On June 3, 2020, Walter, Lincoln and other students testified in front of the Minnesota House Jobs Committee, the first of five times youth campaign leaders would testify at the State Capitol. Despite bipartisan support, the campaign's efforts to pass state legislation in the June and July special legislative sessions stalled because of disagreement between the Republican-controlled State Senate and Democratic-controlled State House on how to pay for benefits. Inspired by the youth-led campaign, in August of 2020, Minnesota's U.S. senators Smith and Klobuchar and four U.S. representatives introduced legislation in Congress to clarify high school student eligibility for benefits.[6]

Walter presented his letter to the governor and testimony to his advisors at HSRA in his demonstration of learning at the end of the project as real-world examples of his growing mastery of politics at the state level. These artifacts pertained toward HSRA validations in social justice, public speaking, and the humanities.

In October of 2020, Walter wrote and presented a keynote speech to the opening session of the national teacher-powered conference alongside his advisor Haben and HSRA executive director Tony Simmons.[7] Although the conference focused on highlighting teacher-powered schools, where educators have more agency than in administrator-powered schools, Walter and his copresenters challenged the absence of students in conversations about power. The keynote addressed the ways in which schools can either disrupt or perpetuate systems that have oppressed Black and Brown communities for centuries. In his portion of the keynote, Walter talked about how his strong relationship with staff, his Personal Learning Plan (PLP), and his flexible schedule at HSRA enabled him to pursue his passion for social justice and leadership.

The youth-led campaign for student benefit-access achieved success beyond Walter's wildest expectations. After partisan bickering had blocked action at the state capitol, Walter and his colleagues filed a lawsuit against the state in October 2020 with the pro-bono support of a Minneapolis law firm, Youthprise, HSRA and, later, Minnesota attorney general Keith Ellison. On December 1, 2020, the State Court of Appeals unanimously reversed the state's denial of pandemic unemployment benefits to eligible high school students.[8]

The court ordered the state to immediately begin paying benefits to all of the 20,000+ eligible youth. As a result, by early March 2021, young people throughout the state had received at least $30 million in benefits, with at least $40 million more yet to be processed. The court's decision cited many of the same points that Walter had stated in his public letter to Governor Walz seven long months earlier. Governor Walz invited Walter and four youth teammates to meet with him, Lieutenant Governor Flanagan, and Commissioner Grove in late December as they publicly pledged that permanently repealing the law denying student access to benefits would be a top priority of the Walz Administration in the 2021 Legislative Session.

By early 2021, Walter and his teammates had recruited a board of directors, a fiscal sponsor, and raised an additional $150,000 to support the team's activism and social entrepreneurship of eight Bridgemakers youth ambassadors into 2021 and beyond. HSRA's role throughout Walter and the Bridgemaker's incredible journey has been to catch whatever balls the young people threw their way, support them in their mission, and validate the strengths they demonstrated. In many ways, the school got out of the way of the learning the young people were already doing on their own, offered its support and resources, then said, "Yes, you did that. We see you. You deserve the following recognition for your work . . ." As a school that's designed to adapt and respond to students' interests, HSRA was ready, willing, and able to support the work of Walter and the other HSRA Bridgemakers through the advisory model illuminated by Lil C's story and in the Hip-Hop High chapter update added to this edition.

Walter, the Bridgemakers, and their amazing organizing and legislative successes are in some ways unusual. Most HSRA students did not organize dozens of peers, change laws, garner press attention, or raise hundreds of thousands of dollars during the pandemic. But, while some of the outcomes are exceptional, this story says a lot about HSRA's current work: hustling hard to support students' work outside the school building and unapologetically focusing on social justice. This update shows what it looks like when instead of focusing on forcing students to follow school rules, a school follows students to change societal rules.

NOTES

1. Walter Cortina, "Walter Cortina: We've Lost Our Jobs. Many of Us High School Students Need Unemployment Benefits to Get Through This," TwinCities.com Pioneer Press, May 8, 2020, https://www.twincities.com/2020/05/08/walter-cortina-weve-lost-our-jobs-many-of-us-high-school-students-need-unemployment-benefits-to-get-through-this/.

2. Frederick Melon, "Young Workers Campaign for MN Unemployment Benefits," TwinCities.com Pioneer Press, February 14, 2021, https://www.twincities.com/2021/02/14/young-workers-campaign-for-mn-unemployment-benefits/.

3. Susan Davis, Claudia Grisales, and Kelsey Snell, "Senate Passes $2 Trillion Coronavirus Relief Package," National Public Radio, March 25, 2020, https://www.npr.org/2020/03/25/818881845/senate-reaches-historic-deal-on-2t-coronavirus-economic-rescue-package.

4. "The Civic Spring Project," Youthprise, 2021, https://youthprise.org/civic-spring/.

5. Cole Stevens, "Take Five Minutes to Help High School Students Fighting for Workers' Rights," MinnPost, April 5, 2021, https://www.minnpost.com/community-voices/2021/04/take-five-minutes-to-help-high-school-students-fighting-for-workers-rights/.

6. Press Release, "Congresswoman Angie Craig and U.S. Senator Tina Smith Introduce Legislation to Help High School Students in Minnesota Who Lost Jobs Due to COVID-19: Senator Amy Klobuchar, Raps. Dean Phillips, Ilhan Omar, Betty McCollum Join Effort to Make Unemployment Assistance Available to Eligible High School Students During Pandemic," Congresswoman Angie Craig Second

District of Minnesota, August 18, 2020, https://craig.house.gov/media/press-releases/ congresswoman-angie-craig-and-us-senator-tina-smith-introduce-legislation-help.

7. Education Evolving, "Our School, Our Community: Collective Action In These Revolutionary Times," YouTube, November 2, 2020, https://www.youtube.com/ watch?v=L8UdO_JZjYs.

8. Melissa Turtinen, "Appeals Court Rules Minnesota High School Students Can Get Unemployed Benefits: They've Been Denied the Benefits, and Some Were Even Asked to Pay Them Back," Bring Me The News MN, December 2, 2020, https://bringmethenews.com/minnesota-news/ appeals-court-rules-minnesota-high-school-students-can-get-unemployment-benefits.

Chapter 9

Hip-Hop Leadership 2.0

Soon after the release of the first edition of this book, the title and responsibilities of Executive Director of the High School for Recording Arts (HSRA) were bestowed upon Tony Simmons. Tony had not only played a significant role in assisting TC in the formation of HSRA, but also came from a hip-hop music background. Despite that similarity and their closely aligned education and youth development philosophies, TC and Tony's leadership styles have important distinctions.

Two hip-hop artists can collaborate musically yet bring a wholly different energy and vibe to their work. Consider Public Enemy's Chuck D and Flava Flav. Or, perhaps a better analogy would be Black Star's Yasiin Bey (better known by his stage name, Mos Def) and Talib Kweli. Like these groups, TC and Tony build better by bouncing bars off each other.

In the original edition of this book, TC describes himself as "rough around the edges" compared to Tony's "pretty boy" attorney style and recounts inviting Tony to join him to balance his brashness. TC positions Tony as the legalistic thinker and smooth talker: a real compliment to his style and a perfect partner in his plan to grow and operate HSRA.

During the early years of the school, Tony worked alongside TC with each focusing on their respective strengths—TC maintaining strong community relations, sharing his core learning philosophy, and keeping track of the school's budget and finances; Tony focused on helping the school's staff internalize and embody TC's learning philosophy. Tony also focused on creating opportunities to showcase the artistic acumen and business brilliance of his students. Instead of band concerts and art fairs, Tony crafted creative content campaigns for various clients such as businesses, government agencies, foundations, and community based organizations. Tony also built relationships with aligned education leaders, schools, think tanks, and policymakers in the region and across the country.

In naming Tony the school's Executive Director, TC bestowed upon him the responsibility of the future of HSRA. Just as the first edition of *Hip*

Hop Genius highlights hip-hop leadership lessons from TC's approach to building HSRA, this update shares additional lessons from Tony's tenure as Executive Director.

Tony is a great school leader. This is *in spite of*, not *because of*, his relative success in the traditional public school system and having taken a career track that had high regard for process, precedence, and tradition. So, how did Tony's past prepare him to be the leader of a creative and progressive urban school when, although sharing identity and culture with the young people HSRA serves, his life was never as close to the margins as theirs?

PEEP THE SWAG

I was born in Brooklyn, NY less than one year after TC came into the world in the Twin Cities. Like him, I had two loving parents and a community that wrapped their arms around me and each other despite the challenges of being Black in America during the 1960s. As a child growing up then, I bore witness to and learned the importance of embracing community and my identity in the midst of the civil rights and Black empowerment movements.

As a third grader, I had already checked out from the formality of the industrial model of education with desks lined up in rows and white women teachers who I had never seen in my neighborhood. They had the unreasonable expectation that I would never move from my desk, let alone talk to my best friend Dewayne sitting next to me. One day, while I focused on being quietly compliant, my teacher caught my attention with the announcement that a new music teacher was soon going to arrive.

I recall waking up from whatever daydream I was having. Music was already a big part of my life and a major contributor to how, even at that young age, I saw and felt culture and a sense of place. A good part of this clearly came from all the records my parents played at home, from Nat King Cole, Miles Davis, Jackie Wilson, Lena Horne, and Motown artists, to the music I heard at my cousin's house like James Brown, Marvin Gaye, and the great Puerto Rican and Dominican salsa and merengue artists of my Puerto Rican neighbors. These sounds mixed to cultivate in me a love for music that ran deep. So, when I saw a tall, handsome, impeccably dressed Black man walk through the door of my third grade classroom to teach me music, not only did I wake up, I sat up! This was the first time I had even seen a Black man in a classroom who wasn't emptying the wastebasket.

At that point, the teacher introduced Mr. Williams, a local jazz saxophone player and a licensed music teacher. Mr. Williams brought with him a cardboard box filled with plastic flutes. He and the teacher passed them out. Once

I had a flute in my hand, I watched Mr. Williams write scales and music notes on the blackboard. He explained how to read notes and the proper fingering to produce a desired sound.

But Mr. Williams was more than a music teacher. He was sharp! He carried himself with quiet pride and dignity. He spoke softly but all the kids hung onto every word he said. And when he played for us, man, he blew the room away! That taught me right there the power of presence and disposition.

The way Mr. Williams looked, talked, and the sounds he made come out of that horn were all connected. I remember right then I started caring how I spoke, dressed, and carried myself.

By the time Tony first visited HSRA, his manner of presenting himself had evolved into a hybrid of a jazz musician and a NY hip-hop industry executive. Whether it was the sharp jeans, Timberlands, button up, suit jacket (with obligatory pocket square) and fitted Yankee cap, the early HSRA students saw someone who not only dressed the part, but spoke about the work of *and in the style of* a music executive. Countless students since have said with admiration that they have never met a principal who talked or looked like Tony. The attention and care he has put into his presence and disposition have made him their Mr. Williams.

As a leader, Tony is very conscious of his image and how it impacts both his students and those within the wider education community. "At first it didn't dawn on me how different I come across from most educators. To me I was just being me." However, during a visit to HSRA a guest from rural Minnesota said he thought Tony might have been one of the students. (Tony was in his forties at the time.)

"I took it as a compliment," Tony smiles. "But more to the point was what my look meant to that person as he was experiencing, perhaps for the first time in his education and perhaps overall life, a school full of mostly young Black men, being fully their authentic selves and roaming the halls of their school building with all the freedom and agency they could possibly possess." The students' kinetic energy, bold and sometimes loud voices, bravado, strong attitudes, and their dress and overall steelo was just a generation down from Tony's. "I knew that what that educator and others saw without saying was that these young people were me; and I was them. I wasn't trying to have them see me as a model for assimilation or rejection for who they were but if anything a model for what to grow into that didn't reject where they were starting from."

STAY FRESH

I've always been a geek for whatever is new and futuristic. Whether it was in music, dress, or technology. When I was at Howard University, everyone was listening to funk and R&B. Rap was on the rise, but George Clinton, Cameo, and Maze were everywhere! One day, one of my fraternity brothers, Chico, asked me if I wanted to go with him to see Prince at the Warner Theatre. This was like 1980 and Prince was this rising cat from the Twin Cities that had a couple of cool songs out by this time . . . "I Wanna Be Your Lover," "Uptown," "Controversy." They were cool songs, but I asked Chico how much the tickets cost and he said something like $10 or $15 and I was like, "Hell no!! That's way too much!" Chico got serious and said, "Look dude, this cat is blowing up right now and I'll pay for you if you don't want to. . . . That's how bad I think you should check him out."

That night, a group of five or six of us got seats in the balcony to see Prince. The crowd was cool—a different vibe than what I was used to. Then this band called "The Time" came out and tore it up! We were all blown away with their music, stage performances and attitude. We danced like crazy and had the best time! When they ended we were all like, "No way Prince can top that!" Then Prince came out . . .

What we witnessed blew our minds. This dude had on a purple raincoat, nothing but black panties under it, high heel boots, and he sang and danced his ass off, and played the electric guitar like he invented it. Throughout his performance, we were transfixed! No dancing or any movement. We were stuck! After it we were like, "What the fuck was that??!" I said, "I think it was the future."

These early, indelible experiences stuck with Tony. In his role as program director prior to being named Executive Director at HSRA, he sought to bring forth the inspiration to do things differently, to explore and experiment. He first took on the challenge to facilitate a Business of Music class that he and a friend of his who was a teacher developed, wherein students learn how to distribute, license, copyright, and monetize their music, as well as how to write press releases to promote their own art. Tony took note from hip-hop's growth process, examining the examples created through innovative partnerships like that between Run DMC and Adidas to connect his students' music and business sensibilities. This has led Tony to craft successful partnerships like a multiyear collaboration between HSRA and State Farm. Far from a typical relationship between a school and the corporate social responsibility wing of a business, HSRA's partnership with State Farm generated gains on four fronts simultaneously: providing creative learning opportunities for students (including album production, social media campaigns, and a TV advertisement with Lebron James), making social impact in areas of seat belt safety and the national dropout crisis, reaching the insurance company's community engagement goals, and generating revenue for HSRA. Early lessons on the potential of remixing culture to produce new and innovative forms of expression, and building paths where there were none, inspire Tony to lead the HSRA team away from traditional dynamics of teaching toward a more learner-centered approach. Tony knows neither he nor his staff can ever be caught sleepin' on their students (one of whom could be the next Prince) or where the music industry and education sector are headed.

One example of how this ethos of staying fresh has manifested in Tony's leadership came through an opportunity initiated by a major local foundation invested in creating opportunities for African American boys and young men within HSRA's city of St. Paul. The foundation presented the many disparities between these young men and white and even other BIPOC young men, and made the case that St. Paul's future was tied to dramatically improving opportunities for young African American men in the city.

This case was specifically put out to African American founders and leaders of community-based organizations, including HSRA. Tony reached out to an extremely talented recent graduate to ideate on what he and his peers could do to address the crisis.

Known by his artist name, Lewiee Blaze, Lewiee made a name for himself while a student at HSRA for being an extremely creative and prolific rapper/lyricist/poet/speaker. Lewiee wrote and recorded numerous songs with strong social justice themes. He also spoke at numerous conferences and was a keynote speaker at major education institutions and convenings including Harvard University Graduate School of Education and the Deeper Learning Conference in San Diego.

"Lewiee was excited about taking on this challenge to address the conditions that was working against him and his peers but also to create creative and innovative opportunities that didn't just prepare him for a job but to help him to become an independent business creator and operator," Tony recalls. "He told me that he and his boys had already come together as a group doing the work and that they called themselves Individual With Dreams." This group consisted of mostly HSRA students and graduates, all Black, and mostly male. They used their knowledge of creative content creation, multimedia equipment skills, proficiency with social media, and importantly their street cred to recruit and transform themselves and their friends who often thought that society didn't have positive plans for them. Lewiee himself was already on probation and out of school by the time he enrolled at HSRA. He often talked about while in jail realizing he was at a crossroads in his life and at that moment decided to give HSRA a shot. It worked for him and his friends at HSRA. He said he had the chance to utilize the hustle and resiliency skills he built in the streets while he was producing projects at school. And once he realized he could do that just for himself, he decided to explore how he could use his skills and insights to help others and transform his community. Tony explains: "To me, knowing all this about him, it was a no-brainer to put Lewiee and his crew at the helm of coming up with a winning proposal to address the problem that was being presented. I think Lewiee Blaze is the future."

Lewiee and his crew soon came up with a proposed campaign called N4 (New Mindsets, New Media, New Leaders, and New Narratives) that received a grant award from the foundation. They started speaking to their peers who were still in the streets about how they could change their hustle, access knowledge, and build with others to create sustainable work that they owned. They began to speak on this message at various local schools and hosted peer-led community talking sessions. They also visited the Stanford d.school to learn about design. They collaborated with the designers there to iterate on the concept of design thinking and make it accessible to their community. d.school Designer-in-Residence, Louie Montoya later visited Lewiee and his team in Minnesota to learn from their implementation of community-based design practices. All of this work culminated in a major creative multi-and social media campaign aimed squarely at the demographic that the foundation targeted. It was viewed as a big success by the foundation and the community, and Lewiee has become a well-known and well-respected activist and artist who supports himself through his community work.

What Tony recognized as a leader with a focus on innovation was that the future could not just be passed to the youth through talk, case studies, and hypotheticals. The future and the solutions to the matters that threaten young Black men had to be put into the hands of those young men. In other words, as Tony puts it, "When you get a glimpse of the future and it requires letting go, you must trust in what you see, even if it looks way different than what you may have offered. If you get a glimpse of the future and it looks promising, trust in it and as some cats in jazz say about improv, 'just let it be what it be.'"

SHOW AND PROVE

My sister coincidently moved to the Twin Cities around the same time I did and sent her daughters to private school in the Minneapolis suburbs. For the most part they did well there. However, as a teenager, once one of my four nieces became restless and uninterested in school. Her behavior started to get her in trouble both at school and home.

So, one weekend I took my niece to HSRA. Needless to say, she loved it, especially the recording studios. She also immediately bonded with the students who were there that weekend working on a recording project.

When I took her home, she immediately told her mom that she wanted to go to "Uncle Tony's school." She couldn't stop talking about it. As my sister listened, she got more and more agitated, until she finally blurted out, "There's no way my daughter is going to that school of yours, Tony!"

I couldn't believe my own sister would say that. I never brought up the idea again.

Sometime later, my niece got in trouble for shoplifting. Her grades had gotten worse, she had begun cutting school, and her relationship with her mom had deteriorated. After my sister told me about all of this, she blurted out: "Maybe she should go to your school."

I was shocked yet again. That next week my sister enrolled my niece at HSRA and immediately she began to thrive. She not only loved going to school, she began to record and collaborate on group projects. Her grades improved and she began making friends. Within two years, my niece graduated. At HSRA graduations anyone in the audience can speak to the graduates. My sister took the mic, tears streaming down her face, she declared how proud she was of her daughter, and how deeply she believed in the school.

Over the coming years, Tony's niece met a record producer at HSRA, they got married, moved to Atlanta, and built one of the most popular recording studios in that mecca of Black music. Their studio was featured on the reality TV show, *Love and Hip-Hop* and they continue to have a successful business and a growing family.[1] In the end, Tony knew his sister's heart had always been in the right place and that she had simply had an outburst driven by her love of her daughter when she was first presented with the idea of her daughter going to HSRA. She has made yearly donations to the school since her daughter's graduation.

For Tony, this story provides a great lesson: He never assumes anyone understands the work, not even people in his own community—or even his own family! People on his team tell him negative things being said about the school, suggesting he should respond. However, that isn't his style. Instead, his approach is to stay focused on the school's mission with faith that ultimately the students' successes will say everything that needs to be said about the school's quality and impact.

Despite the earnestness of their work, their desire to adopt best practices in progressive education, spending above average amounts of school funding towards resources that directly reached their students, and working tremendously hard to produce better results than the traditional system, HSRA is still frequently under fire. "It feels like the system has a plan for our students and anyone who tries to disrupt that plan also becomes a target," Tony reflects. According to Tony,

> We have been audited by every possible auditing group known to even have a tangential connection to education. At times it would come in like waves! Financial audits, curriculum audits, IRS, suspicious press, people from the community trying to attack us. It felt as if the suspicion, marginalization, and oppression our students experienced were being directed at us for having the audacity to engage them.

Some of this can perhaps be explained by anti-Black racism. It is possible the school has received disproportionate scrutiny because it has Black leaders and serves Black students. But some of it is likely explained by *how* it serves its students. Perhaps if HSRA had a "no excuses" approach that demanded its students walk the halls quietly with their hands behind their backs or was more akin to Joe Clark's school in the movie "Lean on Me," the suspicion and pushback might not occur to the extent it does. Instead, HSRA does not treat students like suspected juvenile delinquents, but as human beings deserving of the right to be known and to be free to explore their passions and interests—and for that the school pays a price in terms of perception and performance accountability.

Rather than focusing on what other people claim they are doing wrong, Tony stays focused—and works to keep the whole HSRA community focused—on what they are doing right. Day in and day out, he reminds them to keep doing good work with good intentions, to collect the appropriate data to demonstrate it, and to have faith that this will ultimately speak louder than anything he could say in an argument with a detractor.

In hip-hop culture, there is an ethos of "show and prove." This is similar to the adage, "the proof is in the pudding." One doesn't show they are a good b-girl or b-boy by filling out a multiple choice test on the names of dance moves; expertise is demonstrated on the dance floor. The best way to prove HSRA is a good school is not to plead or debate with haters, it is to be undeniably great.

FIGHT THE POWER

Chris Lollie was "that student" most teachers acknowledge having—a rambunctious body of energy, a bit mischievous but with a huge heart. Chris was also smart as a tack and incredibly creative, but had been kicked out of multiple schools. What other schools saw as smart-mouthed, insubordinate, and incorrigible, HSRA saw as a brilliant student that needed love and a supportive community.

By the time Chris graduated in 2004, he was a rising independent hip-hop artist with multiple jobs to support his family and music career. One day after a midnight shift, he decided to pick up his daughter from her morning daycare in downtown St. Paul's skyway level. Every winter, St. Paul's urban bustle moves from the streets into the skyways. Next to the daycare was a bank with a lounge located within the common area of the skyway. On this particular day, Chris sat down on one of the bank's sofas to wait for his daughter to be let out of daycare. While there, he was approached by the bank's security guard who told him he had to leave. Chris asked why and told the security officer he had seen many people sit on that sofa without visiting the bank. The security officer told Chris he still had to leave. Chris told him "no." That's when the security officer left and came back with the bank manager who reiterated the security guard's message: Chris had to leave, or else.

Chris told the two that he was refusing to leave because he had done nothing wrong. The bank manager, in a response that has become all-too-familiar to Black residents of St. Paul, told Chris that if he did not leave he was going to call the police.

After the bank manager and security officer left, Chris went to pick up his daughter. While walking to get her, Chris was confronted by a police officer who asked Chris for his name and ID, which Chris refused and asked why he was being questioned. The officer asked him for his ID again. Chris said, "The only reason why you're questioning me is because I'm Black." At that point, another officer had arrived. The officers physically grabbed, tased, and handcuffed him. All the while, Chris was shouting for help. He informed the officers that his daughter was within eyesight of the arrest. He also recorded the entire interaction.

Chris was arrested and booked. Once he was released from jail and his phone was returned, Chris uploaded the video on YouTube and it immediately took on national attention. In the end, all charges were dropped and Chris sued the city of St. Paul, winning a settlement and claiming his victory as a rare admission of guilt from the city's police department.[2]

I reached out to him to give him support and love. After the lawsuit was settled, I invited Chris to work with the school to create a KnowYourRights creative workshop.

I also reached out to St. Paul police, criminal defense attorneys, the business community, and others so that our students and staff could get diverse perspectives on what happened to Chris and what was happening to many of them.

Music initially drew Tony to his leadership role at HSRA, but after the unlawful arrest and detention of Chris Lollie in the midst of an ascending reckoning around the unjust killing of Black and Brown people by the police, Tony no longer saw his work as a progressive education leader rooted solely in music and the recording arts. From that point on, Tony saw himself as a warrior for social and racial justice. This work has informed the way he has led, not just at HSRA, but at the High Tech High Graduate School of Education as well, where he is the codirector of the New School Creation Fellowship.

Tony often references this, one of his favorite quotes, which comes from the education philosopher Paulo Freire:

> If the great popular masses are without a more critical understanding of how society functions, it is not because they are naturally incapable of it—to my view—but on account of the precarious conditions in which they live and survive, where they are "forbidden to know." Thus, the way out is not ideological propaganda and political "sloganizing," as the mechanists say it is, but the critical effort through which men and women take themselves in hand and become agents of curiosity, become investigators, become subjects in an ongoing process of quest for the revelation of the "why" of things and facts.[3]

Tony says that if HSRA had a true purpose to its existence and work, it would be to honor this quote with the unapologetic focus on the conditions and lives of its students, and with the aim to engage them in learning to confront, disrupt, and enact positive and meaningful change.

NOTES

1. "CSP Studios on VH1's Love and Hip Hop Atlanta Season 2 Episode 3 & 5," CSP Music Group, 2021, https://www.cspmusicgroup.com/atlanta-recording-studios/blogs/yung-la-old-post.

2. Marino Eccher, "St. Paul Will Pay $100,000 to Chris Lollie, Tased in Skyway Arrest," TwinCities.com Pioneer Press, February 18, 2016.

3. Paulo Freire and Ana Maria Araújo Freire, *Pedagogy of Hope: Reliving Pedagogy of the Oppressed* (London: Continuum, 2004), 90.

Chapter 10

Society's Sucker Punch 2.0

In the ten years since *Hip Hop Genius* first came out, the societal problems touched on in this chapter have changed. But not much. Now twenty-two years into its existence, the High School for Recording Arts (HSRA) still serves young people on the short end of society's most insidious systems and the school's leaders still encounter many of the same barriers—although sometimes cloaked in new disguises.

SO, WHAT'S CHANGED AND WHAT STAYED THE SAME?

Since the book's first edition was released in 2011, the school and those who make it what it is have become recognized national leaders in education reform and reengagement practices. One way in which the school has done this has been through the advocacy of alternative accountability policies for schools serving formerly out-of-school young people. As David "TC" Ellis and Tony Simmons came to a clearer understanding that traditional metrics of accountability (attendance, four-year graduation rates, and standardized test scores) posed a continuing threat to their commitment and approach to serving overage and undercredited students, they realized that they would have to go on the offense to rewrite the rule book to more realistically appraise the successes of the school and its students.

As a result, Tony started sharing publicly how HSRA was fighting to avoid being declared a "persistently low-achieving school" on the basis of test scores. Mentors, such as Dr. Wayne Jennings, Joe Nathan, Ted Kolderie, and Dr. Howard Fuller, helped him garner the attention of an even wider group of national education reform leaders. At a high profile roundtable discussion put on by the National Association of Charter School Authorizers, Tony had the opportunity to infuse HSRA's learning, which was ultimately included in a groundbreaking report called, "Anecdotes Aren't Enough: An Evidentiary

Based Approach to Alternative Accountability."[1] With this report, HSRA began representing itself more confidently to its students, their families, and the national community of educators interested in serving young people through alternative approaches. Perhaps not surprisingly, the same hip-hop heads who had flipped something outta nothing and started a school out of a recording studio have brought that energy to the whole industry, becoming known for their work in helping to create standards for use in nontraditional schools across the country.

BILLIONAIRES AND BULLSHIT

Perhaps the most egregious sucker punch society throws at the students of HSRA comes in the form of this nation's widening socioeconomic divides. In a recent episode of *The Daily,* a podcast from the *New York Times*, the news outlet reported on the tax-dodging practices of the ultra-wealthy, demonstrating how through legal loopholes in tax laws, billionaires have regularly been able to pay nothing or next-to-nothing in taxes.[2] This has enabled an increasing concentration of wealth in the hands of an elite few, which has led to less resources for the rest of the world, especially those who were already locked out of the halls of money and power.

Data shows that the share of wealth held by upper-income families in the United States has increased dramatically over the last ten years while the middle class has shrunk.[3] This widening of the wealth gap is tied to an ever-growing climate crisis that unequally impacts Black, Brown, Indigenous, and low-income populations. The more the earth is exploited for material gain, the more the climate deteriorates; and the more the climate deteriorates, the larger the wealth gap grows.[4] These challenges have not only persisted since the release of the first edition of this book, they've grown worse.

Imagine a world where young people had all of their basic needs met, a world where schools serving previously out-of-school young people could focus on providing engaging educational programming and not on scraping and scrapping for dollars to help provide students with food, clothes, and shelter. Unfortunately, current trends are moving in the opposite direction, and this is compounded by the ways in which the education system measures success, the ongoing impacts of the criminal punishment system, and the public and private funding mechanisms on which schools depend.

GRADUATION RATES RISE, BUT GAPS PERSIST

Perhaps because of their widespread use as a measurement of the success of high schools, four-year graduation rates can be helpful in contextualizing the school in the landscape of secondary education. The nation's four-year graduation rate has improved somewhat since this book first came out—from 71 percent in 2008 to 85 percent in 2018. But as of 2015, there were still well over 1,200 schools where 60 percent or less of students who entered as freshmen actually graduated[5] out of roughly 23,500 public high schools nationwide.[6] Data on the "dropout" and pushout phenomena carry important caveats.[7] For example, young people who are pushed out before entering high school are often not counted as part of the "dropout" rate. In Minnesota, young people who leave one school and then later enroll at another (like many at HSRA) are not considered in data regarding "dropouts," despite having already experienced being labeled socially as "dropouts." The implications of this label have been shown to have harmful effects on the self-esteem of young people regardless of the systemic factors at play.[8] So, while the national "dropout" rate has gone down, uncounted numbers of young people still battle the effects of a broken system as they attempt to reengage in their learning. If educators don't know a student has dropped out or been pushed out, how can schools begin the difficult work of reengaging them? And, for schools like HSRA that serve students who have already experienced pushout and the damaging labels that come with it, what will it take to get the system to recognize the different, more difficult work being done for and by those students?

While improvements in America's graduation rates have been demonstrated nationwide, Black, Brown, and Indigenous students are disproportionately affected. Although 89 percent of white students now finish high school in four years, for Black students that number is 79 percent and for Latinx students it's 81 percent nationwide.[9] Other indicators such as socioeconomic status and gender still influence whether or not students graduate "on-time." Students from economically disadvantaged backgrounds finish at a rate of 79.5 percent and the 2018 graduation rate for young men was 6 percent lower than that for young women.[10, 11]

Changes in support of lesbian, gay, bisexual, transgender, queer/questioning, intersex, two-spirited, and additional forms of gender nonconforming (LGBTQI2S+) peoples' rights have occurred in the last decade, but many institutions do not collect high school completion rates for the LGBTQI2S+ cohort. Thus the overall statistics, while seemingly representing some positive change for the bottom line of the country's graduation rate, also remind us that education systems have work to do to even be able to measure whether everyone has the same opportunities to succeed.

THERE'S NO JUSTICE; THERE'S JUST US

Just as the last ten years have seen an improving overall graduation rate but persistent gaps along the lines of race, class, and gender, the country has followed a similar trajectory when it comes to students' involvement in the criminal justice system. In the last decade, the nation has cut its rate of youth incarceration by almost half.[12] Despite this reduction though, in 2017, of every 100,000 incarcerated young people, 55 were white, 226 were Black, 71 were Latinx, and 149 were Indigenous.[13]

Some high school students also get caught up in the "adult" prison system. While the nation's overall prison population has been declining since its peak in the late 2000s, the country still holds more people in prison than any other nation in the world and related expenditures continue to rise. According to The Sentencing Project, the United States spent $56.6 billion to incarcerate 1,380,427 people in 2019.[14] Of these, 32.9 percent were Black and 23.4 percent were Latinx, despite representing only 13 and 19 percent of the national population respectively.[15] Although the prison population has been decreasing, the number of people on probation sat at 3,673,100 in 2016 bringing the number of people under the control of the U.S. prison system to 6,613,500 people the same year. This extension of the U.S. prison system through the long arms of probation—increasingly supported by new digital technologies—has allowed this country's carceral reach to grow in new ways since this book first came out.

Monique Morris's research on high school "pushout," shows a strong correlation between being pushed out of high school and becoming incarcerated at some point in life.[16] At HSRA, the average student has attended 4.5 other schools before enrolling. Morris's research helps explain the corollary statistic that 65 percent of newly enrolled HSRA students are already system-involved. HSRA's social justice-oriented, relationship-based approach brings that number down to 13 percent by the time students graduate.[17]

POCKETS OF SUPPORT

The first edition of this book noted the challenges schools like HSRA have faced in the past as they pursue funding to support and expand their programs. While various forms of the same challenges persist, the school has become more financially secure. This is due in part to HSRA developing its own new revenue streams. For example, when the school purchased its current building and prepared to move into the new location, the school's leaders cleverly chose to zone the swimming pool housed within the building as a condominium so that a popular swim school could lease the space and offer its services to students of HSRA at discounted rates. With the revenue generated from the pool area, the school was able to construct its basketball gym.

In addition to generating revenue, HSRA has also seen an uptick in philanthropic support. In 2020, HSRA received a grant from the Hewlett Foundation for ongoing support over three years with the explicit goal of further establishing the school as an exemplar model for other schools and educators worldwide. The school also recently received a grant from the NewSchools Venture Fund in part due to its existence as a Black-founded, Black-operated institution serving young people on the wrong end of a system designed to overpolice, oversurveil, and incarcerate Black and Brown youth.[18]

This increase in grant-funding from national entities may serve as an indication that education funders have been waking up to the reality of America's racist past and the implications it has on the education system's present ability to serve students. Schools like the Living School in New Orleans and Empower Academy in Colorado have also made social justice and liberatory approaches to teaching and learning explicit components of their program.[19, 20] These schools also received funding from major philanthropic donors, representing increasing support for schools seeking to actively disrupt and dismantle systemic forms of violence.

While financial support for social justice-oriented school models seems to be en vogue, in an equitable world, schools would be far less dependent upon a benevolent philanthropic sector to appropriately serve their students. To firm up and spread these approaches, policy-level shifts are necessary.

Meanwhile, policies that support culturally responsive and sustaining educational approaches are being kicked back and forth across the field. Arizona banned ethnic studies in 2010. In 2017 a federal judge declared this ban unconstitutional. Then, under the governance of the 45th president, the White House threatened to investigate any school teaching the Pulitzer Prize–winning *1619 Project* from Nikole Hannah-Jones of the *New York Times*.[21] Conversely, in 2019, the state of California passed AB 331 requiring every school to teach ethnic studies at the high school level by 2025.[22] It seems at least for the moment that these contradictory changes don't indicate so much a changing of the guard as they do a widening of the gap between what some view as a high quality education and what others view as a threat to the status quo.

MEASURING WHAT MATTERS

The first edition of this chapter also pointed out the detrimental impacts of high stakes testing. These tests still exist and HSRA students must take them despite research showing the damaging effects of high stakes testing.[23] However, like HSRA, more schools have turned to or added competency-based measures to assess learning through project-based, experiential, hands-on demonstrations of academic and social-emotional knowledge. For example, the Mastery Transcript Consortium has established a cohort of 350 schools, roughly one-third (public), to implement a holistic set of assessment tools that replaces transcripts and grade point averages with learner profiles and portfolios of learning.[24] As well, fewer post-secondary institutions require SAT and ACT scores at all when it comes to accepting students to their institutions. Basically, the world is catching on to what HSRA, Big Picture Learning, High Tech High, and other student-centered, project-based programs have already known: there is no one-size-fits-all tool that can accurately assess student achievement.

Ten years ago, data from the National Research Center for Career and Technical Education reported boredom as one of the primary reasons students left school. In the summer of 2020, HSRA conducted a youth participatory action research study funded by the Center for Policy Design that trained HSRA students to conduct qualitative, semistructured interviews. HSRA student-researchers interviewed fellow HSRA students. Their findings identified not just boredom and irrelevance in their former schools as causes of departure, they also identified racism, a lack of caring relationships between school staff and students, a lack of safety, and school cultures that felt inauthentic or unrepresentative.[25] Participatory action research methods like this are being used by students, educators, and researchers to better understand and design around students' experiences. The better we all understand students, the better we can collectively imagine new educational approaches.

The current systemic context within which HSRA operates still sends the same signal it did ten years ago: students are being trapped in or kept out of traditional, mainstream schools. And, until education systems are reconfigured to engage all students in holistic and affirming ways, HSRA and other schools will be essential in getting the drop on the "dropout epidemic" and shielding students from society's sucker punches.

NOTES

1. Alison Bagg, Cliff Chuang, Chuck Cook, Chase Davenport, Naomi DeVeaux, Jody Ernst, Tony Gerlicz, David Greenberg, Patricia Hayes, Mikayla Lytton,

Heather Mauzé, Vasy McCoy, Telca K. Porras, Ronald Rizzo, Ernie Silva, and Tony Simmons, *Anecdotes Aren't Enough: An Evidence-Based Approach to Accountability for Alternative Charter Schools* (Chicago: National Association of Charter School Authorizers, 2013).

2. Podcast: Why Billionaires Pay So Little Tax. *New York Times*, June 15, 2021, "The Daily."

3. Horowitz, Juliana Menasce, Ruth Igielnik, and Rakesh Kochhar. "Trends in U.S. Income and Wealth Inequality." Pew Research Center's Social & Demographic Trends Project. August 17, 2020. Accessed June 22, 2021. https://www.pewresearch.org/social-trends/2020/01/09/trends-in-income-and-wealth-inequality/.

4. Sam Phan, "Wealth Gap Widening for More than 70% of Global Population, Researchers Find." *The Guardian*. January 22, 2020. Accessed June 22, 2021. https://www.theguardian.com/global-development/2020/jan/22/wealth-gap-widening-for-more-than-70-per-cent-of-global-population-researchers-find.

5. Tony Sanders, "User Clip: Mapping the 1,235 Dropout Factories: Short Discussion of the Socio-Economic and Other Factors of Where the Dropouts Are Taking Place," C-Span, November 14, 2015, https://www.c-span.org/video/?c4562051/user-clip-mapping-1235-dropout-factories.

6. Fast Facts, "Educational Institutions," IES National Center for Education Statistics, 2019, https://nces.ed.gov/fastfacts/display.asp?id=84.

7. We use the term "pushout" instead of "dropout" in order to maintain a focus on the system's role in students' departure, as opposed to placing the onus on students.

8. Anya Kamenetz, "Delinquent. Dropout. At-Risk. When Words Become Labels," nprEd How Learning Happens, npr, April 28, 2015, https://www.npr.org/sections/ed/2015/04/28/399949478/delinquent-dropout-at-risk-whats-in-a-name.

9. Digest of Education Statistics, "Table 219.46. Public High School 4-Year Adjusted Cohort Graduation Rate (ACGR), By Selected Student Characteristics and State: 2010–11 Through 2017–18," IES National Center for Education Statistics, 2020, https://nces.ed.gov/programs/digest/d19/tables/dt19_219.46.asp.

10. Common Core of Data: America's Public Schools, "Table 1. Public High School 4-Year Adjusted Cohort Graduation Rate (ACGR), By Race/Ethnicity and Selected Demographic Characteristics for the United States, the 50 States, the District of Columbia, and Puerto Rico: School Year 2017–18," IES National Center for Education Statistics, 2019, https://nces.ed.gov/ccd/tables/ACGR_RE_and_characteristics_2017-18.asp.

11. Richard V. Reeves, Eliana Buckner, and Ember Smith, "The Unreported Gender Gap in High School Graduation Rates," Brookings, January 12, 2021, https://www.brookings.edu/blog/up-front/2021/01/12/the-unreported-gender-gap-in-high-school-graduation-rates/.

12. The Sentencing Project, *Fact Sheet: Trends in U.S. Corrections* (Washington, D.C.: The Sentencing Project, 2021).

13. The Sentencing Project, *Fact Sheet*, 6.

14. The Sentencing Project, *Fact Sheet*, 2.

15. "QuickFacts United States," United States Census Bureau, https://www.census.gov/quickfacts/fact/table/US/IPE120219.

16. Monique M. Morris, *Pushout: The Criminalization of Black Girls in Schools* (New York: The New Press, 2016).

17. Letitia Basford, Joe Lewis, and Muffet Trout, "It Can Be Done: How One Charter School Combats the School-to-Prison Pipeline," *The Urban Review* (2020), https://link.springer.com/content/pdf/10.1007/s11256-020-00583-x.pdf.

18. More information on the NewSchools Venture Fund grant that HSRA received can be found in the update after the Flip-Hop Education chapter.

19. "Home," Living School: Learn by Doing, https://www.livingschoolnola.org/.

20. "Empower Community High School: The World Is Ours," Empower Community High School: The World Is Ours, https://empowerhighschool.org/.

21. Connor Perrett, "Trump Threatens to Investigate and Pull Federal Funding from Schools That Teach NYT's 1619 Project on the Consequences of Slavery," *Insider*, September 6, 2020, https://www.businessinsider.com/trump-pull-funding-california-schools-1619-project-2020-9?op=1.

22. Dustin Gardiner, "Ethnic Studies Requirement for California High School Students Passes Legislature," Microsoft News, San Francisco Chronicle, September 1, 2020, https://www.msn.com/en-us/news/us/ethnic-studies-requirement-for-california-high-school-students-passes-legislature/ar-BB18zGFE.

23. Alfie Kohn, *The Case against Standardized Testing: Raising the Scores, Ruining the Schools* (Portsmouth, NH: Heinemann, 2000).

24. "MTC Member Schools," Mastery Transcript Consortium, 2021, https://mastery.org/mtc-member-schools/.

25. Ryan Evans, Michael Lipset, Bunchung Ly, Joey Cienian, and Amanda Galloway, *"Nobody Ever Asked Me Why I Left High School." Let's Ask Them* (St. Paul, Minn.: Center for Policy Design, 2020).

Chapter 11

Trends in Hip-Hop Education 2.0

While the original Trends in Hip-Hop Education chapter acknowledged that it could not adequately recognize all the existing roads cutting through the intersection of hip-hop and education, it attempted to capture the major thoroughfares. In the ten years since the first edition of *Hip Hop Genius* was published, the research, writing, and practices related to hip-hop education have multiplied almost exponentially. Approaches to bringing hip-hop into learning spaces have been tried, tested, remixed, and built upon. There are now several museums, archives, academic centers, and nonprofit organizations dedicated to hip-hop education. Dozens of universities hold conferences on hip-hop education. Hundreds of educators participate in weekly hip-hop education chats on social media. The field of hip-hop education has grown so big and diverse that there's no possible way to document every single piece of work encompassed within it. As part of his doctoral studies, one of this edition's coauthors, Michael Lipset, wrote a review of the literature on hip-hop based education in academia and, despite producing sixty-five pages of documentation in the process, he admits it nonetheless fell short of being comprehensive. And that's just the academic literature. An unknown number of community-rooted initiatives have not yet been researched at the university level. Instead of attempting to document everything this section recognizes some of the new trends that have emerged with regard to hip-hop and education. Where the original edition ended its discussion of the trends in hip-hop education by calling into question "not only what happens in classrooms, but also whether classrooms are needed at all," and calling for "entire institutions to be reimagined and reconfigured," this update offers brief examples of efforts in the past decade that might be referred to as *hip-hop based school design and school change.*

THE LIBRARY

The first edition of *Hip Hop Genius* acknowledged the handful of books on hip-hop and education that had been published at that time. This catalog has grown. Marc Lamont Hill and Emery Petchauer published *Schooling Hip-Hop: Expanding Hip-Hop Based Education Across the Curriculum* in 2014, which discusses important developments in the study of hip-hop aesthetics in learning spaces and engaging aspects of hip-hop culture for student learning.[1] In *Youth Culture Power: A #HipHopEd Guide to Building Student Teacher Relationships and Increasing Student Engagement*, Jason D. Rawls and John Robinson focused on relationship-building and student engagement through hip-hop based education.[2] *Slam School: Learning Through Conflict in the Hip-Hop and Spoken Word Classroom* by Bronwen Low examines the use of hip-hop and spoken word in one high school classroom. Low's ethnography analyzed the collaborative work of one teacher and one hip-hop based teaching artist, laying bare many of the challenges and opportunities of bringing hip-hop and spoken word into formal high school classrooms.[3] In *For White Folks Who Teach in the 'Hood . . . and the Rest of Y'all Too: Reality Pedagogy and Urban Education*, Chris Emdin offers "reality pedagogy" as a framework for many of the lessons he has learned at the intersections of hip-hop and education.[4] This book is a *New York Times* best seller and has driven much interest in and shaped many peoples" understanding of hip-hop education. Emdin has launched a series of edited volumes with collaborators, Edmund Adjapong and Ian Levy, entitled *#HipHopEd: The Compilation on Hip-Hop Education*, which includes two recently released books: *Volume One: Hip-Hop as Education, Philosophy, and Practice* and *Volume Two: Hip-Hop as Praxis and Social Justice*.[5] These volumes feature peer-reviewed academic work covering a broad range of topics relevant to hip-hop based education.

CULTURALLY SUSTAINING PEDAGOGY

When Gloria Ladson-Billings introduced the concept of "culturally relevant pedagogy" in 1995, she identified an approach to teaching that puts students at the center of their learning, celebrates their cultural identities, and doesn't just subject them to lectures on old white men.[6] Since then, Django Paris and Samy H. Alim built upon Ladson-Billings' work with what they call "culturally sustaining pedagogy," which Ladson-Billings has acknowledged as the next step toward a more equitable school system.[7]

Through culturally sustaining pedagogy, Paris, Alim, Ladson-Billings, and others call on educators to celebrate, support, and strengthen those parts of students' cultures that have stood tall in the face of Eurocentric curriculum and irrelevant lessons. As a culture that evolved to become the predominant youth voice globally, hip-hop remains loaded with opportunities for the execution of a culturally sustaining pedagogy. In the era of #BlackLivesMatter, culturally sustaining pedagogy has become a rallying cry for educators who hope to harness the energy of revolution in their work and Paris, Alim, and Ladson-Billings each write about working with and honoring hip-hop in classrooms.

HIP-HOP THERAPY AND YOUTH ORGANIZATIONS

Ian P. Levy and Ahmad Washington, along with other practitioners and researchers of school counseling, have pioneered hip-hop based school counseling, focusing on the use of recording studios in schools as opportunities for therapy. This builds on Marc Lamont Hill's work on "wounded healing" described in the first edition, channeling young people's need to express themselves for healing purposes. Raphael Travis, Jr. trains social workers who work in other settings beyond schools through the use of and engagement in Hip-Hop.

In 1996, Edgar Tyson diagnosed the term "Hip-Hop Therapy."[8] He trained JC Hall in the practice of hip-hop therapy as it had been developed up until that point. Since then, the Beats, Rhymes and Life crew in Oakland, California, have taken up the charge[9] and, along with scholars like Elliot Gann and Raphael Travis, use beatmaking to channel the therapeutic effects of creative processes in hip-hop.[10] These practices are plenty and developing, but the broad lesson learned from the work of those wielding hip-hop to support the growth of young people is that hip-hop, when unpacked with critique and honesty, can heal.

Perhaps it's for these reasons so many youth organizations centralizing hip-hop in the lives of young people have sprung up over the years. Hip-hop coding programs for young people like EarSketch from Young Guru and Georgia Tech encourage young hip-hop and musically inspired people to learn how to code by making music.[11] The Girls Make Beats program empowers aspiring young women producers by providing mentorship from more established women in the game.[12] And Michael Ford, founder of the Hip-Hop Architecture Camp, brings together hip-hop and architectural design in order to develop a new generation of architects capable of literally building the future they want to see.[13]

RECLAIMING SPACE: HIP-HOP CONFERENCES, ARCHIVES, AND MUSEUMS

Hip-hop has always understood the politics of space. A concert venue, a corner cipher, a subway car—these are all spaces that hold unique importance. Museums, archives, and conferences are seen as some of the most staid spaces in society. Hip-hop educators have started reclaiming these spaces and flipping their scripts. Today, hip-hop archives, conferences, and museums represent some of the freshest intersections of hip-hop and learning.

Coauthor of the first volume of the *Hip-Hop Education Guidebook*, Martha Diaz is one of the first people to hold a graduate degree in hip-hop archiving.[14] Along with Pedro Noguera, Diaz also led the first team to do a national scan of the spaces where hip-hop and education collide and collude.[15] For almost a decade, Diaz has led the Hip-Hop Education Summit, which has since evolved into a think tank, and has hosted convenings at New York University, Columbia University, and Stanford University.

In 1991, Timothy David Jones, Ceeon D. Quiett-Smith, and Sherri D. Warren, organized what is recognized by many as the first ever hip-hop conference at Howard University.[16] Now, thirty years later it seems as though every academic setting from community colleges to those in the ivy league has hosted a hip-hop conference. Timothy David Jones, Christopher Emdin, Edmund Adjapong, and collaborators from their organization #HipHopEd now host an annual hip-hop education conference at Columbia Teachers College, which has included Science G.E.N.I.U.S. rap battles between students. The HipHopEX Lab, founded by Aysha Upchurch at the Harvard Graduate School of Education, puts on an annual conference on hip-hop and education called the Can't Stop Hip Hop: The Education Movement.

The Hip-Hop Based Education Special Interest Group at the American Education Research Association annual conference could be considered evidence that hip-hop has reached the summit of academic recognition. This conference is perhaps the largest and most prestigious academic conference on education in the world and now includes a hip-hop special interest group among hundreds of other special interest groups covering a range of topics such as school leadership, teacher training, urban education reform, education policy, and more.[17]

Cornell and Harvard Universities have built Hip-Hop Archives over the past ten years. Cornell's archive houses flyers for early hip-hop parties in NYC in the same climate controlled safe as a copy of the Gettysburg Address. Harvard's archive has an endowed fellowship named after hip-hop legend Nas. In Canada, Mark Campbell, a professor at the University of Toronto, founded the Northside Hip-Hop Archive, which holds the archives of hip-hop as it has grown across that country.

The Hip-Hop Education Center, founded by Martha Diaz is now housed at the first museum dedicated strictly to hip-hop culture, The Universal Hip Hop Museum in the Bronx, New York.[18] Founding members of The Universal Hip Hop Museum include Kurtis Blow and Grandmaster Melle Mel. The museum is chartered by the New York State Department of Education Board of Regents. Hip-hop's long tradition of mix tapes now has its own museum, The Mixtape Museum, founded by Regan Summer McCoy. As this edition is being written, the "Writing the Future: Basquiat and the Hip-Hop Generation" exhibition at the Boston Museum of Fine Arts has just been extended in response to high demand.[19]

The spread of hip-hop education throughout mainstream and elite institutions carries the risks of dilution and cooptation, but simultaneously holds potential for new stages to honor the brilliance of hip-hop educators and students, and to build bigger with broader coalitions. What began as sporadic conferences across the country almost thirty years ago have since sent shrapnel fragments of hip-hop culture throughout academia and public learning spaces, a trend that will hopefully result in the values and practices of hip-hop culture reclaiming and claiming spaces not yet known.

BUILDING AROUND THE WORLD
AND AROUND THE CLOCK

On May 3, 2010, Dru Ryan sent the first tweet using the #HipHopEd hashtag. On June 15 of that year, one of this book's authors, Sam Seidel sent the second. A few months later on November 16, 2010, Brandon Frame and Chris Emdin kicked off the first #HipHopEd chat. The handful of heads who joined that conversation has grown over the past ten years to include thousands. With leadership from Timothy David Jones, Chris Emdin, Amil Cook, Edmund Adjapong, and Ian Levy, each Tuesday at 9 p.m. Eastern, the chat engages hundreds of people and makes millions of web impressions. Versions have started in other countries. People share ideas, links, and lyrics all week using the #HipHopEd hashtag and through a Facebook group. Recently, the #HipHopEd team has taken the chat to Instagram, where Emdin hosts live video discussions on the topics of each week's Twitter chat. #HipHopEd itself has become an organization with an annual conference and a book series.[20] The online conversations stretch beyond this hashtag. As new digital platforms emerge, hip-hop educators utilize them to connect. Recently, Martha Diaz created a group on Clubhouse for live audio discussions about hip-hop education. Thousands of people joined and have connected through this new platform demonstrating that as quick as new technology platforms emerge, hip-hop educators will find ways to use them to connect and build.

HIP-HOP SCHOOL DESIGN

Institutionally, hip-hop has been incorporated as the core for the design of entire new schools. Jamaal Bowman—now a U.S. congressman for New York's 16th Congressional District—and a team of artists and educators teamed up to start Cornerstone Academy for Social Action (CASA) in the Bronx. CASA, a middle school rooted in what its founders understand as the five elements of hip-hop—MCing, breakdancing, DJing, graffiti writing, and knowledge-of-self, is a hip-hop-based new school startup. This school takes a project-based approach to teaching and learning that reimagines core content areas through the five elements.[21]

Hip-hop has also been engaged as a vehicle for school transformation. For example, in Montreal, Québec, Dr. Bronwen Low and a team of researchers and research assistants, including one of this edition's coauthors Michael Lipset, examined one English-speaking public school that had been identified for "turnaround." The school fit all the characteristics of public schools identified as failing in the United States—it served mostly students of color, employed an almost entirely white teaching staff, and experienced decreasing enrollment, failing test scores, high leadership turnover, and a lagging school culture. In collaboration with hip-hop teaching artists, the research team turned to HSRA as its model for change and embarked on a three-year effort to revitalize the Montreal school. What they found was that the main change agents they introduced—hip-hop teaching artists—were able to bring important opportunities for learning to the students, helping to heal some of the wounds felt throughout the community by providing opportunities for self-expression and therapy through the arts. Students marveled at each others' talents, which they noted as a shift from the familiar culture of bullying and harassment. The teaching artists built projects incorporating community organizations and community members, bridging gaps between the school and community. Through this work, the teaching artists became partners in the development and practice of project-based learning experiences rooted in hip-hop.

The team also found serious challenges to what Michael started calling "hip-hop based school change"—the practice of working with hip-hop to bring a school that hadn't been serving its students well closer to doing so. Working with hip-hop at a school that had been operating for more than twenty years meant bringing a culture to which some students felt closely connected and expanding its impact to an entire student population that may not have identified with it. Despite efforts from teachers and teaching artists to diversify options for students' artistic expression, some students felt the implication of the new programming was that they should enjoy learning through hip-hop because that's what some adults had assumed would be of interest to them. Teachers without previous experience with the culture were also resistant, concerned about the appropriateness of bringing hip-hop culture into a school context.

The first edition of this book predicted such challenges, noting that "given the right set of conditions, [schools] can spawn new, highly successful sibling schools, but they cannot be cloned." This is true of any school, but especially a school steeped in hip-hop, which puts a premium on freshness (and has little tolerance for biting). HSRA's Executive Director and one of this edition's coauthors, Tony Simmons summarizes some of the challenges with educators seeking to model their school design or school change efforts too closely on what HSRA has done or too explicitly on hip-hop culture:

We never meant to call ourselves "hip-hop" or "hip-hop high." In fact, when Randy Fielding first coined that term for us, David ["TC" Ellis] and I asked each other, "Is that good??" What we meant was that we didn't need to name ourselves being "hip-hop" or to teach it explicitly, we just were hip-hop. It was a way of being, our culture and dedication to see the genius of each student, honor their creativity, and provide them with the space to grow and practice being free, in furtherance of our hope that they become change agents in their communities and beyond. I could see the issue a kid would have being told that is what they are and will be doing. David and I are now cool with being referred to as "hip-hop high" 'cause people authentically see that in us. But you rarely if ever hear us or anyone else at HSRA use that term or explicitly say we are about to do "hip-hop."

As the trends of youth programming, museums, archives, conferences, courses, books, articles, school change, online communities, and more evolve to give breath and breadth to the world of hip-hop based education, educators should always consider how and why they're working with hip-hop. Too often, in and outside of educational environments, the cultural practices of young people of color get appropriated. When this happens in schools, instead of helping students learn, it can end up making them feel more like outsiders. Asking questions like, "Do my students really want this?" "Am I the right person to do this?" "What messages might I be sending by teaching this lesson this way?" And, "who benefits from me doing this?" can help aspiring educators avoid causing harm and move toward more culturally affirming and sustaining approaches to engaging with their students.

For educators considering engaging aspects of hip-hop culture in classrooms, counseling offices, school design, youth programs and beyond, it is important to do the knowledge to the work that has come before. The previous sections of this update and the original Trends in Hip-Hop Education chapter can serve as springboards for studying the work of countless educators who have already danced at the intersection of hip-hop and education. Focus on honoring not just the content and technique of the art, but the ethos of the culture. Most importantly, don't pretend to be someone you aren't or to know things you don't. In other words, keep it real.

NOTES

1. Marc Lamont Hill and Emery Petchauer, *Schooling Hip-Hop: Expanding Hip-Hop Based Education Across the Curriculum* (New York, N.Y.: Teachers College, Columbia University, 2013).

2. Jason D. Rawls and John Robinson, *Youth Culture Power: A #HipHopEd Guide to Building Teacher-Student Relationships and Increasing Student Engagement* (Bern, Switzerland: Peter Lang, 2019).

3. Bronwen E. Low, *Slam School: Learning Through Conflict in the Hip-Hop and Spoken Word Classroom* (Stanford, Calif.: Stanford University Press, 2011).

4. Christopher Emdin, *For White Folks Who Teach in the 'Hood . . . And the Rest of Y'All Too: Reality Pedagogy and Urban Education* (Boston, Mass.: Simmons College/Beacon Press Race, Education, and Democracy Lecture and Book Series, 2016).

5. Christopher Emdin and Edmund Adjapong, *#HipHopEd: The Compilation on Hip-Hop Education* (Leiden, The Netherlands: Brill, 2018).

6. Gloria Ladson-Billings, "Toward a Theory of Culturally Relevant Pedagogy," *American Educational Research Journal 32*, no. 3 (1995): 465–91.

7. Gloria Ladson-Billings, "Culturally Relevant Pedagogy 2.0: a.k.a. the Remix," *Harvard Educational Review 84*, no. 1 (2014): 74–84.

8. Edgar H. Tyson and J. C. Hall, "About Us," Hip Hop Therapy, 2018, https://www.hiphoptherapy.com/about-us.

9. "Contact Us," Beats Rhymes and Life, http://brl-inc.org/contact/.

10. Raphael Travis Jr., Elliot Gann, Alexander H. D. Crooke, and Susan M. Jenkins, "Using Therapeutic Beat Making and Lyric for Empowerment," *Journal of Social Work 21*, no. 3 (2020): 551–74.

11. "Georgia Tech Works to Attract the Next Generation of Scientists and Engineers," Georgia Tech Research Horizons, August 20, 2013, https://rh.gatech.edu/news/230771/georgia-tech-works-attract-next-generation-scientists-and-engineers.

12. "Girls Make Beats," Girls Make Beats, 2021, https://www.girlsmakebeats.org/.

13. "The Hip-Hop Architecture Camp," The Hip-Hop Architecture Camp, 2021, https://www.hiphoparchitecture.com/.

14. Marcella Runell and Martha Diaz, *The Hip-Hop Education Guidebook Volume 1* (New York: Hip-Hop Association Inc., 2007).

15. Jason Koebler, "Teachers Use Hip-Hop to Engage Students," *U.S. News and World Report*, November 7, 2011, https://www.usnews.com/education/blogs/high-school-notes/2011/11/07/teachers-use-hip-hop-to-engage-students.

16. Lil' Nikki Duncan, "30-Year Anniversary of Howard University's 1991 Hip-Hop Conference," The Shadow League, March 30, 2021, https://theshadowleague.com/30-year-anniversary-of-howard-universitys-1991-hip-hop-conference/.

17. "Hip-Hop: Theories, Praxis & Pedagogies," American Educational Research Association, 2018–2021, https://aerahiphopsig.wixsite.com/hiphopsig.

18. "Education Center," Universal Hip-Hop Museum, https://uhhm.org/education-2/.

19. Times Staff, "'Basquiat and the Hip-Hop Generation' Exhibit Extended," *East Boston Times-Free Press*, April 20, 2021, https://eastietimes.com/2021/04/20/basquiat-and-the-hip-hop-generation-exhibit-extended/.

20. More information about the book series can be found above and more information on #HipHopEd can be found at HipHopEd.org.

21. "About Jamaal," Jamaal Bowman for U.S. Congress NY-16, https://www.bowmanforcongress.com/about.

Chapter 12

Flip-Hop Education 2.0

In the last decade, almost every approach discussed in the Flip-Hop Education chapter in the first edition of this book has been tried and tested by the High School for Recording Arts (HSRA). From generally working to increase impact across the landscape of education to formally working to replicate itself, HSRA's lessons gleaned through these efforts offer valuable insights to anyone interested in applying hip-hop's sensibilities to transforming education. As noted in the update to the Society's Sucker Punch chapter, HSRA has received support from the Hewlett Foundation to establish itself as an exemplar model from which other educators might learn. This concept could also be considered a version of becoming an open source lab school as envisioned in the first edition of this chapter. Certainly, the school remains open to serving as an inspirational burst for visitors.

REPLICATION

This chapter's update shares the story of the High School for Recording Arts Los Angeles (HSRA LA), a pilot program that operated for two years in Los Angeles. The story of HSRA LA serves as testament to the transferability of the HSRA model as well as yet another example of the challenges of school replication and the sucker punches society serves.

The HSRA LA project began in 2017 when the NewSchools Venture Fund selected HSRA as a grant recipient for authorship of a charter petition and opening of a full school. HSRA's previous experience working with a school in Los Angeles mentioned in the original edition demonstrated that an HSRA-style school in Los Angeles could provide a welcome education option and could interface with LA's entertainment industry in exciting ways. Their initial experience building a recording arts program in LA had led to working with Tyler the Creator as a student before he became the internationally known artist he is today. As a student, Tyler cultivated his recording artistry under the tutelage of the HSRA OG Studio Director, Phil Winden. Beyond Tyler's meteoric success, the HSRA team had seen the potential for a recording arts school in LA both because of its expansive entertainment industry that could serve as internship sites, project partners, and future employers for students and because of the large population of students not being well-served by the current educational options. This time, the HSRA team felt confident they could operate successfully if they guided the school's creation from the start rather than taking on a school that had already been in operation for three years before they took control.

The proposed model for the new HSRA LA was the same as the St. Paul program, but with added attention to details to ensure responsiveness to what HSRA knew would be a predominantly Latinx student population. This included connecting with local Indigenous youth advocacy groups to partner on recruitment, identifying Latinx community workers to play important mentorship roles at the school, and building learning opportunities around historic sites of Latinx resistance in a state that was once a part of Mexico. Rather than simply use the grant funds from NewSchools Venture Fund to author a charter application and plan for the following year, HSRA utilized the resources and partnered with a commercial property owner in their network to open a small school space immediately. Just as David "TC" Ellis had operated under St. Paul Open School's charter in the early days, HSRA LA partnered with the YouthBuild Charter School of California to operate in full credit-granting capacity without a charter. Small-scale piloting of this nature was a successful strategy at the beginning of HSRA and has since become a best practice of new school creation shared by organizations such as 4.0 Schools.[1] Such programs have found that starting early and small with what they call "micro-schools" allows new school founders to prototype a model, iterate on early designs, and establish a proof of concept quickly and inexpensively.

To recruit students for their new micro-school, the HSRA team would pull up to parks where young people were hanging out, set up a generator, a mic, and an amp, and host informational freestyle ciphers to engage potential students. Young people would join in, dropping bars, and accepting flyers that held information about the school.

While rocking these ad-hoc ciphers, the team simultaneously built partnerships with the Gang Reduction Youth Development Taskforce, the Juvenile Justice Departments of Probation and Parole, youth housing service providers, school counseling service providers, and other arts organizations serving similar populations.

HSRA's director of social impact, Michael Lipset, was tapped to lead the school. Well-regarded local hip-hop artist and Spanish teacher, Daniel "D Smoke" Farris was hired as Studio Director. D Smoke's identity as a Black man who grew up in Inglewood (home to hip-hop artists such as Pac Div, Mack 10, Big Syke, Blu, and Ab Soul) with no direct Latinx heritage but who had majored in Spanish studies as an undergrad at UCLA and was a highly skilled rapper made him a rare and valuable team member in the LA context. Sir Philip Bailey, the son of Earth, Wind & Fire's lead singer and TC's long-time friend Philip Bailey, was brought on as the school's first licensed high school teacher.

Michael and Sir hosted a two-week pilot program in the summer of 2017 to engage the students they had recruited through the park ciphers. For additional help, they called some HSRA alumni who had relocated to Los Angeles and were on their own grinds in the music business. These included TRY Bishop (self-identified as "The Real Young Bishop" in the original edition), Aaliyah Lenee, D'meetri, Ellen Harris (self-identified as "Fat Ellen" in the original edition), and Mia Rosner to round out the crew. Through this summer pilot, the team once again demonstrated the viability of the HSRA model within the context of LA and used the results of this program to raise further funds in support of the LA school.

To build out the recording studio for the new school, Michael and HSRA student support team member Malik Holon loaded up a U-Haul with an old whisper room soundproof recording booth that HSRA had been given when a local post-secondary recording program was shut down. Malik and Michael drove from St. Paul to LA with iMac's, midi controllers, sound cards, desks, and the sound booth in tow.

In September of 2018, HSRA LA opened its doors. Nine students showed up on the first day of a total of twelve who had enrolled.

That year proved difficult for HSRA LA on a number of levels, but also produced positive student outcomes, some of the drivers of which have now become promising new elements of the HSRA model in St. Paul. The school doubled its average daily attendance from the first trimester to the third, more than quadrupled its overall enrollment numbers over the year to finish with a total enrollment of 37 students, and graduated every eligible senior. In addition to these accomplishments, HSRA LA established a partnership between the school and the state of California that allowed it to hire students, pay them minimum wage ($13.25/hour at that time) for up to 120 hours of internship work, and grant them credit for their experiences. The school was able to hire just over half of its students into paid internships as the operators of their own record label to produce promotional content for their music, write press releases, contact media outlets, and distribute their work digitally. To operate this program, Scott Herold of Rock the Cause Records, a contractor hired to instruct HSRA's Business of Music program in St. Paul, joined remotely every morning and evening to teach the class. The school-state partnership was possible through the federal Workforce Innovation and Opportunities Act (WIOA) and has since been adopted back home by the school in Minnesota.[2]

In this single year, students visited legendary recording studios and sound stages throughout Hollywood, including the Canon Soundstage, one of the largest sound stages in North America, and Westlake Studios where Michael Jackson, Rihanna, Prince, and many others have recorded. They took school trips to the University of Southern California and the Los Angeles Recording School. They hosted guest visits and master classes from DJ Qwess Coast, the OG Arabian Prince (an original member of NWA), Sickamore (Senior Vice President of A&R from Interscope Records), Silky D (known as the first woman DJ of the West Coast), Dave Hampton (studio designer and sound engineer), Sheldon Reynolds (guitarist and vocalist from Earth, Wind & Fire and the Commodores), Maxwell Benson (producer and animation artist), and more. The school was also visited by H. Samy Alim, Pedro Noguera, and Martha Diaz, all leading scholars at the intersections of race, culture, hip-hop, and education.

To ensure the transmission of the school's vision from the flagship to the new site, D Smoke flew with three students from HSRA LA to HSRA in St. Paul. On that trip, D Smoke and the students—Rodrigo "Drezz" Hernandez, Empress Hill and Sebi Ali—collaborated with HSRA, St. Paul students to produce original songs. By the end of the year, the students of HSRA LA were asked to provide the keynote performance at the 2019 Deeper Learning Conference hosted at High Tech High in San Diego. Their performances, which can be found on YouTube, were received with standing ovations.[3]

In many ways, the HSRA LA experiment in expansion only served to validate the predictions made in the original version of this chapter ten years ago. The opening of HSRA LA provided important new learnings that made their way to the flagship school in Minnesota, as seen with the WIOA sponsored internship program and new, long term connections in the industry. LA also provided a wealth of opportunity given the magnitude of difference between the size of the recording industry in LA compared to that of Minnesota. But, it meant HSRA's leaders were away from St. Paul frequently, and forced to lead, coach, and fight for their vision in multiple geographies simultaneously.

Perhaps most importantly, the HSRA approach once again was shown to work for students in a radically different location. In LA, one 23 year-old young man enrolled at the beginning of the year fresh off a prison stint. The morning he entered HSRA LA for the first time, Irving "Teflon Don" Alvarez woke up in a park where he had found a quiet place to sleep in recent weeks. Through his experiences with HSRA LA, Irving found housing and a place to exercise his voice. He joined Chuco's Youth Justice Center, a well-reputed youth activist organization centered on prison abolition, and began advocating for the rights of formerly incarcerated people, traveling regularly to

Sacramento for actions with other activists. Over the year, Irving advocated for important systemic changes to the criminal justice system in front of state-level policy-makers; joined the Brothers, Sons, Selves program; and persisted through incredible odds, including a hit-and-run accident late one night that left him in need of a new set of front teeth.

Irving also played an important role in helping HSRA LA survive into its second year. When the state passed a moratorium on new charter schools in 2019 directed at preventing all charter petitions that would serve young people between the ages of 16–24 through alternative approaches to education, Irving used his connection with Chuco's Youth Justice Coalition that was housed at Free LA, another chapter of the YouthBuild Charter School of California, to help forge a partnership that would allow HSRA LA's studio programming to continue. Vital next-stage funding for HSRA LA from the NewSchools Venture Fund had been predicated upon the approval of a charter petition, which was now no longer legally possible. With funds and time both running out, HSRA's leaders faced the difficult decision to either relocate the studio to another YouthBuild school or shut down the program altogether. With Irving's help, they were able to do the former.

That year, student interest in Free LA's programming grew to the point where the school established a wait list for enrollment. When COVID-19 shut schools down across LA in the spring of 2020, HSRA offered virtual programming from Minnesota to Free LA students, but attempts to raise further funds to continue operating at Free LA into the 2020–21 school year proved fruitless. Regardless, the effort to open and operate HSRA LA can be seen as a success from the perspective of continuing to learn how to spread the school's promising practices and so long as experiences like that of the Teflon Don's are the outcome.

4 LEARNING

In reflecting upon the challenges of opening and operating new chapters, HSRA's leaders returned to the vision of expanding HSRA's impact described in the first edition of *Hip Hop Genius*—the establishment of a nonprofit designed to share practices and provide support and consultation to educators interested in implementing HSRA's best practices. This approach protects the flagship campus in St. Paul from mission drift and overcommitment while allowing the school to support others in serving out-of-school youth.

In December of 2020, upon recruitment of an independent board of directors, HSRA ratified a new nonprofit—4 Learning—to serve this purpose. Today, 4 Learning operates under Michael and Tony's guidance to support the incorporation of HSRA's best practices by educators near and far, thus serving one avenue of opportunity identified in the original version of this chapter: supporting the implementation of HSRA-like approaches to education in other schools and learning spaces.

Ten years later, there are still so many societal problems to solve and so many young people poised to solve those problems who deserve validation and education. All of the work and corresponding results described in the last two chapters demonstrate that it would be a mistake to underestimate hip-hop's potential power in these realms. More than ever, we need its creativity, courage, collaboration, and resourceful reflexes. And there is one more aspect of hip-hop culture that this moment demands, which we will introduce in a new and final chapter.

NOTES

1. Matt Candler, "Micro-Schools: What the Future of School Might Look Like—As Long as We Don't Treat It Like a Silver Bullet," *Medium*, June 27, 2014, https://medium.com/future-of-school/agile-in-education-an-intro-to-micro-schooling-c508c3bbc367.
2. "Workforce Innovation and Opportunity Act," Employment and Training Administration, U.S. Department of Labor, https://www.dol.gov/agencies/eta/wioa/.
3. High School for Recording Arts Los Angeles, "HSRA LA Keynote Performance 1 at Deeper Learning Conference 2019," YouTube, May 12, 2019, https://www.youtube.com/watch?v=9U9Q-kyTLA0.

Chapter 13

A Call to Bumrush 2.0

I am taking no prisoners, taking no shorts
Breakin' with the metal of a couple of forts
While we're hearin' that boom supplement the mix
We're gonna rush 'em like the Bears in the 46
Homeboys I don't know but they're part of the pack
In the plan against the man, bum rush attack
For the suckers at the door, if you're up and around
For the suckers at the door, we're gonna knock you right down.
—Chuck D, "Yo, Bum Rush the Show"[1]

In November of 2017, we sat together at a table in a function room at Stanford University's Graduate School of Business. Seven High School for Recording Arts (HSRA) students sat with us, as did Anjel Newman, who had been a student at the AS220 Youth arts program Sam had directed in Providence and who was now the director of the program herself. The occasion was a two-day global symposium and think tank on "The 5th Element: The Future and Promise of Hip-Hop Pedagogy," organized by Martha Diaz, Jeff Chang, H. Samy Alim, and Casey Philip Wong.[2]

A woman stood up a few tables away with a mic in her hand. She spoke about a hip-hop education program she had initiated in East Palo Alto. Apparently, her students loved the program, so she had spoken with the school district—who saw they were not making progress in improving the test scores of the students she was serving—about supporting the program and integrating it into their schools. The district had agreed, but the tone of their response had given her the feeling that they felt they were doing her a favor. The funding was minimal. No scheduling accommodations were made. The program ended up being shoved into one classroom for one block of a traditional school day. She was dissatisfied with the lackluster support—she was giving the district a seed that could be cultivated to renew their whole approach to supporting young people in their community, and they were limiting it to a tiny container and barely watering it. The students were dissatisfied too—something that had felt more connected to their culture than to the institution had gone from raw and limitless to trapped and co-opted. And the district continued to be dissatisfied with their test results.

"This shit ain't hip-hop," Tony said to Sam. No disrespect to her. She was doing her best to bring something beautiful to the young people of East Palo Alto. But "How are we letting each other get played like that?"

Hip-hop isn't sad and doesn't ask for permission. Hip-hop is flipping something outta nothing. Hip-hop is bold and brash. It's "overcharging n****s for what they did to the Cold Crush."[3] And yet, too often, we are allowing ourselves to be divided and conquered. Capitalism has taught us to compete before we collaborate; to behave like crabs in a barrel. For all of us who rely on grant dollars to survive, how can we not end up seeing those doing the most similar work to us as competition?

How can we not resent it when a program that is newer, lighter touch, or less expansive than ours gets more funding? How can we not hate when a scholar discussing the same topics gets a more prestigious position or paid more?

In the face of such comparison and jealousy, showing each other love can be a transgressive act. But taken too far, it can backfire. Bigging each other up for sloppy work can lead to even sloppier future moves. Critique and even friendly competition can be healthy. As is said in the Bible and *many* rap songs, "Steel sharpens steel."

Back in the Stanford conference room, Tony brought another dimension into play. "There's an element of hip-hop culture that we've gotta bring to situations like this," Tony said with a sly smile on his face as he paused for a moment for dramatic impact before landing the message . . .

"The bumrush."

In *Hip-Hop Genius* we pulled metaphors from hip-hop culture to explain the approaches we felt were needed to revolutionize our country's approach to education. The subtitle of this book, *Remixing High School Education*, named one of those metaphors loud and clear: *the remix*. Throughout the book, we looked at how the leaders of HSRA *sampled* elements from across the world of K–12 education, the music industry, and beyond to compose something new and fresh. We looked at other elements of the culture that came into play in the leadership and innovation of the school, too: the way that TC's leadership pulled from the improvisational energy of *freestyle rap*; the way democratized power between students and educators flows from the hip-hop practice of *the cipher*; the way TC, Tony, and Wolfie's bold operational approach to setting up their studio and charter embodied the brash business hustle of *hip-hop entrepreneurship* and mirrored rappers starting their own record labels by selling music out of the trunks of their cars.

To call these "metaphors" doesn't fully convey the proximity of HSRA's founding to the moves hip-hop artists and entrepreneurs were making at the same time. TC was a rapper. While other rappers flipped money earned through street entrepreneurship into recording studios and record labels, TC did the same thing, except he flipped it into an educational program. Remember he took Down 4 Dirt recording equipment and transformed it into the positivity of Studio 4 (the "4" coming to represent Family, Community, Respect, and Education). While this was a literal embodiment of hip-hop's creative resourcefulness for HSRA, it could be a metaphorical inspiration for others. The message of *Hip-Hop Genius* is that the creative resourcefulness embodied by TC and his crew could be embodied by so many more—after all, this country's education system is faced with limited resources and desperately needs creativity and courage. It also needs collaboration.

This is what brings us to the importance of *the bumrush.*

What is a "bumrush?" Picture a bunch of young hip-hop heads outside a nightclub. A rap show is going on inside. Some of the young heads out front are more talented MCs than anyone on stage. They don't have the dollars required to pay for admission, but they outnumber the bouncer. They have hunger and a sense of justice ("We should be in there! We have the talent, the authenticity, and the cultural cachet. How dare they charge us for our culture?!"). They use their numbers and their courage to rectify the situation. All at once, they charge the entrance. The bouncer grabs the first one or two, but pretty soon they've broken through as all their friends stream by pulling them in. The bouncer thinks about going after them, but isn't getting paid enough and doesn't want to attract the wrath of such a bold and coordinated crew.

This is what Wu-Tang Clan did to the music industry. Their style was unorthodox to the pop sounds of their day. At first, Prince Rakeem and the Genius got record deals and followed the major labels' blueprints for them. It led to unsuccessful early releases. So they transformed into the Rza and the Gza, and came back—with seven of their friends who embodied their raw street swagger in even more extreme manners. Instead of one eager, meager MC showing up and begging to bury a little of his style somewhere on an album that was being creatively directed by a music executive, the Wu-Tang Clan came running into the industry with machetes, face masks, and black hoodies. They demanded that a label sign all of them together *and* that the label allow them to each sign their own separate deals with other companies.[4] And they took over and transformed both the sound and business of hip-hop at the time.

If you're dedicated to transforming education, ask yourself: have you been more like Prince Rakeem listening to the record label telling you to make saccharine love songs or the Rza running up in Loud Records' offices with eight members of your crew and demanding they sign you all?

As hip-hop educators we need to stop with the infighting and hateration. We've been getting lip service and been asked to conform to existing structures for too long. Divided, we've taken deals that allowed for progress, but not for the raw power of what we've got.

Hip-Hop Genius is one example of this phenomenon. Chapters are assigned in college education courses. We have been invited to speak all over the world about the concepts in the book. People find inspiration in and utilize lessons from the book. Several other hip-hop education books and initiatives are making a similar impact. And yet the education system remains largely unchanged.

It's time for a bumrush.

Picture our education system as a nightclub like the one described above. Who do you see as the owner, bouncer, performers, and attendees? What are the roles of the school districts, unions, tax dollars, and taxpayers? Where are you in the mix?

In the Twin Cities, you can drive through downtown St. Paul or Minneapolis on any given evening and—weather permitting—see groups of young people gathered on the sidewalks communing in the ways of the hip-hop generation, ciphers popping, laughter bubbling, young couples flirting loudly. . . . When it gets cold, though, you might walk through the downtown skyway system—elevated glass bridges that connect office buildings to office buildings on the second level of skyscrapers—and find these same young people and activities have moved inside to escape the cold. But what you don't see often, because it is rare in the Twin Cities—which offers no exception from the segregated reality of this country that has kept Black, Brown, and Indigenous people from entering positions of power for far too long—are these same faces on any of the floors above the skyway level. Corner offices remain populated by mostly white men.

Classrooms aren't so different. The teaching pool of Minnesota can only claim 5 percent of its teachers are people of color.[5] To bumrush the education system means doing whatever it takes, wherever it needs to be done, to upend the systems of power and oppression that keep Black, Brown, and Indigenous young people only sporadically percolating beyond those second floor skyways.[6] It means shifting this country's paradigm of education so dramatically and so suddenly that those corner offices flip demographically to represent our overall population—and that power is wrested from those offices to be recentered in the parks and community centers of surrounding neighborhoods. It means a new system of education altogether, one that operates on its own standards.

If we return to the scenario in East Palo Alto that prompted our initial conversation about the need for an education bumrush, it means supporters of culturally relevant and sustaining education—whether students, parents, teachers, preachers, hip-hop heads, or otherwise—running up in the next East Palo Alto school board meeting and demanding that the district fully fund and integrate the teacher's proposed program into all schools immediately.

The education system has plenty of gatekeepers. Just as a bouncer keeps out those whom the club owner believes don't have enough resources or the right attire, the standardized testing apparatus, teacher credentialing programs, and others block nonconforming educators and students from our schools.

The performers on stage change. For much of the past ten years, the mic was dominated by "No Excuses" soldiers. Recently, it has shifted and the main act seems to be a group of educators who make "equity" and "innovation" the refrain of every other song. In practice, though, this rarely goes past serving tacos on Tuesdays to "honor diversity" and allowing the highest achieving students to do a project at the end of the school year. They are backed by booking agents and record labels—politicians, lobbyists, policymakers, and funders—who, beholden to the dictates of neoliberalism, only support those artists whose messages they control.

And sadly, while some are fanatic groupies and others are begrudging attendees, much of our society shows up at the club, willing to pay, even though for every ticket purchased, someone else can't afford admission.

As our education system remains relatively stagnant despite the rapidly changing world around it, young learners could do the same thing to the education system that young artists, digital distribution, and at-home recording studios have done to the recording industry—make it obsolete. In fact, post-secondary education faces that exact threat right now. Enrollment has declined each year over the past decade. The percentage of potential students who believe that attending college will help them get a good job has decreased dramatically in the past few years, as has the percentage who believe higher education will be worth the expense.[7]

"The pandemic has rattled the system," HSRA's founder David "TC" Ellis reminds us. "It's done damage to it, but they're trying to quickly reconstruct the same shit. Hip-hop educators better do something quick or else they'll take away all the innovation that was forced by this challenging moment." Part of what TC has modeled in his leadership style has been a brash but beautiful blend of swagger and audacity. The bumrush is a collective manifestation of that *swaggacity*.

Jay-Z demanded record labels "pay us like you owe us," right after announcing that he was "overcharging" the industry for what they did to early hip-hop performers like the Cold Crush Brothers.[8] Bumrushing the education system means Black, Latinx, and Indigenous young people making the same demand of the education industry: "pay us like you owe us." This does not mean "give us more of what you are already giving us"; it means "give us the autonomy and resources to build a new, radically different system." It does not mean breaking down the door to eat at the same table where others feast; it means saying "fuck your table, this is our farm over here, and we're harvesting the most ripe, voluptuous, organic food in the world, seasoning it the way we want, and sharing it with anyone who is hungry."

As we write this, Minnesota policymakers have introduced in the state legislature a proposal for a constitutional amendment that would make providing every student in the state with a quality education a "paramount duty" of the government.[9] This is a bold move; one that recognizes the undeniably important role of our education system to everything else that goes on around it. But we cannot sit back and expect the industry to disrupt itself. If the amendment passes and the state's primary duty is officially oriented to guaranteeing a quality education to all children, there will inevitably be a moment of chaos in the club. We—the authors and readers of this book—can't sit at the bar waiting for someone else to figure it out or for them to listen to our gentle suggestions about what could be different. We have to be ready: gathered in the dark outside the venue, prepared to rush the door.

> Cold bum rushin' doors like at first it's something
> All we realize that the show ain't nothin'
> For the stunts and the blunts, whole world inside
> The reason that the mighty used force supplied
> No comp, we'll stomp all in our way . . .
> Walkin' and talkin,' fist full in the air.
> —Chuck D, "Yo Bum Rush the Show"[10]

We have to make this a nation where education runs this muhfucka, not the other way around. We have to ask, who will have the mic when the change occurs? Or, better yet, who will bumrush the door, grab the mic, and move the crowd? In the wake of George Floyd's murder and in the context of #BlackLivesMatter, people have bumrushed police stations, corporate storefronts, and even locally owned businesses to make their voices heard. This book is not prescriptive. The expectation is not that educators follow this book in stepwise fashion or try to replicate projects verbatim but rather that students, families, educators (credentialed or not), and everyone called to do so, draw inspiration from these pages and mobilize that inspiration in their own way. This is flipping something outta nothing. This is an education call to action. This is Hip-Hop Genius.

NOTES

1. Public Enemy, *Yo! Bum Rush the Show*, The Bomb Squad, February 10, 1987, song.

2. "The 5th Element: The Future and Promise of Hip Hop Pedagogy," Stanford Diversity Works, November 9, 2017, https://diversityworks.stanford.edu/events/5th-element-future-and-promise-hip-hop-pedagogy-0.

3. Shawn C. Carter a.k.a. Jay-Z and Fonce Mizell, *Izzo (H.O.V.A.)*, Kanye West, August 21, 2001, song.

4. Peter Bittenbender, Chris Gary, and Peter J. Scalettar, *Wu-Tang Clan: Of Mics And Men*, Cary Graber and Vanessa Maruskin, Showtime, May 10, 2019, documentary series, https://www.sho.com/wu-tang-clan-of-mics-and-men.

5. Wilder Research and Professional Educator Licensing and Standards Board, *2019 Biennial Minnesota Teacher Supply and Demand* (St. Paul, Minn.: Wilder Research, 2019).

6. Patrick Kennedy, "Among Minnesota's Top Paid Public Company CEOs, Two Are People of Color; Four Are Women," Microsoft News, StarTribune, August 1, 2020, https://www.msn.com/en-us/news/us/among-minnesotas-top-paid-public-company-ceos-two-are-people-of-color-four-are-women/ar-BB17rZsX.

7. "Public Viewpoint: Interested But Not Enrolled: Understanding and Serving Aspiring Adult Learners," Strada: Center for Education Consumer Rights, September 16, 2020, https://cci.stradaeducation.org/pv-release-september-16-2020/#.

8. Shawn C. Carter a.k.a. Jay-Z and Fonce Mizell, *Izzo (H.O.V.A.)*, Kanye West, August 21, 2001, song.

9. "What Is the Page Amendment?" ourchildrenmn.com. May 31, 2021. https://ourchildrenmn.com/about/

10. Public Enemy, *Yo! Bum Rush the Show*, The Bomb Squad, February 10, 1987, song.

Index

About the Authors

Samuel Steinberg Seidel is director of K12 Strategy + Research and an adjunct professor at the Hasso Plattner Institute of Design (commonly known as the d.school) at Stanford University, and a member of the Circle for Justice Innovations.

Tony Simmons is the executive director of the High School for Recording Arts, and cofounder and codirector of the New School Creation Fellowship and Center for Love and Justice at the High Tech High Graduate School of Education.

Michael Lipset is the director of social impact at the High School for Recording Arts, a course lecturer at McGill University in the Department of Integrated Studies in Education, a research associate at the Center for Policy Design, and an avid podcast producer/host.